THE CHRISTIAN STORY

THE CHRISTIAN STORY

A Narrative Interpretation of Basic Christian Doctrine

VOLUME 1

Gabriel Fackre

THIRD EDITION

WILLIAM B. EERDMANS PUBLISHING COMPANY
GRAND RAPIDS, MICHIGAN / CAMBRIDGE, U.K.

© 1978, 1984, 1996 Wm. B. Eerdmans Publishing Co.
255 Jefferson Ave. S.E., Grand Rapids, Michigan 49503 /
P.O. Box 163, Cambridge CB3 9BA U.K.
First edition, 1978
Second edition, 1984
Third edition, 1996

Printed in the United States of America

00 99 98 97 96   7 6 5 4 3 2 1

Library of Congress Cataloging-in-Publication Data

Fackre, Gabriel J.
The Christian story: a narrative interpretation
of basic Christian doctrine / by Gabriel Fackre.
p.   cm.
Includes bibliographical references and index.
ISBN 0-8028-4107-4 (pbk.: alk. paper)
1. Theology, Doctrinal. I. Title.
BT75.2.F33   1996
230 — dc20   95-46995
CIP

To Our Children

Contents

Preface to the First Edition

The seminar table and theological guild are testing places for such a book as this. The rigorous academic scrutiny received there has greatly helped me. But it is working clergy and laity engaged in mission who have provided the most intense learning laboratory for this kind of presentation of basic Christian doctrine. The material made its initial tentative appearance at a Theological Event for United Church of Christ clergy at Craigville, Massachusetts, and took more developed form in the Perkins Lectures at First Methodist Church, Wichita Falls, Texas. Thereafter it received various elaborations and emendations in clergy conferences at La Foret, Colorado, and Deering, New Hampshire; among laity at the Iowa School of the Church; with new Baptist pastors in Maine and missionary sisters at Maryknoll, New York; with members of First Congregational Church, UCC in San Francisco; the First Baptist and Old South Churches in Boston; and in my own congregation, Eliot Church, Newton, Massachusetts, and with its pastor, Herbert Davis. One or another of these chapters of the Story have been explored with colleagues in the Boston Theological Society, with students and faculty in courses and lectureships at the School of Theology at Claremont, Perkins School of Theology, Austin Presbyterian Theological Seminary, Bangor Theological Seminary, Lancaster Theological Seminary, Boston College, in the Christology Seminar of the Divinity School, Cambridge University, and with my classes and colleagues at Andover Newton Theological School. A crucial partner in theological conversation is my family — always my wife Dot, and now increasingly our children.

I am indebted to Kay Coughlin, faculty secretary at Andover Newton, for her persistence and competence in working with the manuscript in its many permutations, and to Gary and Gabrielle Jenkins for their preparation of the Index.

Unless otherwise noted, the biblical quotations are from the *New English Bible with the Apocrypha* (Oxford University Press and Cambridge University Press, 1970).

Preface to the Second Edition

The revisions and enlargements in the second edition are responses to those who have used *The Christian Story* in college and seminary classes, in church discussion groups, or as a resource in preaching, and have let the author know what they thought about it. Also formative has been my use of the book as a text in systematics courses at Andover Newton Theological School and in various schools of theology for the laity. Perceptive reviews have had their impact too.

My original plan to develop in more detail the germinal ideas of this book in a series of volumes on single doctrines proceeds apace, albeit more slowly than I had anticipated. The rise of political fundamentalism prompted an intervening work, *The Religious Right and Christian Faith,* one that employs the doctrinal scheme of *The Christian Story* to assess a religio-cultural phenomenon. As the issue of biblical authority is central to the claims and critique of the religious right, the research for that study made a contribution to the first of the forthcoming single volumes, *Authority and Revelation,* and to this work as well. Also affecting the treatment of that issue in this revision have been the ecumenical discussion of the singularity of Christian revelation vis-à-vis other world religions, the evangelical debates about the Bible, and the increasing attention given to narrative theology.

And again I'm grateful to my daughter and son-in-law, Gabrielle and Gary Jenkins, portents of a vital new generation of faithful pastors, for their work in updating the Index.

Gabriel Fackre
Pentecost 1983

Preface to the Third Edition

Ten eventful years in theology have elapsed since the last edition of *The Christian Story*. A surge in systematics has taken place, chronicled and interpreted in Appendix 2. During that time also the second volume in this projected series has appeared, dealing with issues of authority and revelation. Single volumes on the next chapters/doctrines are in the making. In the same period, my spouse and I wrote *Christian Basics*, a version of this book for laity, one that forced me to say things more clearly and write them more tightly. Learnings from all this have prompted the third edition. Faculty Secretary Sheila Lloyd has helped immensely with its production.

The reader will find new here a development of the "covenant with Noah" as a narrative approach to issues of general revelation and common grace. The "social Trinity" comes to higher profile. A modest angelology has occupied its neglected place. The intensified debate on inclusive language has necessitated further clarifications. A bibliographical essay on the current revival in systematic theology replaces the earlier bibliography. Overworked imagery in earlier editions has been given some rest. And more.

I am pleased that this book continues to be used in seminary and college courses and by pastors in their preaching and teaching. Forecasts in the 1978 edition that basic theology will have its day have proved true. *The Christian Story* and its sequel series on individual doctrines joins the growing company of other books in this genre with its special place as a "pastoral systematics."

Gabriel Fackre
Pentecost 1995

Introduction

This is a book for those struggling with the question, "What is the Christian faith?" The answer given here unfolds in the form of a story. Basic beliefs are interpreted as chapters in the biography of God. We call the narrative "a translation," for whenever the Christian Story is told with the hope of being heard, it is done in the language of a given time and place.

Both the confusions and the possibilities of this particular time and place warrant the telling and hearing. The din of competing religious claims perplexes both the seeker and the ordinary churchgoer. New cults, movements, and religious superstars appear almost daily on the television screen or street corner to hawk their wares. The pious novelty may carry the label "Christian," or very self-consciously reject that identity and offer in its place either a secular nostrum or some import from the East. Who are *we* vis-à-vis these things, and how do we sort and sift their contentions? Confusion is compounded by the hard ethical choices moderns must make, from abortion and euthanasia, ecology and energy, to racial and ethnic justice, hunger, poverty, and war. While one cannot draw a straight line from basic Christian beliefs to particular stands on these questions, a knowledge of the Christian Story illumines them and points in a direction where answers may be found.

If the perplexities of the hour argue for the clarification of faith, its possibilities make that task even more urgent. Within some segments of the faith community a rising self-confidence about Christian identity asserts itself, as does a corresponding determination to share it. Hence the

1

current interest in evangelism. But if we are to get the story *out,* we must first get the story *straight.*

The Christian community must get the story straight also because the world is aggressively telling its own tale. Assailed by its messages on every side, we are tempted to believe they are true: that we live on the "mean streets" of the violent and promiscuous film or in the vapid bourgeois suburb of the television commercial, or that we await the impending nuclear holocaust without hope or God, on the one hand, or, on the other, that we can confidently expect that the virtue and wisdom of the race assure upward mobility for all toward a Disneyland of joy and plenty. To these half-truths and full fictions must be juxtaposed another scenario. It will be strange to the ears and eyes of modernity, a counter-word and counter-vision. Christian Storytelling keeps alive this set of counter-perceptions so that the Church may be what it is, rather than be made over in the image of the regnant culture.

As we engage here in the task of recovery and reinterpretation, we again find some of the long-lost language and enter some of the forgotten, cobwebbed passageways of ancient Christian thought. The arcane and the underground of atonement theories and eschatological motifs require an intensity of interest in the fundaments, a theological will and way. This is not a book for browsers. It is for the student of faith, either clergy or lay — particularly those responsible for forming the community of counter-perceptions — who in private study or classroom dialogue is ready for intellectual struggle with ultimate concerns. The religious gurus and philosophical sages avidly read by the frequenter of the shopping mall bookstore expect as much from their devotees. And now the laity of the Church in their pleas for Bible study and examination of the faith issues are sending the message: "No more pap and gruel!" Work is expected here, mastication and digestion. Not the work, however, of the professional cook or connoisseur. The volume carries detailed footnotes only in the appendix on current systematics, the apparatus of scholarship is modest, and the exposition of each chapter of the Story is limited. Further, some undeveloped themes and neglected areas and assertions demand much more adequate defense, all of which reflect the author's own struggle and inadequacies, as well as the incommensurability of the project with the space chosen to encompass it. This overview will be followed by separate volumes on each basic Christian doctrine. In these individual inquiries deeper probes will be made and the important work of documentation done. What is here suggestive will be there more exhaustive. For all that, this study of the range of Christian doctrines grows out of extensive research and longtime reflection and makes its own demands of comprehension.

The Christian Story is primarily "from faith to faith." But just as an interesting building project in midcity attracts its sidewalk superintendents, so the Church when it is about its business of constructing its basic faith may attract some interested onlookers. Students in introductory courses in religion will find here an orientation to basic Christian belief. Further, good systematics may be the best apologetics.

My own first perception of both the need and readiness for exploration of the faith prompted a modest effort in 1972 in metaphorical storytelling, found in the Appendix. This short tale of deeds of God from creation to consummation, told in the imagery of light, found its way into the mission training programs of several denominations, onto film, and into the preparatory materials of the Nairobi Assembly of the World Council of Churches. The reception given "Dawn People" strengthened my conviction that work on basic Christian faith needed desperately to be done. While metaphor is a particularly apt way of grasping and communicating faith, as today's exponents of "metaphorical theology" point out, it is also necessary to distill *meaning* from metaphor. Indeed, something is always lost in the distillation, for rich imagery, especially in piety, puts us in touch with reality in a way that the more ascetic language of theology cannot. The parables of Jesus, the images of the prophets, the atonement pictures of Paul, and the eschatological symbols of John are examples. But there is a "truth of the symbol" as well as "symbolic truth," as the philosopher of language, Wilbur Urban, long ago pointed out. We have the obligation to say what we mean as well as sing what we say.

This book explores the meaning in the metaphors. And it does so in a certain orderly way, attempting to see Christian faith as a network of beliefs. As such, it is an effort in *systematic* theology. A frightening phrase! Some reject even the possibility of that kind of careful articulation today, declaring that theology is too much in disarray to be any more than bits and pieces. Others are put off by the hint of overrationalization in a time when the experiential and visceral are so much to the fore. Extensive testing of the materials of this book among students, clergy, and laity makes me believe otherwise. This is a ripe time for going beyond both timid *ad hoc* theologizing and too-easy acquiescence to the feeling fads of the day.

3

Mindlessness is no Christian virtue. This volume is obviously not an architectonic presentation of Christian belief. It is an outline of the rudiments of faith, a "mini-systematic," for those who want a working knowledge of the reference points of Christian conviction.

Coring

Martin Marty suggests that the task of the Church has to do with both "coring and caring." Clarity about the ABC's of faith is what we are about here. But is there really a core of Christian faith? The bewildering variety of current assertions as to what Christianity really consists of seems to indicate otherwise. Moreover, both the biblical scholar and the church historian regularly point out the diversity of belief in both Scripture and Christian tradition. There seems to be a multiplicity of stories rather than *a* Christian Story. The strong sense of relativity that marks our time, the assumption that what we believe is rooted and shaped by who we are and where we come from, makes any talk about a common core suspect. Pluralism is the order of the day. The most that many are willing to affirm is a theology from a particular ethnic, sexual, geographic, or socioeconomic perspective.

The truth in this perspectival view of Christian belief we shall attempt to honor in our conception of this effort as *a translation*. It is a recounting of the Christian Story from one angle of vision, not from a God's-eye point of view. Its language and accents are those of a particular time and place. We shall examine what this idiom is in the next section, on the *how* of theology.

However, we do not assume here that basic Christian belief is mired in one's stream of history, nor can it be servile before pluralism. There is an out-thereness of biblical truth that is to be seen, whatever the angle of vision and however our view of it is affected by the glasses we are wearing. There is an object with which our subjectivity deals. There is a story that our translation seeks to communicate. There is a hard core of affirmation at the center of our perceptions and interpretations.

In times of perplexity and possibility in Christian history renewed efforts are made both to locate the outlines of this Story and to translate it into the concerns and language of the day. In the second century, when the Church was beset by pressures from within and without to set forth its identity, there emerged a "rule of faith," a simple statement of the funda-

4

mentals for those making a first profession of faith and for the general purpose of distinguishing between the basic Christian vision and its distortions. Later, this time in the midst of debate about the uniqueness of Christ, the Council of Nicea drew up some definitive articles of belief. From these two epochs of clarification we have the Apostles' Creed and the Nicene Creed. Subsequent eras produced their own statements of the Story. All bear the marks of the time in which they were formed, from the substance philosophy that influences ancient confessions to the masculine language that dates many modern credos. But the translations and accommodations circle around and return to a core of conviction. It is made up of refrains that run through the charter of the Christian religion, the Bible, and recur in the classic and contemporary formulations of faith. They represent the abiding skeletal framework for the flesh and blood of any statement of faith.

In the most elementary of terms these refrains are the chapter headings of *The Christian Story:* Creation, Fall, Covenant, Jesus Christ, Church, Salvation, Consummation, with their Prologue and Epilogue, God. These are the acts in the Christian drama, the chapters in the Story, the exposition of which constitutes the beliefs of the Christian faith. They might be diagrammed simply by the varied relationship of two hands representing the main characters in this Story, God and the world.

God brings the world into being, the stretching of one hand toward the other as captured in Michelangelo's painting of God's reach toward Adam, creation:

The response of the world is the rejection of the divine invitation, the fall:

The recall of God, the new reach of the Creator toward creation, takes place in the covenant with Israel:

The depth of human alienation requires a correspondingly deep plunge into a resisting world, issuing in the suffering Love at the center of human history, Jesus Christ.

The new age from Christ to the end is the time of the Church, salvation, and consummation, when that drama through which we now are living proceeds toward the intended unity of God and the world.

The fundamental beliefs of the Christian faith are the chapters of this tale: Creation, Fall, Covenant, Jesus Christ, Church, Salvation, Consummation. And their source and end is the triune God: Prologue and Epilogue.

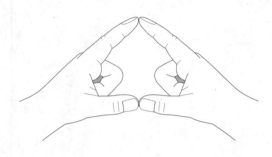

That there is a God who creates, reconciles, and redeems the world is the "Storyline" in its bare bones. But there is a body of belief as well as a skeletal structure. The creation of the world by God entails a conviction about the goodness of nature, the dignity of humanity, the reality of "principalities and powers," and the freedom to respond to the divine invitation. The fall of the world means the abuse of the freedom granted to us, with effects everywhere to be seen in the estrangements in humanity, the groaning of creation, and the havoc wrought by demonic powers. The liberation and reconciliation of a broken world mean a covenant to bind up the wounds, an Incarnation to deal firsthand with recalcitrance, a struggling, suffering, death, and resurrection that bring at-one-ment to alienation, the birth of a community that participates in and serves the new freedom and points to the healing power released into history and the cosmos, and the promise of a coming of the final victory for the Purposes of God. This is the flesh and blood that covers the bones. To know who we are is to be familiar with this body of faith as it is set forth in the biblical language and preserved in the tradition of the church universal. The work of theology is the exploration of the *what* of the matter.

The body and bones of belief are the truth claims of Christian faith. As assertions about reality to which a "Yes" or "No" is appropriate, they are sometimes called "propositions." However, they are a special kind of truth claim more aptly described as "affirmation." Christian faith is a life-and-death credo held by a "believer," not to be had outside this personal involvement. Further, the "I believe" of affirmation bespeaks the modesty appropriate to declarations about ultimate reality. They are couched in analogical language that presupposes sufficient convergence of our idiom with divine intention to render communication possible, but also calls for an honoring of the distance between our words and God's ways.

Translation

When this core Christian tale is told in a given time and place, it is always related in the language of that setting. The worldview of the era and its particular issues and sensibilities shape how the narrative is set forth and heard. That version of the Story will also influence the accent given to one or another chapter, as well as the manner in which the message in its entirety is communicated. In the science of an earlier century the *how*, *when*, and *where* of creation and consummation will be conceived in a fashion very different from the cosmology of this day. And in the society of another time and place the issues that are to the fore may be quite different from our own, calling forth from the body of Christian belief different themes and adapting the thought forms of the time to express those themes. We shall speak more about this in discussing the perspective from which the Story is viewed. The crucial task of translation is to find ways in each generation and location to bring the basic convictions of the Christian faith into the thought world of its hearers. Following the analogy of the human organism, the body must be clothed, fed, and housed with materials available in the land in which it seeks to live.[1]

In this volume the metaphor "translation" is used for the systematics task of communicating Christian faith in a given time and place. As a

---

1. Two of the four features of the teaching of systematics in seminaries and university divinity schools discovered in the writer's research are "retrieval" and "contemporaeneity." The other two are attention to the church context of theology and the fact of diversity. See Fackre, "Reorientation and Retrieval in Seminary Theology," *The Christian Century* 108, no. 20 (June 26–July 3, 1991): 653-56.

literary term, it fits our "story" theme. Some comments on "translation" are in order. What is entailed can be misunderstood if we are not clear about *what kind* of translation is meant.

Those whose lifework is translating texts say translation comes in three varieties:

1. "Literal" translation seeks to find exactly equivalent words in the new language for those from the old language. If the original text says that sin "takes its toll" — meaning dire consequences ensue — then translation requires finding those words in the new language. But what if "taking tolls" in the new context means money dispensed to authorities at certain places along a road? Literal translation can then be very misleading.

2. The problems with a consistently literal approach drive some translators to "take another tack" (there's another tricky metaphor). Hence we have a second way of translating, called "paraphrastic." In the effort to make the original understandable to new readers, the translator resorts to paraphrase, not being bound closely to the grammar, sentence structure, or figures of speech of the original language. *The Living Bible* is an example of how this works in the translation of Scripture.

   Great problems soon become apparent in the paraphrastic approach, *The Living Bible* being a case in point. What happens is that so much attention is paid to the idiom and ideas of the new language and culture that the translation turns into a revision of the ideas of the original. The context takes charge of the text.

3. Most translators, especially Bible translators, aware of the difficulties of the first two approaches espouse the way of "dynamic equivalence." That is, they stay as close to the original grammatical structure as they can, being wary of summaries of a passage in the language and thought forms of the new setting. They follow the original content line by line — "equivalency." Yet, at the same time, they are not tied to the exact repetition of the original words, changing them with modest alternatives that reflect original intent, attempting thereby to be "dynamic." All this is hard work!

This book — and the series growing from it — is a venture in theological "dynamic equivalence." It is grounded in the language and ideas of historic Christian faith. These are constants throughout. At the same time, modest interpretive moves are made that seek to relate the ancient formulations to our contemporary context. "Modest" means the use of motifs such as "story" — hence a "narrative" interpretation of basic Christian doctrines, and the use of metaphors — hence "vision" as well as "word." The option being avoided — the equivalent in theology of paraphrase — is the wholesale rereading of historic teaching in terms of the premises of this day and age: a philosophical system, an economic or political theory, a social theory, a school of psychology, a point of view in literary criticism, and so on. Systematic theology cannot avoid drawing on cultural language and themes. But they must not exercise control over Christian belief. To both acknowledge their presence and yet relativize their role and resist their take-charge tendencies means using cultural idiom in this reserved way. It appears "eclectically," not systematically, the latter taking its signals and content from Scripture. Thus the modest motifs and metaphors employed here have their very meaning transformed by their location in the language world of the Christian community and its Charter.

Translation, so understood, does not mean rewriting the Christian Story. In the zeal to be understood it is sometimes tempting to make this strange tale fit snugly into the stories with which the new land is already familiar. When this happens, faith's perceptions of life, death, and destiny become just another way of saying what is already believed by the philosophy, politics, economics, science, poetry, and common sense of a particular time and place. We thus eliminate the radical, the disturbing, the unmanageable in the Christian faith by fitting it into our terms. The awesome biography of God becomes our autobiography. The Stranger settles in as a pliant citizen of our country, who not only knows our language but also adopts our ways.

While requiring translation, the Gospel is always distanced from our ways, always a norm to which we are accountable, never subservient to our agenda. To know this critical line between translation and accommodation is the art of authentic communication.

Packed into the word *translation* is much more than the idea of a verbal crossover. Translation surely includes the employment of other terms to convey the meaning of the Christian saga. But this language is rooted in profound experience. To tell the Christian Story in one way rather than another is to ask the hearer to relate it to the agonies and ecstasies that have marked the era in which we live and to connect it

11

with deeply shared premises and perceptions. As the recounting of the Story in its biblical form strives for inclusiveness of all its chapters, so this translation attempts to be an ecumenical one that honors the richness of contemporary experience. Thus when "freedom" is referred to as a way of understanding one aspect of the Vision God has for the world, it includes liberation from the enslavements experienced in our time by the black, the poor, the woman, the Third World, the "in-the-middle" citizen, the liberation of the individual from personal and spiritual oppressions that characterize our era, and beyond that the freedom of nature from its technological tyrants.

Whether one's translation of the Gospel is really heard and understood by those who speak the intended language depends on how deeply the translator is really immersed in that world and has learned its idiom. Has the communicator lived and suffered and rejoiced alongside those with whom the word of faith is being shared? Telling the Christian Story *of* liberation is best done from *within* the contemporary struggles for liberation.

To strive for an ecumenical translation is particularly demanding. One cannot be a native of all the lands in which one seeks to live — black, red, white, brown, female, male, young, old, First, Second, Third, and Fourth Worlds. That fact, and the heightened sense of particularity that characterizes contemporary Christian thought, has produced a spate of perspectival theologies — black, feminist, Third World. While our finitude precludes what eternity promises — "neither male nor female" — the universal Vision of the Kingdom calls us to participate as deeply as possible in the places where that realm is making its presence felt. While we cannot *be* native, we can *go* native. We can do our theology in and with those who are struggling to be free and reconciled. When that involvement takes place, the reflection that rises out of it bears the marks of authenticity. And when that engagement is wide-ranging, then the catholicity of experience is productive of ecumenical translation.

Translation means that we go native, "in all things *but* faith and morals." This addendum from classical missionary lore distinguishes translation from accommodation. Because the freedom of the Kingdom of God is not just another word for the going perception of freedom — current liberation movements, whether political, personal, or ecological — the effort to translate means the need to transmute as well. Thus freedom becomes, in translation, liberation from *sin* and *death,* as well as liberation from the political, social, and economic powers of evil that afflict a generation. Authentic translation finds the points of contact with contemporary sensibility, but it also seeks to enlarge the meanings of the language of the new land by infusion of fresh perception from the biblical faith.

What then is the systematic theology we undertake in these pages? It is ordered reflection that seeks to elaborate and render intelligible the faith of the Christian community. It is the explication and interpretation of the chapters of the Christian Story.

Whether we both state and translate the Christian Story responsibly depends on how we go about our task. The matter of procedure, the "how to," is the question of theological method. This is more than the way we arrange the subject matter. In that simplest sense we use here the story form of organizing Christian belief. We employ a narrative method of theology in the community model to be described. More basically, method has to do with what we rely on for setting forth the Christian faith. What are the sources and standards of Christian belief? How do we *get to* the Christian faith? This is the question *of authority.* Because of the erosion today of some of the traditional religious centers of authority — the Bible and the chief spokespersons of the church or traditions — the issue of authority has become an insistent one. In fact, a good deal of contemporary theology is so preoccupied with this question that its attention to the *what* beyond the *how* is minimal. While this book gives primary attention to the what of Christian belief, it must also honor the importance in our day of the issues of authority and its tandem question, *revelation.* Authority deals with the identity, and revelation with the veracity, of the Christian faith. We cannot discuss one without assumptions about and references to the other, but they are distinguishable aspects of the question of theological method. We begin here with an inquiry into the authority for the Story we have to tell.

Authority

What are the authoritative materials for the work of theology? How do we pursue the goal of communicating the Christian faith in the language and thought forms of our time?

In broadest outline, the answer we give to that question in these pages has three elements.

1. First and fundamentally, we go to the *source* of the Story, the Scriptures of the Old and New Testaments.
2. As an aid in interpreting the Scriptures we make use of a *resource*, the life and lore of the church, or the traditions, conversations, and practices of the Christian community.
3. Whatever exploration is made of source and resource goes on in the *setting* of the world of our experience. Within each of these components are these important defining features:
    a. the *substance* of the Gospel to which the source bears witness;
    b. the *norm* of Jesus Christ, before which all our efforts to tell the Story are judged;
    c. the *guide* of classical Christian tradition in the life of the church;
    d. the *aid* of "signs" in the cultural setting; and
    e. the *perspective* in which we view Christ and the Gospel.

What these elements and features are, and how they are interrelated, is suggested by the diagram below and explored in the following pages.

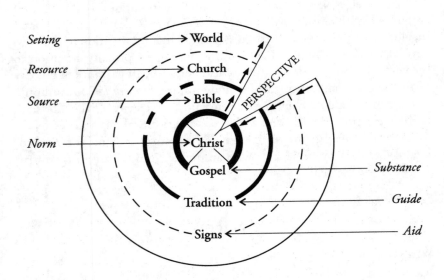

The Bible as Source

The ultimate source of the Christian Story is the Scriptures of the Old and New Testaments. (The apocryphal material is "edifying for the people of God," as ecumenical statements have it.) Our theological work begins and ends in this canon, which emerged in the early centuries from the Christian community as it struggled with its identity, and which that community has since maintained as the fundamental reference point of Christian doctrine.

The authority of the Bible rests in its testimony to the decisive events in the faith narrative. Here we learn about both their happening and their meaning. In its role as recorder and interpreter, the Bible is part of these redemptive events themselves. As such, the Scriptures are agents of liberation and reconciliation, and therefore the work of the Spirit (Rom. 16:25-26). The relationship of inspiration to revelation we shall investigate in the following section. For the time being, we note that the authority of the Scripture is grounded in its gift of disclosure.

The authority of disclosure is inseparable from the nature of what is disclosed. The Storybook exists to tell the Story (2 Tim. 3:15-16). It is not an encyclopedia of general knowledge, authoritative in matters of physics and chemisty, astronomy and geology, sociology and psychology. It borrows the language and thought forms of its own time to state the Christian faith. One of the artful evasions of the Word to be heard and the Vision to be seen in this book is to use the book for purposes for which it is not designed. This is the error of fundamentalism. The Gospel is not to be confused with the multifarious and changing accounts of the processes and patterns of cosmic and human life. For information about these we turn to the natural and human sciences and not to the book of the Story. On the other hand, no modernity adept at making this point about the Bible as earthen vessel with its transient thought forms should cause us to fall into the other trap of relativizing all the perceptions of the Bible and replacing them with the categories of contemporary experience. Thus we are faced with the delicate task of identifying the abiding and distinguishing it from the transient.

The perennial truth to be found in the Scriptures has to do with the Storyline within the Storybook, the Gospel *substance* of the biblical source. This is the Good News of God's Purpose and Work from creation to consummation, with its center point in the life, death, and resurrection of Jesus Christ. Here and there this narrative is sketched in luminous passages in the New Testament, such as the proclamation addressed to the people of Israel (Acts 2:14-36; 3:12-26), or as the saga expressed in Greek idiom (John 1:1-18). In the main, it appears in segments, act by act, as the drama unfolds from Genesis to Revelation, with the total plot manifest as the Bible is viewed in its entirety.

In the early struggle to define itself vis-à-vis alternative worldviews, the Christian community set forth its substance in baptismal rules of faith. A common pattern of belief following the narrative structure took form as "the apostolic teaching," transmitted to us in subsequent edition as the Apostles' Creed. Thus the earliest expression of "tradition" fixed on the Christian saga as its confessional identity. We shall return to this in the later discussion of the church as resource in the interpretation of the biblical source.

Apostolicity was indeed the criterion for selecting the books of the New Testament canon. Critical scholarship has demonstrated that these writings cannot be thought of as the simple report of one or another apostle. But the rationale for the inclusion of this book rather than that one is its reliable transmission of original apostolic testimony. The layers of subsequent tradition have not obscured the proclamation of salvation, and its apostolic authority therefore remains.

The centrality of the paragraph about Christ in the Creed reflects the decisiveness of the christological norm within the biblical source. The New Testament witness to the turning point of the Christian drama, the deliverance wrought in the life, ministry, death, and resurrection of Christ, is the prism through which the light of revelation is to be seen and understood. The meaning of the events in the whole sweep of the biblical narrative — the depth of the fall, the width of the covenant, the length of the whole drama — is read from this reference point. What is relevant in the Old Testament and what is definitive in the New are determined by this disclosure of the divine Purpose, the eternal Word of God enfleshed in Jesus Christ. Thus the 77 percent of the Book that is the Hebrew Bible, our Old Testament, is to be understood not only on its own terms but also within its New Testament context. How the law and the prophets are appropriated in the Christian faith is determined by how their promise is illumined and fulfilled in the New Testament. The full depth of the fall and the full width and length of the covenant are measured from a future vantage point. The Word of God, enfleshed in Jesus Christ and interpreted by the eye and ear witnesses to the

Incarnation, is the center from which the whole range of biblical data, the whole Work of the eternal Logos from creation through covenant to consummation, is perceived.

To describe the Bible as the source of the Story could mean that Christian thought starts with this material, or does its work with an eye on its origin, or uses it to provide the symbols of this tradition, but then takes off on the wings of human experience to spin out more adventurous themes. Our conception of the source, however, is more encompassing. Faith is grounded in and *returns to* this orientation.

The Bible is the source of authority in the sense of standard as well as beginning point for theological reflection. The Scriptures of the Old and New Testaments are the guardian of faith. Claims made that this or that assertion is Christian theology must be adjudicated before this bar. How important this is to underscore when conversation partners are given a role in the authority structure of Christian faith, in this case the church's presence as a resource, and the world of general human experience as setting.

In acknowledging the Bible as the premier factor in authority, we must keep in mind our earlier principles of interpretation. The Scriptures' status as source has to do with their faithful recounting of the Christian narrative. The Bible is witness to this *substance* of faith, the fundamental affirmations of the Gospel. These fundamentals, having to do with the being and doing of the God of liberation and reconciliation, constitute the apostolic standard within the great variety of materials that make up the Bible. They comprise the Good News of the deeds of God, the defining characteristics of the Gospel. In our diagram the Storyline is indicated by the thickened inner edge of the biblical circle. And our grasp of the meaning of this Gospel substance in the time and place in which we live and witness is always guided by the christological norm. Source, substance, and center together constitute a circle of authority that gives focus to the task of theology.

Issues of "inerrancy" and "infallibility" attend the contemporary discussion of the authority of the Bible. They come up when the question is asked, "Why is the Bible authoritative?" We have dealt with that query by implication only in this section, focused as it is on the what rather than the why of the matter.[2] We shall turn to it, and the family of concerns related to it, when examining the underside of authority, revelation.

---

2. *The Christian Story*, vol. 2: *Authority: Scripture in the Church for the World* (Grand Rapids, Mich.: Eerdmans, 1987), investigates in detail these and related issues.

The Church as Resource

"How are they to hear without a preacher?" asks Paul (Rom. 10:14). How can the Vision be seen without a seer? Preachers and seers are not only the ordained and gifted, but the whole Christian community wherever it helps to unstop our deaf ears and open our blind eyes. The improvement of our hearing and the sharpening of our sight come from the people of God, past and present. The fathers and mothers of faith bequeath us the result of their own struggle to hear and see, and the brothers and sisters, our present companions in the Church, also make for clearer hearing and seeing. This gift of the Christian community comes to us in creed and council, catechism and confession, dialogue and proclamation. It meets us in the ancient lore of the Church and the present learnings of the Christian community. This common life and its wisdom, brought to us by the constant activity of the Holy Spirit, is a fundamental resource in our engagement with the biblical source.

Its resource role expresses itself in two ways:

1. Where we stand on matters of Christian faith is influenced by where we sit in the pew. That is, our particular church heritage shapes our way of thinking about who God is, what Christ has done, and how we read Scripture. To understand this is to be grateful to God for whatever light is given from this angle of vision, but also to acknowledge the limitations of partial perspective.
2. Because the Body in its entirety belongs to Christ, and because the Spirit gives manifold gifts (1 Cor. 12:4-6), we are called to open ourselves to the insights of the *full* Christian community.

Catholicity of church encounter with the Bible makes for wideness of vision, and therefore depth of insight. A thickening of the inner line of the church band on our diagram indicates those points of ecumenical consensus inherited from the past, "tradition," which functions as "guide." Found in both official documents and formal statements of the undivided Church, such as the Apostles' and Nicene Creeds, the doctrines of the Person of Christ and the Trinity, and patterns of affirmation implicit in the worship and working faith of the church universal, tradition is a weighty resource in Christian theology.

The circle of tradition is not closed, for the Spirit's ecclesial Work is

18

not done. Traditional doctrine develops as Christ and the Gospel are viewed in ever fresh perspective. Old formulations are corrected, and what is passed on is enriched. This open-endedness, however, does not overthrow the ancient landmarks. As tradition is a gift of the Spirit, its trajectory moves in the right direction, although it has not yet arrived at its destination.

The relation of the church circle and its defining inner line to the outer ring of "the world" and the perspectival arrow that issues from it is suggested by the image of Christ's face viewed from different angles. As different generations or locations view him from varied angles, new perspectives are added to the characterization of who he is, and a more encompassing grasp is given of the physiognomy of faith. Ever new light and truth break forth from God's holy Word, as John Robinson expressed it.

By identifying the Church as resource, and placing it within the second ring of authority, we recognize its accountability to the Bible. The Church precedes Scripture, chronologically. But by its own choice, in creating the canon to which it is responsible, the Church itself has given Scripture theological precedence, faithful to the source's own self-testimony. Thus tradition is ministerial while Scripture is magisterial (Clark Pinnock). Or in more formal theological terms, tradition is the *norma normata* (the rule that is ruled) and Scripture is the *norma normans* (the rule that rules).

The World as Setting

By "world" we mean general human experience in all its variety, richness, and ambiguity. Who we are, what we think, how we feel, and where and when we live are factors in the theological task. This experiential environment includes the rudimentary intuitions and encounters of day-to-day living and the most sophisticated use of reason by empirical inquiry or the canons of logic. It encompasses the arts as well as the sciences, the full range of philosophical, aesthetic, moral, and universally religious sensibilities and constructs. As we follow the course of the biblical narrative, we shall see that there is more than one chapter to our Story just because this human venture as such, our general experience of the world in its plenitude, cannot be counted on to give us ultimate life and light. Pervaded as it is by the powers of sin, evil, and death, the world is not self-sufficient or self-saving. Hence the unfolding drama, in which a fallen world is challenged by the singular deeds of God and general human experience, is confronted by the particularities of divine disclosure.

But we have still included the world in our authority structure. Why? There are two reasons, descriptive and normative.

1. Because theology is done by finite human beings living in the skin of a given time and place, it will be influenced by that habitation. A traditional theology of another era that believed it was preaching only the pure Gospel can be seen by a later generation, with the benefit of hindsight, to have introduced into its formulations cultural assumptions, whose unacknowledged presence can confuse the Gospel or whose incongruence can compromise it. Better then to acknowledge the presence of the world in the work of theology, carefully relativizing it as a factor in authority — as the setting, not the source or resource — making use of experiential idiom and themes that are coherent with the Gospel and thus fit instruments for its translation. We will attempt to show how this can be done in the comments on "perspective."

To interpret the descriptive role of human experience in this way is to part company with the absolute relativizers, who believe we are so mired in our historical contexts that no transcultural assertions are possible. This latter view makes its presence felt in theology in several ways. For some it means that there is no access to the Gospel as it is found in Scripture (or no unity to Scripture itself, since it is an awkward amalgam of various gospels, themselves the products of various religious communities) because of the unbridgeable gap in context between the reader and the writer. For others it means that because every theology is conditioned, we are free to make our own history determinative for our own faith, and free as well to reject the views of other Christians, creatures as they are of alien and sometimes oppressive contexts. The view that all truth claims are relative is, finally, impossible to sustain, for it denies what it presupposes. If there are no absolutes, then the declaration that this is so is also suspect. Further, it puts a historically conditioned philosophical thesis in charge of Christian faith. And when carried out methodically, the absolutizing of this position renders open discourse within the theological community impossible, since all other conversation partners are presumed to be imprisoned in their historical contexts, and one can be faithful only to one's personal location and history as "true for me."

The view set forth in these pages accepts the facts of temporal and spatial conditioning as the beginning point of critical self-understanding in theology — knowing who you are, what time it is, with what you must deal. That social existence, however, in turn must stand before the Gospel as it comes to us in the scriptural source and the traditioning resource. The word of truth as it comes to us through these media by the power of the Spirit can cut through the boundaries of time and space and be heard cross-culturally and cross-temporally. We are not so imprisoned in our *context* that we cannot be addressed by the biblical *text*. This engagement we shall explore when looking at the dynamics of perspective.

2. Not only the claims of finitude but also those of faith place human experience in the authority structure of Christian theology. As the Holy Spirit makes the christological center and the biblical source supremely authoritative, and gives the Church and its tradition a subsidiary role, so the same Spirit puts the world into the conversation of faith as the setting in which the Gospel must be communicated. The God of Christian faith takes time and place seriously, having brought them to be in creation, having become enfleshed in their midst at the Incarnation, and moving the world to its fit end at the consummation. Into this stream of divine glory are released the powers of sustenance, a universal grace that contests the world's self-destructive tendencies. A narrative understanding of Christian faith will view this grace of preservation as the power necessary to keep the saga moving toward its destination, furnishing humanity with enough of a grasp of its purpose and sufficient power to pursue it to keep life livable. Therefore, the world is capable of certain *preceptions* of truth and *questions* of truth. A theology that connects with the world in which it does its work can be edified by those perceptions and must answer those questions. In the former case they help to render patent what is latent in the Gospel. Because the Spirit that flings these clues into human experience is the Spirit of the Son, the eternal Word that forms the world, whatever is true in human experience is of a piece with Jesus Christ, the incarnate Truth. Yet that Incarnation would be rendered irrelevant, and the biblical story

21

foreshortened, if the grace in general human experience were sufficient to overcome the powers of sin, error, suffering, and death. Necessary it is, but not sufficient; for the chapters from Exodus to Easter tell us of a need for the subsequent decisive moves of a gracious God.

The world, with its factuality and its sturdy but slender graces, lies on the circumference of the circles of authority. Its "signs" are an *aid* to understanding. Giving the world this position acknowledges that the theology must take its setting seriously. To do so is to make a pilgrimage from setting to source to center. Here lies the role of perspective in the journey of faith.

Perspective

Rising out of our contemporary experience and reaching toward an understanding of Christ and the Gospel is our "perspective." No one is exempt from this fact of finitude; the views we hold are shaped by where we stand. Further, Christian theology must identify those aspects of contemporary experience that represent the real questions posed by that time and place and the genuine perceptions of truth that cohere with Christian faith and can enrich our understanding of it. These constitute our effort to translate the Christian faith into the language and thought forms of our time and place. Again, a properly self-critical theology will bring to light covert influences from the world about us that distort our perspective by confusing a segment of cultural opinion with the Gospel itself. And it will test carefully overt claims made by one or another current philosophical, political, psychological, biological, or aesthetic view for its faithfulness in translating the Gospel. Is "self-esteem" (Robert Schuller) the modern equivalent of justification by grace through faith? Does "liberation" equal salvation? How does the "mighty man" view of family, church, business, and government (Jerry Falwell) fit in with the cross? Can "process philosophy" do justice to the once-happenedness of redemption in Jesus Christ? Can "storytelling" as a mode of theological discourse do justice to the truth claims of Christian faith?

To answer these questions and to find a viable perspective for contemporary theology one must proceed along the angle of vision so chosen and follow a route toward the center of faith. How does a theological proposal from a stated perspective relate to the thinking and decisions of the Church universal? Is there resonance with contemporary church thought and action? More importantly, how does its claim fit with the great consensus points of classical Christian faith? If they conflict with the letter of that tradition, do they yet fit the spirit and intent and represent a possible development of doctrine along the arc of ancient teaching? To answer that latter question, and finally establish the veracity of a perspectival claim, are there clear warrants from the biblical source of faith as it bears witness to the cardinal affirmations of the Gospel and its center, Jesus Christ? A viable perspective must pass all these checkpoints in its journey inward.

And it must face them again in its journey outward. The interpretation of the Christian faith is a ceaseless task. Do the affirmations that have passed through the refining fires of ecclesial, biblical, and christological inquiry still connect with contemporary questions and perceptions? Has the proper refinement of a perspective by Scripture and tradition at the same time brought it into a new captivity to either untranslated code language of the ancient faith or past ecclesial formulations that are no longer channels for hearing the Gospel in a new setting? To find this out, the pilgrim must carry the learning from the center to the circumference again. Responsible translation must be both faithful and fruitful, a trustworthy account of the Gospel and effective communication with the world. The arrows inward and outward along the perspectival lines represent the movement here described.

Effective communication does not mean "success" in the worldly sense, for the word may often fall on deaf ears because of hardened hearts. Yet the same word never returns barren. It may reap hostility as well as commitment, but it will be heard. To return to the world is to discern that effectual encounter. To be in touch with contemporary experience is part of the perspectival movement, but not its resting place. The journey begins again to the center for definitive adjudication of all our efforts to tell the Story to our contemporaries. This descent and ascent we here set forth (one that does not always take place in such an ordered way, since there are many zigs and zags, leaps over stages, etc.) is sometimes referred to as "the hermeneutical circle." While retaining the dynamic movement suggested by the circulation between cultural fact and biblical faith, we use here the arrowhead, or perspectival wedge form, to indicate more clearly than the circle does the priorities in the translation process. The truth about ultimate issues is finally tested against source, substance, and center, the tip point of the perspective, while the personal and social meaningfulness of its translation is measured in the field of human experience. Confusion about what happens at each pole of the movement leads either to the captivity of faith by culture or the denial to faith of access to culture. As we are primarily concerned in the authority question with the correspondence of what we say to what is so, truth claims in this sense, the importance of the center as the decisive point of testing is stressed.

Distortions

We cannot leave the subject of authority without passing reference to the vulnerability of the three rings of authority. The power of each has exercised a fascination in Christian history that has lent itself to inordinate claims. The preeminence of the biblical ring has given rise to *biblicism*, which severs it from the other rings and claims it to be the sole route to the Gospel. Thus the lively presence of the Spirit in the Church and the world is denied. Correspondingly, among those impressed by the deliverances or vitalities of creed or council, bishop or preacher, charismatic or community, some emerge who insist that the Church alone is to be heard on ultimate matters. So appears *ecclesiasticism*, which either denies partnership with source and setting or calls into question the fundamental character of the community. And finally, the worldly matrix in which Christians find themselves — the opinions, current sensibilities, regnant philosophies, moral and spiritual experiences — becomes so alluring that the world defines the faith, and the Bible and Church become marginal. Thus *secularism* both disdains its companions in the quest for the truth, the Christian community and its Book, and replaces the biography of God with its own autobiography.

The elements of authority do their work in getting the Story straight when they are bound together and when each is honored for the gift it brings to the rest — a source, resource, and setting.

The form perspective has taken in the history of Christian theology has varied. It has appeared by way of a modest use of a term from the world that has resonance in the faith community — "Logos" in the early Fathers' dialogue with ancient culture, or "homoousios" to interpret the unity of Jesus with God in Nicea's statement about the meaning of Christ.

Or it may be represented by a fighting word that the Church writes on its banners in the struggles with the errors and oppressions of its time — "justification by faith" in sixteenth-century Europe, "liberation" in Latin-American countries today. Sometimes a slogan, at other times a carefully worked out set of commitments to the meaning of the Gospel for that time — they attempt to relate and even restate the Christian faith, seeking in the process to be faithful to the Christian Story. On yet a more ambitious scale, the Christian faith has been reformulated wholesale in terms of either a dominant cultural premise or a powerful philosophy or political ideology. In the former case, an Enlightenment Christianity seeks accommodation with modernity, or a secular Christianity seeks to redo the Christian Story in essentially this-worldly terms. In the latter case, the philosophy of Aristotle in the high Middle Ages or existentialism and process thought in our own day have been offered as frameworks for reinterpreting the whole of Christian faith.

One of the lessons in this variety of experimentation in perspective seems to be that the more exuberant and encompassing efforts in restatement — by either cultural premise or philosophical reformulation — carry with them a tendency to domesticate the Christian faith in the categories of the time, rendering it incapable of doing the critical work it must do vis-à-vis that time, and eroding the Story's own distinguishing features. The art of perspective therefore is to learn to *relate* but not to *capitulate* to the culture out of which that perspective grows.

Uneasiness about the tendency toward captivity to the world in the history of perspectives has prompted some to reject the need for this kind of principle of interpretation, putting in its place the assertion that all that is required is the simple setting forth of the Story from the Storybook. This is an understandable reaction to the manifest dangers of skewing faith in the interests of being understood and acceptable. However, such formal declarations of independence from cultural influence carry a hollow ring. The feeling tones, premises, and even philosophical themes of the worldly matrix in which all theology takes place still exercise an influence on those would-be escapees from the facts of theological finitude. To ignore the context simply means the importing of many unexamined assumptions from the world into theology without benefit of close scrutiny and critique. Better an examined perspective than an unexamined one. Better, too, modest relationships to cultural creativity than wholesale adaptation to the culture's fevers and philosophies, with its attendant captivity of faith.

25

What we are calling *perspective* functions as a principle of selection and organization of biblical material, formed from these materials and relating them to the tradition and contemporary experience. While it gives contemporaneity to the Bible, it is, however, *not* a canon in the sense of passing judgment on the biblical materials, being ultimately answerable to this source and norm. Perspective suggests not only the formative nature of a point of view, but also its relativity.

We turn now to our own perspective for this particular translation of the Gospel, seeking to locate modest but meaningful cultural awarenesses to which our theology must be alert. In identifying these, we make an attempt to formulate them with sensitivity to our cultural setting and accountability to the biblical source and in continuity with the churchly resource. A viable principle of interpretation will open up the Story to be found in Scripture and tradition in such a way that it may be seen by and speak to the people of this time and place.

Narrative

Already, the perspective in which basic Christian beliefs are interpreted in this book has made its appearance. The earlier discussion of "coring" characterized the standard loci as chapters in a story. "Narrative," therefore, is our way in, through setting and resource, to source, substance, and center. A perspective related to features of our contemporary context, it is also no stranger to Scripture itself. With credentials in both setting and source (in this respect it is like the durable *logos* motif), it serves well our modest effort in "dynamic equivalence" translation.

Our structuring of Christian teaching in terms of its development from creation to consummation is not an uncommon procedure in the exposition of doctrine. The statement of faith as something of a story makes an appearance in the early baptismal "rules of faith," which later grew into the ecumenical creeds, Apostles' and Nicene. In them appears the unfolding of a drama in paragraphs on creation, reconciliation, and redemption. Here are the three "missions" of the economic Trinity, about which we shall subsequently speak. The ordering of Christian teaching continues this way in many of the standard works of dogmatics. Yet the dynamism that characterizes this movement, the point-counterpoint of the action, and all that this implies about the One with whom we have to do, are easily obscured by the abstract form in which it is often presented. The doctrinal "loci" are just that, places of action in the drama.

While the storytelling theme has deep roots in the history of Christian thought, as just noted, its use in theology has been a subject of extensive discussion in recent decades. The theme of narrative has many and varied expositors in contemporary theology. To prepare for its deployment here, a survey of the main views is in order.

Types of Narrative Theology

What is a story? The answer is not so simple, for the term is employed to describe a variety of different things, from a news report to a prevarication. As literary form, story or narrative refers in the broadest sense to the account by a narrator of events and participants moving in some pattern over time and space.[3] In this inclusive sense a history book and an accident report in a newspaper are narrative. But the word "story" as it is used in theological inquiry is related to the narrower literary meaning: an account of characters and events in a plot moving over time and space through conflict toward resolution. As such, a story in its more delimited sense is to be distinguished from history and any other kind of "empirical narrative," whose essential purposes are to report discernible happenings. While no history is without its selectivity, determined by the chronicler's frame of reference, a story in the narrow sense is narration self-consciously controlled by narrator vision, in which the flow of events becomes a plot and participants become characters in a storyline marked by conflict and moving toward resolution. The set of lines on 5-8 visualizes how Christian faith is, in this elemental sense, a story.

Story by no means excludes history. The Christian recital could not exclude empirical narrative or it would cease to be Christian, for its central events presuppose hard empirical claims — Jesus did live, Jesus did die on the cross, and on that elusive boundary between empirical and transempirical reality Jesus did rise from the grave. But as story, the description of these and other events is patterned according to a larger meaning. The narrator who gives this overall signification is, finally, God, whose Purposes

---

3. A more detailed treatment of narrative theology appears in Gabriel Fackre, "Narrative Theology: An Overview," *Interpretation* 37 (October 1983): 340-52.

are dimly perceived by the seers whose accounts constitute the Scriptures. But we are ahead of ourselves, anticipating in this description of macro-story one form of narrative theology. The main point is that Christian faith is being discussed today in the context of a literary form — story in its delimited sense — with its characteristic features of tension and vision, pain and hope, movement and consummation.

Why narrative now? The climate is right, storytelling thrives in times and places where imagination, intuition, and affect assert themselves. The relative atrophy of these dimensions of selfhood in a culture dominated by modern science and technology, giving pride of place to the rationalized, cerebral, abstract, and didactic, evoked a reaction — a quest for the re-covery of the spontaneous and intuitive, and their expression in symbol, metaphor, ritual, and story. The challenge of left-brain dominance by right-brain sensitivities was given further impetus by the feminist protest against male hegemony. And television has had its impact with its barrage of instant stories.

The recovery of imagination in the work of theology must not be juxtaposed to rational inquiry and conceptual formulation. In this book, story, metaphor, and visual symbol make their appearance alongside dis-cursive exposition. Wilbur Urban, anticipating many of these modern developments in *Language and Reality,* argues for the complementarity of "symbolic truth" and the "truth of the symbol." The power of symbol and saga enables us to make our way into the Reality who meets us in a commensurate mode of engagement (symbolic truth), and the latter is the conceptual assertion of the fact, not the fiction, of the One who comes (the truth of the symbol).

Narrative theology may have had its most decisive stimulus from the drama of the times. In this case the products rather than the process of technology have their effects, in the perils of modern warfare and the promise of economic plenty. Weapons of mass destruction have come into increasing use in the twentieth century, with some now so awesome as to cause a generation to contemplate the possible end of human life on the planet. At the same time, the have-nots of the world are increasingly aware of their plight and the disparity between them and the haves, thus bringing the battle for justice alongside the struggle for peace as the twin dramas of our era. In a community of faith that has no illusions about human nature, response in kind could be expected. Thus the "conflict and victory" or "dramatic" model of atonement (Christus Victor) rising in the Nazi era and given expression by Aulén or Barth, the hope theologies of Moltmann and Schillebeeckx in the time of utopian visions, the liberation theologies in a period of raised awareness about oppression, and the peace theologies in a time of latent consciousness of the threat of nuclear war are all variations on the narrative theme of biblical faith.

Narrative theology comes in three distinct yet often overlapping forms. We shall identify these views as *canonical stories, life story,* and *community story.* Each point of view has recourse to narrative in its exposition of faith but does so within its own framework and primary set of materials. These varied perspectives on narrative correspond to the three components in the authority structure of Christian theology, to which we shall presently turn. Canonical stories focus on the biblical materials, life story on human experience, and community story on the classical Christian tradition. The use of a given context as the principal arena for narrative does not necessarily entail its primacy as theological authority, however. Canonical storytellers can employ biblical tales for their morally transformative or disclosive power, or "symbolic truth," but reject their cognitive claims, or "the truth of the symbol." Community storytellers may rely on Christian tradition for the explicit formulation of a "world-plot" but declare its final warrants to be in Scripture. An exposition of life story may hold religious biography or autobiography to be the way to communicate Christian faith today, but hold at the same time that Scripture and/or tradition constitutes the norm of Christian belief.

Theological narratology in the *canonical* mode works with the biblical text. From structuralist methods of textual analysis through the use of computers to the "new literary criticism," biblical scholars explore the nature and meaning of their narratives. Thus a canonical narratologist holds that in the Judah and Tamar tale in the Joseph drama, the adventures of Abraham and Moses, the apocalyptic scenarios in Daniel and Revelation, the parables of Jesus, and the journey to Golgotha, the truth conveyed is inseparable from the story form in which it comes to us. Some speak of disclosure, insight granted in the responsive hearing of a tale that is similar to our aesthetic experience before and with a great painting. Others point to personal transformation with its "jars" and "jolts," stressing thereby the ethical impact and reorientation effected in narrative encounter. More specifically, in canonical story each of the features of narrative is seen to embody the very character of biblical faith, the open-endedness representing the freedom of both humanity and Deity, conflict

29

and the power of negativity reflecting the foes of the divine intent, the coherences of the tales in both the Scriptures of the Hebrew people and the New Testament expressing the purposiveness of existence, the movement over time and place showing a faith inextricable from temporality and earthiness, and resolution manifesting an ultimate hope. Thus the story form takes its shape from biblical faith, and we in turn are found by that faith only as we are engaged by its narrative form.

The practitioners of theological *life story* reach beyond the biblical canon to human experience as such for their narrative materials. Attention is turned to personal story in its depth, richness, and variety, your journey and mine. While the feelings and events of individual journeys play a prominent role in this mode of narrative theology, some also point to the importance of the story of a people, the memory and retelling of which preserve its dignity and identity in the face of social and economic tyrannies.

The exposition of life story in theology maintains in practice its protean theory. One group holds autobiography as the key, the telling of one's own story in the context of therapy, in the tradition of personal testimony, in the setting of religious education, or in the combination of personal narrative and Bible study. Another view, in continuity with introspective spirituality or Kierkegaardian self-examination, stresses the exploration of one's own personal odyssey. Yet another variety finds a significant place for hearing another's story, "biographical theology"; it sees the confessions of Augustine or the life and letters of Martin Luther King, Jr., as ways of encounter with the ultimate truths of faith. The moral power of story is stressed by others, who believe that ethnic communities can preserve themselves through its mode of discourse or that the power of moral vision communicates itself best through narrative. For others, the very act of verbal storytelling, from Bible stories to personal stories, is the way to faith, hope, and love. In the coherence, concretion, surprise, tension, movement, and resolution of life narrative, God wills and works disclosure and transformation.

Canonical stories and life story are narrative in microcosm, personal and textual accounts in human scale. Our third type expands to macrostory with its cosmic scenarios. Here *community story* brings us to a kind of narrative theology in which a people identify an overarching plot reaching from Alpha to Omega, gathering up within its sweep all the particulars of canonical tale, and finding a place as well for the experiences of life story.

Indeed, the very order of the canon suggests a storyline, but only occasionally does the flow of events get set forth as such, as for example in passages that record the earliest kerygma. We have to do here with "cult-epic" — the tracing by the Christian community of the saga that brought it to be, and out of which it lives.

As noted before, the early baptismal rules of faith, by which entrance was made into this people and its singularity declared, were among the first signs of community story, preserved for us in the subsequent credal tradition. They appeared in the liturgical life of the church, and continue to be found there as a natural habitat for the metastory, as in the sparse and profound narrative of the eucharistic prayer. Also in the first efforts in dogmatic definition, as in the economic Trinity, we find the drama in capsule form reflecting the paragraphs of baptismal symbol and creed. So, too, the Story emerged in the "classic" motif of the atonement, with its dramatic character. Later, as doctrinal formulation took on greater complexity, the structure of the great narrative appeared in the traditional loci. In subsequent centuries, covenantal, salvation history, and dialectical theologies self-consciously developed the narrative trajectory. In contemporary discussion, the movement of biblical theology and its heirs and the theologies of hope and liberation work within an overarching narrative framework.

The features of narrative appear here in a macrocosmic setting. The plot is conceived in eternity itself and unfolds in history with God and the world as its principals, moving through formative and finally climactic events. Since *The Christian Story* is an exercise in this kind of narrative theology, we shall reserve further comment on the specifics of community story for the pages that follow.

As an expression of the third type, "narrative" in this book is a key part of the perspective for presenting and patterning the distinctives of Christian belief. With the other types, drama, concretion, and affect are viewed as integral to Christian faith and its appropriation. Ultimate truth is grasped in a mode commensurate with God's own way of engaging us in the maelstrom of living and dying. Its aptness is further warranted by the experience of negativity so pervasive in the late twentieth century, and thus the tandem of peril and promise integral to story. Again, a narrative interpretation of Christian doctrine that is not bound to the language of bloodless abstraction characteristic of a rationalized and technocratic society or the mass-speak of pop culture stays close to the rudiments of

31

human experience, addressing affect as well as intellect. Community story differs, however, from the other forms of narrative theology in that it seeks to do these things vis-à-vis the orientation points of historic faith. And in its systematic form it must deal with the basic propositions of Christian tradition (we shall call them "affirmations," since Christian truth claims cannot be separated from personal commitment), as well as attend to the play of imagination and the intuitions of the heart. As narrative, it cannot succumb to a heartless propositional*ism,* but as theology it cannot fall prey to mindless imagination*ism.* A collegiality of the three types of narrative theology would be mutually enriching, bringing together the power of the text, the drama of life experience, and the lore of the Christian community.

In contrast to perspectives that employ a philosophical system, a political or economic theory, or a psychological construct as the framework for interpreting faith, we understand perspective in terms of the root metaphor and dominant motifs of narratives. Allied to it are comparably modest symbols and themes.

Metaphors and Motifs

Allied to a narrative perspective, as that is here understood, are some symbols and themes that further serve the translation process. Like narrative, they are familiar to the setting, resource, and source of authority.

"Vision" is a metaphor and theme with roots in Scripture and a long history in Christian tradition.[4] It appears in the dreams and prophecies of the Old Testament — particularly the projections of future hope in the prophetic tradition — and in the New Testament — particularly

---

4. H. Richard Niebuhr associates the vision of God with the contemplative-rational-Greek tradition in Christian thought, in contrast to the prophetic-Hebrew theme of "the kingdom of God" (*The Kingdom of God in America;* New York: Harper & Bros., 1937, 20-21). While our interpretation of vision and dream here is taken from a decidedly historical usage — the vision of God *is* the Kingdom of God — and does not depend on the *visio Dei* tradition in theology and spirituality, it is interesting to note the case made by A. H. Curtis for the biblical meaning of the term *vision* (A. H. Curtis, *The Vision and Mission of Jesus;* Edinburgh: T. & T. Clark, 1954). He shows that in the Old and New Testaments the presence of vision is always conjoined to a summons and commission to action.

the future-oriented visions in Jesus' teaching about the Kingdom of God and in John's Apocalypse. And in Christian tradition, both ancient and current, it exercises its power in a variety of ways, from the *visio Dei* teaching of saints and theologians to the "I have a dream" legacy of Martin Luther King, Jr. Indeed, a narrative reading of Christian doctrine is oriented to the "Vision of God" as the future toward which the divine drama moves.

Vision and light are related metaphors in Christian tradition. Light and dark are pervasive images in the Bible as well as in theology, liturgy, and hymnody. However, its usage must be scrutinized with a sensitivity to its historic and still potential abuse. Racism has made a simple equation: light = white and dark = black. As light is good and dark is its opposite, white is identified as good and black as bad. But the praying, singing, and preaching of black churches challenge this equation. We do here as well. Light is *not* white but the full spectrum of color, and darkness is the absence of color. Ironically, white religionists of good intention strive to purge hymnody, liturgy, and theology of light/dark imagery, thus tacitly accepting the racist equation and impugning the practices of black churches.

Liberation movements and theologies have given currency to another metaphor and motif in Scripture and tradition. From Exodus to Easter, the themes of freedom and justice come to the fore. The central chapter of the Story begins with Mary's song praising the God who "has brought down the powerful from their thrones, and lifted up the lowly" (Luke 1:52 NRSV), and throughout testifies to the liberating Work of Jesus Christ (Luke 4:18; Rom. 5:8-11; Gal. 5:1; Eph. 2:16; Col. 1:20).

Through biblical lenses, the worldwide struggle against economic, political, and social tyranny is an inclusive liberation. The lowly that God exalts encompasses every disinherited race, class, sex, age, and condition. Such freedom includes as well the release of the air, the water, and the soil from their exploiters and our animal neighbors from their wanton destroyers.

As with all aids to interpretation, so with the "fighting word," liberation: cultural usage is accountable to the biblical substance and center. Liberation in the Story includes, but is not reduced to, its horizontal dimension. God liberates from sin and death, before God, as well as from evil structures and oppressive human relationships. And the way the liberation struggle is undertaken is always under the norm of Jesus Christ:

the enemy to be resisted is also to be loved and prayed for (Matt. 3:43-45). Thus the metaphors and motifs meaningful in our setting are transfigured by the Story and so serve in its translation.

"Reconciliation" is another bridge theme from source to setting and vice versa. It is at the very heart of the New Testament and classical Christian teaching as the description of Christ's saving Work (Chapter 4). At the same time, reconciliation is a life-and-death matter in human affairs. The world is imperiled by the fires that rage in and among nations, the turmoil among religions and races, the possibility of a nuclear conflagration.

The quantum leap in the technology of modern warfare that has put the future of the human race in question begins to evoke in agents of reconciliation a commensurate determination to end nuclear peril. And the crusade for ecological wholeness is another sign of the present longing for the unity of all creation. The search for wholeness can be found in inner as well as outer journeys toward peace, as in the multifarious movements to heal the divided self through a deepened spirituality. These various searchings of the spirit and organizations dedicated to change may indeed express their dreams in strident rhetoric or unacceptable ideology, but their glimpse of the horizon of wholeness cannot be gainsaid.

Reconciliation in harness with liberation, both in their fullest senses, are pointed to in the biblical vision of *Shalom* (Ezek. 34:25-39). While its meaning must appear in the actual recounting of the narrative of the deeds of God, we identify it here by our key terms. Shalom is the liberation (Luke 4:18; Gal. 5:1) and reconciliation (Rom. 5:8-11; 2 Cor. 5:18-21) of all things. It is *freedom from sin, evil, and death* and *the life together of God and the world.* Found originally in the prophetic pictures of a liberated and reconciled world, and climactically in the eschatological hopes of the New Testament, Shalom envisages the end of every bondage and the overcoming of each alienation. As such, Shalom begins with the personal, societal, and natural perceptions of liberation and reconciliation that mark our culture and transfigures them by both a deepening of the understanding of the slaveries and alienations to which they are juxtaposed and a lengthening of the vision of their resolution toward the future of God. To this end our Story presses.

Authoritative Translation

A statement of Christian faith, a translation of the Christian Story, is authoritative if it has passed the tests we have set forth. To summarize, it must be

1. rooted in the biblical source and accountable to the Gospel substance and christological norm,
2. continuous with the traditions of the Church, past and present, and
3. intelligible to those to whom it is addressed, connected to the realities of their time and place, and illuminative of their lived experience.

If a perspective leads us through the circles of authority in this fashion, its outcome will be a responsible and compelling recounting of Christian narrative. Our goal in the pages that follow is to follow this method in the exposition and interpretation of the Christian faith.

Revelation

Auhority establishes the *identity* of our faith. Implicit in this but as yet unresolved in our discussion is the question of the Story's *veracity*. The Story is not just the language that distinguishes our community from others; it is an affirmation about the way things really are. It makes truth claims. That is, God discloses through it the ultimate nature of authority. "Revelation" has to do with that deep-down state of affairs. The doctrine of revelation has to do with why we go *where* we go to discern what is so.

Any exploration of the "why" inevitably touches on some of the "what" of the matter. Form is inseparable from the content. So our talk about revelation anticipates what is believed about the agent of revelation, the Holy Spirit. The Work of the Holy Spirit in classical Christian thought includes "illumination." (Martin Luther says that the Holy Spirit "calls, gathers, enlightens and sanctifies"; the ancients speak of the spirit as giving "life and light.") Therefore when we examine the meaning of revelation as the bringing of truth about God, we are assuming that the power that furnishes this light is the Holy Spirit. Revelation is "seeing the light," the truth of the Christian Story, by the gracious action of the divine Spirit.

The subject of revelation has been hotly disputed in recent Christian thought. The word and concept were used as a key to much neoorthodox interpretation of Christian teaching in its effort to establish the validity of faith in a nontraditional or nonfundamentalist fashion. Diverse as this movement was, it was marked by

1. the assertion of the Bible as a vehicle for personal encounter with God rather than as a catalogue of theological propositions,
2. a view of God as active in history, decisively so in a line of key events chronicled in Scripture with their climax in Christ,
3. the acceptance of methods of critical scholarship in the interpretation of Scripture, and
4. recovery of many orthodox doctrines on sin and salvation, as well as the authority of Scripture in the way described.

The reinterpretation of revelation in neoorthodoxy meant, therefore, the disengagement of it from the words of Scripture as if they were protected from error of any sort, and the denial that biblical or ecclesial propositions about God or the ways of God were as such univocal divine statements. Revelation was conceived to be what God does in the events of holy history with its center point at the Incarnation, and how we are encountered and transformed by the One who in them and through them calls us to personal response.

From a narrative point of view, the neoorthodox view of revelation gives due attention to the deeds of God, although the Beginning and End are sometimes obscured in this account, and the proper focus on the particular covenants of Israel and Christ does not do sufficient justice to universal grace (the covenant with Noah). Further, neoorthodoxy understood that revelation is not disengaged information given by God to the disincarnate minds of data-gatherers, but knowledge shared by an engaged God, inextricable from the divine self-giving and receivable only by those who come with like self-involvement.

The revelational theology associated with neoorthodoxy has been subject to sharp attack. Some critics question whether the Bible conceives of revelation the way neoorthodoxy does. Others doubt the validity of the experience of personal encounter. Still others assert that neoorthodoxy ends in a morass of subjectivism because the propositional nature of revelation is denied. Yet others claim that the deeds of God are too drastically separated from the interpretation of them. And some believe that "holy history" is a scheme imposed on essentially diverse and even contradictory biblical materials. While these criticisms do not consistently strike home, enough of them do to cause us to look for another way to take account of neoorthodox insights and avoid its pitfalls.

The Pilgrimage of Revelation

The origins of revelation lie in the Godhead. The eternal Vision, as the intention of God, goes forth as the Word among us. Already the *what* of the matter enters into the questions of *why* and *where.* We shall return to this Christian teaching about the Trinity — the relation of an Envisioner to a Vision, a Speaker to a Word, a Father to a Son. For now, we affirm that the journey of the Word of disclosure takes rise from the very inner being of God. God is, by nature, self-communicating, self-giving, self-revealing.

Revelation is a story within the great Story. It is constituted by the places of disclosure along the path of God's creating and redeeming deeds. Its first chapter is a creation bathed in the divine light. An Edenic world is willed and declared as good by God, with all its participants called to "see the Light" and to love and serve one another in the light "that enlightens everyone" (John 1:9).

Chapter 2 tells of a willful world and the descent of night. How much light remains? Especially so for those given the "divine image" to mirror it? Christians disagree about the state of revelation after the fall. Is the original Vision completely lost, with no clues to God's Purposes and no power to pursue them? Perhaps the fall was not so damaging, and the image remains essentially intact, with reason and goodwill unimpaired? These are subjects and points of view to which we shall return. In this reading of the Story, the world's stumble does damage the divine image. We cannot see, in our fallen state, the true Light, nor live by its radiance. But in our prone position, we can still glimpse its reflections.

The rainbow sign of Noah's covenant is a vivid image in Scripture, portraying the divine persistence in the face of the world's rebellion (Gen. 9:8-17). The full radiance of the sun must await another day, but God gives a rainbow sign, the promise of enough light to sustain the world in its fallen state, and to point it toward a better day to come. Under this arch, humanity can still see indications of what it takes to make and keep life livable (Gen. 9:6). So God keeps the Story going forward, preparing it for decisive deeds of deliverance and disclosure.

Earlier theologies have called these fragmentary clues to God's Purposes in a broken world "general revelation," and the universal power that sustains them, "common grace." Indeed, one of the meanings of Providence is the divine watchcare of the world after the fall. Here we understand these varied themes — general revelation, common grace, Providence — narratively, as the beginning of a covenant chapter in the Christian Story, the "covenant with Noah."

The universal Noachic grace of God is the revelatory warrant for the "setting" in our structure of authority. Human experience, as such, cannot be the organ of revelation. Our human powers are in thrall to the No! we have said to God's original Vision. We do not want to know who God is, who we are, and where we are called to go. This is the "bondage of the will" of which we shall subsequently speak. While human experience cannot be the source of authority, its subsidiary role as setting is made possible by a common grace, a modest *impartation* of the Holy Spirit to those aspects of our human experience that sustain creation. Thus the gifts of the mind that enable us to think and act coherently (without agreement on a universal "law of noncontradiction" communication one with another would be incoherent) and pursue inquiry in the natural and social sciences enable human life to go forward. The gifts of moral discernment, including movements of social and personal challenge and change, make and keep life human. The gifts of the heart in poetry, music, and literature open up vistas to the future without which life would be impoverished. So Providence sustains us, prepares us, and with all the manifest incompleteness of these gifts does make our minds, moral sense, and hearts restless for the chapters of the Story yet to be.

The covenant chapter on revelation only begins with the Noachic rainbow. Yet to come is a "pillar of fire" (Exod. 13:21) with its *special* leading of a particular people, and with that the beginnings of "special revelation." In this mysterious particularity God chose to show a people the way toward Shalom. In the push and pull of Israel's community life — the initial journey of Abraham and Sarah, the liberation from Egyptian bondage, the giving of the Law, the raising up of prophets, the ministrations of priests and kings, the wisdom of sages, the powers of faithful women — an "election" took place and a disclosure was made. The writings that grew out of these engagements are the Scriptures of the Hebrew people, now the "Old Testament" of the Christian community.

We have this treasure in earthen vessels. Our text is an assembly of national chronicle, cosmic saga, personal story, song, prayer, wise saying, catalogue of moral mandates and ritual code, prophetic vision, and apocalyptic expectation. How can these varied genres attached to social need and personal agenda, which have come to us over a long traditioning process in which fragments were assembled by an editor here and a redactor there into respective wholes and finally the canon of the Hebrew Bible, be "revelation"? To say that this is so is to believe that the power of God, the Holy Spirit, has broken through the clouds of human ignorance and given those responsible for this lore a glimpse of ultimate light. "Those responsible" are the authors individually, and collectively as well, for the fuller meaning of a biblical assertion can often be grasped only when it is situated in the environment of the whole Bible, in this case the New Testament as well as the Old. Those who are so granted a vista on the truth are, therefore, "seers." The gift of the Holy Spirit opens their inner eye, and their capacity to see and say what they see becomes "in-Spirited," inspired. This "prophetic" testimony of the Old Testament visionary, together with the apostolic testimony of the New Testament about which we shall presently speak, constitutes the divine inspiration of Scripture.

As words are inseparable from ideas in great literature, so the vivid language of the Bible is integral to its powers of disclosure. In this sense, biblical inspiration is verbal, and all theology must return to the code language of its charter. Because the Holy Spirit honors the earthen vessel and does not seek to make it a golden casket, verbal inspiration does not mean divine dictation, or a mechanical protection of each sentence from flaws. What Old Testament seers had to say about the relation of the sun to the earth, the sequences of personal events and social history, the recommended stoning of blasphemers, or *sheol* as our destiny after death are all marks of its earthiness. However, these judgments in science and history, morals and theology, that cannot be accepted literally are still part of a record in which the Vision is seen, even in these dimly lit pages, to whatever degree each statement illumines the substance of the Good News and coheres with its norm.

Because the thirty-nine books of the Hebrew Bible are part of a drama in the making, their revelatory significance lies beyond them. Yet these writings provide the necessary horizon for grasping the meaning of what is to come. As Christians make a place in their faith for the Old Testament, they read it with the eyes of expectation, raising questions yet to be answered, hoping for someone and something yet to come. But who and what the significance of the latter is can be grasped only in the light of the prophetic seer who transmits the visions gained from this stage of the narrative. Let us follow its trajectory and see how the New both fulfills the promise of the Old and is at the same time filled out by it.

The spark and pillar become the presence of Light. The Vision becomes a Word that takes flesh and dwells among us. The powers of darkness here meet their match. The eternal Sun of God shines in Jesus Christ and the everlasting glory is made known. In the life, death, and resurrection of Christ, the Purposer discloses the Purpose by the ultimate Power — Father, Son, and Holy Spirit. Revelation at this definitive point in the outworking of salvation is Jesus Christ, the Logos — the Word saying it, the Vision showing it.

Who he is in our history is unveiled in the figure of Jesus — what he was and said in his Galilean career and what happened to him in his death and resurrection. But more, the risen and ascended Lord continues to disclose the truth as he moved the minds and hearts of the apostolic community after Easter. As we have the record of God's dealings with Israel by the Work of the Spirit in the *prophetic* seer, so we have the account of God's indwelling in Christ and its issue in the testimony of the *apostolic* seer.

Here then is the *new* testimony, attestation, testament to the way things are and shall be. In these twenty-seven books the apostle tells us the Good News that the Purpose of God has won his way in the world. Their newly sighted eyes see what God is doing in the life, death, and resurrection of Christ to defeat the powers of sin, evil, and death. And their eyes of faith are opened, in every sense of the word, to see the meaning of these events, conveying to us the whys and wherefores as well as the whats. In all the disclosures made to them, and through them, the Light of God illumines the outer event and its inner significance. As the luminous center of the revelatory process, Jesus Christ is what he says and says what he is. The developing narrative with its direction and outcome now becomes the *Gospel,* a promise fulfilled and a consummation assured. "Christ has died. Christ is risen. Christ will come again!"

The revelatory process continues to make its way from the divine source through the biblical event and inspired seer to the believing receiver. The Christian community is given its own pentecostal tongues of fire to light up the landscape, enabling it to glimpse the truth and tell its Story. The Holy Spirit so gives the gift of *illumination* to the believing community, sight into the Vision of God — *insight.* Neither the ultimate sight, the one that comes only with the rising of the final sun and the passing of all the clouds of sin, evil, and death, nor the eyewitness vision of the biblical seer, this insight of faith is partial and clouded, seen "through a glass darkly" (1 Cor. 13:12 KJV). It admits enough light, however, to make the journey of faith.

The illumination of the community of faith happens along the path of its pilgrimage through time and place. Thus the Light is perceived from different angles of vision, and the illumination provides new perspectives on the old story. The community's way of translating the ancient tale is commensurate with the varied locations through which it passes. And further, the community's understanding is enriched as it widens and lengthens its viewpoint. So the portrayal of what is seen in each generation builds a storehouse of wisdom, a dictionary of root metaphors, a body of theological meanings, which constitute the tradition of the Church. This harvest of perspectives does *not* give us a series of new revelations, but rather new *perceptions* of the one definitive revelation. That is, God's special deeds in Israel climaxing in Jesus Christ as these are interpreted by prophetic and apostolic witness illumine the Church, and its traditions are the result of that illumination.

The end point of revelation is the final disclosure when God is all in all and insight becomes sight. In this movement from grace to glory, the scales of finitude and sin fall from our eyes and we meet "face to face" (1 Cor. 13:12). Here is the *visio Dei,* when "the pure in heart . . . see God."

The sweep of the revelatory process that is the linear counterpart to the circular authority structure described earlier can be visualized in this way:

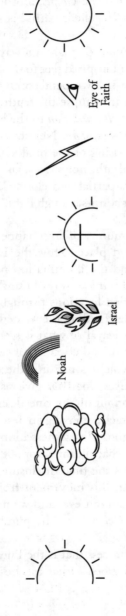

DEEDS: (narrative of reconciliation)	Creation	Fall	Covenant	Election	Christ	Church	Salvation	Consummation
DISCLOSURES: (narrative of revelation)	Intention		Preservation	Inspiration (prophetic-apostolic testimony)	Incarnation	Illumination (ecclesial and personal insight)		Illumination (eschatological sight)

Noah   Israel   Eye of Faith

GENERAL REVELATION   SPECIAL REVELATION

The Way to Insight

Illumination has its personal as well as ecclesial side. The receiving of revelation is not only the corporate making of tradition, but also the singling-out ray of Light that opens the eye of faith. This individuating insight comes by the same route as that just reviewed. Special revelation is a process, not a product. Its origins lie in Deity, and its issue is constituted by the acts of God in pursuit of the Purpose of God, and the perception and transmission of them by visionaries. Its end point is insight, sight into the primal Vision by the eye of faith. Like its analog from the aesthetic or intellectual sphere, the special insight of the Spirit is marked by a eureka experience. This connection, this Yes! that erupts in the encounter with any profound truth cannot be programmed, arranged, manipulated. In wider human experience it is recognized as an event that mysteriously happens when circumstances are right. Indeed, one may arrange the conditions, but the insight takes place "out of the blue." Either you see it or you don't. In the insight of revelation the comparable affirmation is couched in the language of grace. Insight comes as an unearned gift, "by the grace of God." Put another way, insight as truth in the sense of illumination, the Christian eureka experience, is the Spirit's self-authentication. The grace of insight is prevenient: it is not manufacturable or manipulable by us, but goes before us. The Holy Spirit blows where it will (John 3:8).

Yet there is an environment in which the process of revelation is known regularly to take place, a time in which the Spirit promises to be present. Preparations can be made for its arrival. When we ask what that is, we are called back to the orbs of authority: the Bible, the Church, the world. It is in the Bible, within the Church, as it is immersed in the world, that the Holy Spirit pours out light and power. In our familiar pilgrim image, when we are on the road (in the world) traveling in the pilgrim band of the Christian community (in the Church), consulting the map (searching the Scriptures), we are positioned to receive Light on our path.

The Cone of Disclosure

The doctrine of revelation is the basis for the concept of authority. The Work of the Holy Spirit is *why* the rings of authority are *where* they are and *how* they are interpreted in relation to one another. To visualize the revelatory underpinnings of the places and relations of authority, we can turn the concentric rings on their side and view them as a cone. Continuing the light imagery: the eye of faith "sees the Light" of truth as it is pressed to the revelatory scope. The cone that directs it to its proper end is made of materials shaped by the power of the Holy Spirit according to their proximity to the Light: the biblical source, substance and center, the ecclesial resource and guide, the worldly setting and aid.

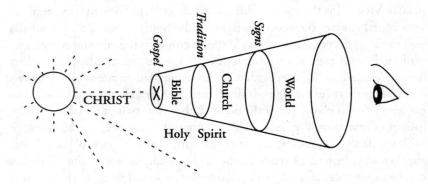

What is the role in the revelatory process of the Christian doctrines to be explored in this systematics? As part of the present tradition of the Church, they constitute a "guide" to the faithful, "guidelines" in the circles of authority and cone of revelation. To the extent that they are *derived from* the biblical source, *expressions of* its substance and *in accord with* its center, *continuous with* the trajectory of the Church's classical tradition, and *intelligible to* the world in which we live, they can be a "glass of vision" (Austin Farrer) that directs our eye to its goal. Whether they are *revealing* truths transparent to the Light — "for us" as a Christian community put by God in a given time and place, or "for me" in my own "seeing the Light" — depends on the mysterious Work of the Holy Spirit. Making for further doctrinal modesty, Scripture teaches that all such "*in*sight" granted to us in this world is still "seeing through a glass darkly" (1 Cor. 12:13 KJV). Only in the final eschatological radiance is all disclosed, and we see "face to face" (1 Cor. 12:13).

The pilgrimage of revelation? With its origins in the inner being of the God in whom there "is no shadow or turning," the divine Light is shed on a creation and is rebuffed by a world enamored of night. God does not give up on us, setting a "bow in the clouds," a sign of the gifts of common grace, then opening the eyes of a chosen people to the sights of Shalom, then entering our very world as the Vision and Word made flesh, then inspiring a company of prophetic and apostolic seers to witness to the saving deeds of God, then illumining a community of believers to receive and interpret ever anew what has been seen and said, and finally promising a great day when all the shadows pass and God will be "all in all."

Until the coming of day, Paul's hope for the church at Ephesus is also our plea: "I pray that the God of our Lord Jesus Christ, the all-glorious Father, may give you the spiritual powers of wisdom and vision, by which there comes the knowledge of him. I pray that your inward eyes may be illumined, so that you may know what is the hope to which he calls you . . ." (Eph. 1:17-18).

Prologue: God

The Christian Story of what God does rises out of who God is. Yet what we know about who God is comes from what God does. The "ontology" — the being of God — is grounded in the "epistemology" — the knowing of God — from the divine deeds done among us. So we must anticipate some of the drama of the *knowing* (the Story ahead) to speak in this Prologue about the *being* of God.

The central act in the great Story is *Jesus Christ*. The opening chapter of the Gospel of John (itself a "prologue") puts all this tersely:

> In the beginning was the Word, and the Word was with God, and the Word was God. . . . And the Word became flesh and lived among us, and we have seen his glory as of a father's only son, full of grace and truth. (John 1:1, 14 NRSV)

The "Word" spoken to us in Christ tells us about the Word *in* God — the Word *as* God, related so intimately to Another as a "father" to an "only son." Here we have the outlines of the remarkable, mysterious, and fundamental Christian teaching about God called "the Trinity" — "Father, Son, and Holy Spirit." While the Bible contains few references to these names so associated (Matt. 28:18-20; 2 Cor. 13:14), and no simple statement of the Trinity on its surface, the "deep structure" of Scripture discloses to Christian eyes a doctrine of the Trinity.

The full meaning of the Trinity becomes clear *after* the Story is told. As noted, who God *is* depends on the knowledge of all that God *does* in the unfolding drama. So we shall return to the doctrine of God in the

46

Epilogue. However, to launch the narrative, to understand the "plan" (Eph 1:10) and "purpose" pursued in it, a basic truth about God as revealed in Christ must be identified. That trinitarian truth is the Life Together that God *is,* disclosed in the Life Together that Jesus Christ *was.* Jesus Christ *preached and taught* the coming Reign of God as the *Shalom* of a creation ruptured by sin, *embodied* it in his ministry, and *overcame* the final obstacles to it in his death and resurrection. The characters that appear throughout this story within the Story are "Abba," "Son," and "Holy Spirit" in the very oneness that is manifested in Christ's words and deeds. Christ is "our peace" (Eph. 2:14). So the Word comes to us in Christ that God *is* Peace, Shalom, the oneness of Father, Son, and Holy Spirit.

Can we do a modest dynamic equivalence interpretation of the trinitarian God who from "the beginning" had a "Word"? The Greek term *logos,* appearing in the Gospel of John as "word," had over thirteen hundred meanings in the ancient world. Some of them suggest equivalents that fit well with our narrative translation of Christian doctrine. Common to its usage in many philosophies and religions of the ancient Mediterranean world is the meaning of an architect's plan for the universe, a design that holds all things together. Christian theologians of the early centuries made use of this concept in their teaching that Christ is the eternal "reason" or "word" of God, become incarnate in Jesus of Nazareth. Alongside these connections made with Greek and Oriental thought was a tradition within Judaism that spoke of Wisdom and Word as connected with God. Some biblical scholars believe that this Hebrew theme may be present in John's use of the word *logos* to interpret Jesus Christ.

Against the background of these variations on the theme of *logos* as architect's design, reason, wisdom, the words from Ephesians take on special meaning. The writer declares that God, "with all wisdom and insight . . . made known the mystery of his will . . . set forth in Christ," having "a plan for the fullness of time, to gather up all things in him, things in heaven and on earth" (Eph. 1:9, 10 NRSV). Similarly, Paul speaks of "God's hidden wisdom, his secret purpose framed from the very beginning to bring us to full glory" (1 Cor. 2:7 NRSV). Thus God had an eternal Plan, an eternal Purpose. God "had . . . a Dream," a Vision. The prologue of the Story, therefore, is the *forevision* as well as the foreword of God. Athanasius, challenging Arius at the Council of Nicea, declared that there never was a time when the Word was not, so we may say there never was a time when the Plan, the Purpose, the Vision was not. God: the

Purposer (Father) with a Purpose (Son), and the Power (the Holy Spirit) to fulfill it. God: the Envisioner, with a Vision and the Power to pursue it to the end.

The Word, Purpose, Plan, Hope, Vision of God — as made manifest in Jesus Christ — is the *freedom* from the powers of sin, evil, and death that makes possible *peace* with God, neighbor, and nature. Jesus Christ is the source of our *liberation* and *reconciliation.* Christ is the *Light* that ends the *night.* So is revealed to the eye of faith in Christ the God who is free . . . to be Together. The Trinity — Persons so freely open to One Another that we have to do with God the Three-in-One. The doing of Christ discloses the being of God, a trinitarian Life Together. God is not just a "loving" Person; God *is* Love (1 John 4:8), three Persons so "coinherent" — so intimate with one another that the Three *are* One. The early church teachers described the social nature of God as the *perichoresis* of the Persons, their mutual inhering and interpenetration, a Unity-in-Plurality.

God, as three free Persons in perichoretic Unity, wills a world in kind. What God is in the divine nature is what God purposes, plans, intends in a derivative fashion for creation. The "vision of God" so understood is "the hope of glory" (Col. 1:27). The inner eye of God is fixed on the future, the *doxa,* the "glory of God." As the "secret purpose" and "depths of God's own nature" (1 Cor. 2:10), this Hope, this "glory of the Father," is the eternal Son of God. He is the "Wisdom from on high" of the hymn writer, the "image of the invisible God" and the "brightness of his glory" of Scripture. The biblical seer shares this vision of the future because of discerning "the glory of God in the face of Jesus Christ" (2 Cor. 4:6). The Nazarene radiates the eternal splendor, "God of God, Light of Light, very God of very God" (Nicene Creed). In the Story, our chief end is to glorify God by living toward and moving in that lucent reality. The pursuit of that Purpose is the Story that unfolds.

Christian teaching about *election* is to be understood in the framework of these themes of forevision. In the widest sense, divine election means the eternal decision to fulfill the "secret purpose" at whatever cost. What God foreknows, God also foreordains (Rom. 8:29-30). Hence the assurance that in everything God works toward that good end (Rom. 8:28). Election is first and foremost eschatological, the unbreakable promise that nothing can separate us from the fulfillment of the divine purpose (Rom. 8:35-39). What of election in the narrower sense, the predestination of particular individuals? How are "God's elect" related to the overall consummation (Rom. 8:33)? In a narrative account of Christian faith the discussion of this is best done retrospectively, with data drawn from the drama itself and the character manifest therein of the God who acts in it. We shall reserve the discussion of particular election for a final analysis of the divine attributes.

The Power of the Purpose

There are fanciful visions just as there are empty words — fantasies that are out of touch with reality, dreams with no hope of becoming fact. God "has a dream," but is no "dreamer." God has the *power* to fulfill the divine Purpose. As the Son is the Wisdom of God, so the Holy Spirit is the Power of God. The Holy Spirit is that busy active presence that connects dream to reality and finally brings them to a point of convergence. The Holy Spirit of God is the Power of God to achieve the eternal Hope.

To speak of the power of God in our prologue is to be reminded that many of the discussions of the nature of God begin with an abstract analysis of the divine perfections and attributes: omnipotence, omniscience, omnipresence, and so on. Not infrequently the exciting story of the history of God gets tuned out by those who cannot get past these abstruse descriptions. But also a fundamental error can be made. Whatever we say about God, the central character of the Christian Story, must be drawn first and foremost from the central event in that epic, Jesus Christ. We do not know the depths of God from general experience, whatever intimations of the divine are to be found there. That stream is too clouded by our own sin and finitude for us to see the bottom. The purpose of God is disclosed in key happenings. And from that same revelation we learn as well the meaning of the power of God. The notion of omnipotence itself, which we get from our general experience outside of that disclosure, contributes to the tendency to interpret the divine power as the ultimate extension of constraint as we know it. God is indeed all-powerful. But the *what* and *how* of that power are redefined by the death and resurrection of Christ. We shall return to this when examining "theodicy," the question of how we hold together a belief in the power of God, the love of God, and the reality of evil. God's power *is* all-sufficient, the power needed to fulfill the divine purpose. But the way it is exercised does not conform to our human expectations.

Analogies for the Trinity

Christian thought about the Trinity has returned again and again to two kinds of analogies, psychological and social. We have already had recourse to them.

Saint Augustine in *De Trinitate* made active use of psychological figures for interpreting the Trinity, such as Memory, Understanding, and Will. Saint John of Damascus spoke of "Intellect, Word, and Breath." Here we have made reference to "Purposer, Purpose, and Power" and to "Envisioner, Vision, and Power." The strength of these analogies is their preservation of the unity of God as One, with memory, understanding, and will, purpose, vision, and power. The Trinity cannot be mistaken for a club of separate selves. The psychological analogy warns us away from polytheism — "tritheism." It is supported by the translation of the Greek term for person *(hypostasis)* as "subsistence," a persisting identity. Some of the traditional symbols for the Trinity make that clearer than our words do, for example, the triangle △ or the trefoil ♣. And, of course, in the life for worship, we instinctively relate to God as the One with whom we have to do, rather than addressing our prayers to a group, or referring to God as they.

For all that, there has arisen another image of the Trinity that is *social* rather than *psychological,* stressing the threefoldness rather than the oneness. The translation of the term *hypostasis* as *person,* and the appearance in Scripture of Father, Son, and Spirit as centers of action and interrelationship formed a community understanding of the Trinity. The richness of that life and communication is captured in the social metaphor, as for example the Father's relations of "filiation" and "spiration" to Son and Spirit in their inner-trinitarian life. Sociality is the presupposition of the Incarnation, the coming of a Son, united with yet distinguishable from the Father, very personal familial imagery describing the eternal being of God. The personal action of the Spirit also reinforces the social metaphor (1 Pet. 1:12; John 16:13-15; Rom. 8:27). And from the patristic period to some contemporary exegesis the pronoun "us" (as in Gen. 1:26 and 11:7) is cited as an argument for the divine intersubjectivity. Jürgen Moltmann has shown the political significance of the conception of God as a divine society. Alongside the triangle and trefoil is to be placed the triquerta ⧓ .

The concept of "social Trinity" is an important corrective to the tendency of the psychological analogy to exhaust the meaning of the triune God, or to allow a too-simple concept of analogy to control theological understanding. The attribution of qualities from our plane to God is never a direct crossover, but entails a baptism and transformation. God as both one and three has no equivalence in human experience.

While the social analogy, pointing to the three eternal Persons that God *is*, relativizes the use of the psychological figure, it also can be taken too literally, leading into tritheism, and must be relativized. There is no human experience like God's unique threeness that is *also* a oneness. Historically, western Christendom has tended to give precedence to the psychological and eastern Christendom has favored the social. Each needs the other for correction and complementarity.

The theme of *perichoresis* earlier noted is an important linkage between the plurality of the social analogy and the unity of the psychological one. The mutual interpenetration of the three Persons assures the oneness of God and at the same time affirms the threeness. But, again, it is a way of saying something for which we have no human experience and thus witnesses to the mystery God is, a Sovereignty that eludes all our feeble attempts at control.

Both analogies are used for *who* God is, insofar as we can hint at that fundamental identity. We have been speaking haltingly, therefore, about the very inner being of God. Being God as Father, Son, and Holy Spirit means having internal relations, those suggested by the two kinds of analogy. This inner life of God is called, in Christian theology, the "immanent Trinity" or the "ontological Trinity." And, in our perspective here, these inner relations put us on a narrative trail. God's inner being as social, as Community — Life Together — sets the Story on its course toward the divine promise and quest for the world's corresponding community in the Reign of God. God as "psychological" — the Purposer — hopes for and presses toward a liberated and reconciled creation that reflects the inner freedom and peace of God.

The Missions of God

In the trinitarian theology of the Church, the "economic Trinity" keeps company with the immanent Trinity. The former represents the *economy* of God, the outworking in our midst of the divine plan, the external "missions" of the internal Persons. Appropriate to the Father (the ancient teaching of "appropriations") is the mission of creating; appropriate to the

Son is the mission of reconciling; appropriate to the Spirit is the mission of sanctifying. The economy, therefore, is the story. Otherwise describable, it is a drama in three great acts: creation, reconciliation, sanctification. The three Persons correspond to the three missions. But the God of the Bible is *one,* and that means *all* the Persons are involved in all the missions. God is Life Together in the economy as well as in the divine inner life. The threefold doing as well as the triune being of God is expressed in the ancient law of the Trinity (Anselm): "All the works of the Trinity are one."

Inclusivity: Humanity and Deity

In the twentieth-century freedom struggles, one after another long marginalized segment of society has fought for recognition. Colonial nations, disenfranchised races, and ethnic communities have challenged their rulers. Those oppressed for their sex, age, class, and condition have also risen to claim their dignity. So the God whose being and will is freedom and unity "brought down powerful from their thrones and lifted up the lowly" (Luke 1:52).

Language has had its place in these struggles. Those "lifted up" have declared their freedom to name themselves rather than being named by "the powerful." So the twentieth-century name changes from Negro to Black to African American, from elderly to senior citizen to elders, and so on. Heightened awareness of the justice of naming also has meant a challenge to patriarchal and androcentric language in Christian theology and elsewhere. The quest for "inclusive language" in telling the Christian Story is high on the agenda of contemporary theology. The doctrine of the Trinity as "Father, Son, and Holy Spirit" confronts us with this issue. Here we examine aspects of inclusive language that affect how we tell the Christian Story today.

The Debate

We are in the midst of a conversation — an often heated exchange — on this subject reminiscent of other controversies, some of which have taken centuries to resolve (the christological controversies). As then, so now there are many different partisans. In *The Christian Story* series, an attempt will be made to understand the variety of views on a given topic and articulate a position in the light of that examination of alternatives. The disputed question of inclusive language is an occasion to illustrate that approach in a preliminary way in this introductory volume. What follows is a description of the conversation partners on the subject of inclusivity. All lay claim to this commitment, yet have different interpretations of its meaning. The author's own view can be determined by the way language for God and humankind is used throughout this book.[1]

An Inclusive Language Spectrum

1. Human Inclusivity

The most conservative view focuses on removal of all male-gendered English language for the human race. Thus "man," "mankind," "brother," "brotherhood," "son," and the like are eliminated and replaced by "humanity," "humankind," "people," "persons," "others," "brothers and sisters," "sons and daughters," and so on. "He" and "she" are sometimes used alternately in reference to humankind, and inherited titles are altered — "chairman" to "chairperson," "mailman" to "mail carrier," for example. These are changes widely accepted in mainline churches and often required by religious publications' writing guidelines. The New Revised Standard Version Bible follows this usage.

In spite of its established place in many church circles and in academia, gender-inclusive language for humanity has yet to take hold in significant reaches of both religious and secular communities. "Man" and "mankind" are still standard fare in the national media and in many local churches.

The warrant given for change is justice for women, with precedents in the language alterations of other struggles for human dignity, such as "colored" to "Negro" to "Black" to "African American." "Man," considered in former times as a generic term for the human race, is a child of patriarchy. With our raised awareness of the latter's imperial history, it cannot be heard as other than exclusivist.

---

1. The material for this section is taken from Fackre, "Ways of Inclusivity: The Language Debate," *Prism* 9, no. 1 (Spring 1994): 52-65. For extensive endnotes that document each position, see that article at 61-65.

2. Language for God: Reinterpretation

This version of inclusivity acknowledges that traditional masculine language for deity has reinforced male hegemony. Changes must be made. But they have to do with the *interpretation* of the inherited language, not the alteration of it. Reinterpretation entails recovery of the *intended* meanings of the ancient terms, meanings that are held to challenge rather than endorse the patriarchy of the host culture.

The argument for reinterpretive inclusivity is a variation on a common theme: the true understanding of such words as "Father" or "Son" comes from the biblical story/the canon/Jesus' "Abba" language for God/ the narrative of Christ/the nature of deity as defined by the cross/the historic discourse about God in the Christian community, *rather than* extrapolation from human experience, past or present. Positions further along the present spectrum are criticized with linguistic, historical, sociological, theological, and biblical arguments. Thus the identity of God so rendered in the biblical context is not the domineering figure of patriarchal culture but one embodying the coequality and reciprocity of Persons within the Trinity, or the divine vulnerability, or maternal sensibility, or partnership, or liberating purpose. With linkages to Barth's argument for the "analogy of faith" rather than "analogy of being," supporters of this view maintain that the Christian God named "Father" shatters all our assumptions about human fatherhood, providing a revelatory critique of, and model for, human fathers. Considering this, the witness to inclusivity is made by emptying the traditional language of its cultural/patriarchal associations and replacing it with biblical content.

The theological argument may also be supported by learnings from a school of cultural anthropology or language theory. On these grounds, as well as theological ones, protagonists retain the given language for deity.

3. Biblical Addition

The next view holds the foregoing standpoints to be short of linguistic inclusion. Moving beyond them entails an active search for transmasculine gender symbols that can balance inherited terminology. The given language for God is not altered by adherents of this position in sacred texts or sacrosanct traditions ("God," "Father," "Father, Son, and Holy Spirit," "Lord"). Advocates assert the need for the *addition* of other imagery for

God from those same sources, characterizing their position as employing "the lead rather than the eraser end of the pencil." The expansion of the range of images is held to relativize the dominant masculine imagery for deity.

The search for feminine and inclusive images for God in Scripture is a key aspect of this program. For the most part, discoveries are recognized to be similes, in which God is "like," or acts "as if," the analog. Figures of speech include a housekeeper seeking a lost coin, the womb-love of a mother, a woman in travail, a birthing mother, a nursing mother, a marriage partner, a she-bear, a mother hen, a mother bird, a female pelican, a yeast-and-flour mixer, friend, gardener, potter, helper, healer, shepherd, deliverer, Holy One, *shekinah,* and Sophia/Wisdom. Nonhuman biblical metaphors for God are also encouraged: fire, rock, bread, way, truth, life, light, living water, lamb, vine. Texts cited for these various biblical enlargements include Exodus 19:4; Numbers 11:12; Deuteronomy 32:11; 18; Job 38:3-9, 29; Psalm 17:8; 22:1; 9–10; 91:4; 131:2; Proverbs 1:20-33 and passim, especially 3:19; 4:13; 8:1-36; 9:1-6; Isaiah 42:14; 46:3-4; 49:15, 16; 66:13; Jeremiah 3:4, 31; 20; Hosea 13:8; Matthew 23:37; Luke 11:5-10; John 15:1, 15.

Institutional struggles for parity, particularly the ordination of women and their achievement of leadership roles in the church, are very much part of the goal of expanding the range of inclusive symbols. When women appear in heretofore male preserves of power, especially the pastoral office, the existing male language for God is resituated in a manner similar to the enlargement of the vocabulary pool for church leadership.

View 3, as in the case of views 1 and 2, may be incorporated into positions further along the spectrum. However, it is treated here as an option on the earlier end of inclusivity, often found among self-defined "evangelical feminists," or among women and men who believe it is necessary to work with the language of Scripture or the historic formulas or images of their tradition.

4. Subtraction and Replacement

A fourth view holds the foregoing three to be short of inclusivity because they do not put to the fore the active alteration in *current* usage of male-gendered language for God. The inherited language for God is maintained, however, in selected authoritative texts (Scripture) or in prescribed liturgies or formularies — eucharist, baptism, the Lord's Prayer, and the like. For many, the retention of the baptismal formula is a critical line drawn for either ecumenical or ecclesial or theological reasons, with the rejection of the language of a functional Trinity as in "Creator, Redeemer, and Sustainer" for baptism. In preaching, teaching, personal prayer, and public worship, however, manifestly masculine language is eliminated and other *standard* terms for deity are substituted. The specifics of this position include:

- With the biblical and liturgical exceptions noted, the word and name "God" is substituted for "Father" when the latter is used for either God as such or for the first Person of the Trinity; another biblical term for deity is found, such as "Holy One"; the familiar transliteration of the names for deity in the biblical languages is used — "Abba," "Yahweh," "Adonai," "Elohim."
- The divinity of Jesus Christ as "Son of the Father" or "Son of God" is expressed by substituting "Christ" or "Jesus" or another title for masculine usages. The male sex of Jesus' human nature is often acknowledged and the associated pronoun "he" accepted in references to Jesus' humanity.
- Male pronouns for deity are eliminated, either by changing the grammar and sentence structure, using alternative terms such as "Deity," "divine Being," "divine Purpose," and such, or by substituting "God" for all pronouns for deity.
- The interpretive reference to God as divine "Parent" is employed.
- Beyond that, neologisms such as "Godself" in the place of "himself," are coined.

5. Collateral Subtraction and Replacement

Sometimes associated with this view, but often espoused by those who want to go beyond it, is the elimination of kindred terms or names that are seen to reflect and support androcentrism, hierarchy, or the demeaning and exclusion of people of color, disability/different ability, or lifestyle. In its most moderate form, the collateral view seeks to eliminate from current discourse such biblical terms as "king" and its derivative "kingdom of God," making use of the substitutes "sovereign" and "reign" or "rule" of God. More aggressive moves include the excision of any ascendancy figures from language and hymnody, such as the removal of "descend to us this day" from "O Little Town of Bethlehem."

Further along the spectrum is the removal of the title and name "Lord" either for God as such or for Jesus Christ. "Lord" is seen as the embodiment of both patriarchal and hierarchical assumptions at the center of the inherited language tradition.

Collaterality includes also the removal in personal and public practice — preaching, teaching, prayer, hymnody — of other biblical and historic terms judged to be demeaning to any other group. For example, the almost universal usage of "dark" as bad and "light" as good is held to be offensive to people of color.

6. Extracanonical Addition

Advocates of this view endorse many of the previous proposals, but hold that a consistent inclusivity requires further linguistic moves. These entail departure from familiar usage by adding noncanonical feminine-gendered terms and titles to the inherited language for deity. Considerations of euphony also enter, as in the repetition of "God" in the place of pronouns or the awkwardness of such neologisms as "Godself." Also taken into account is the issue of lost intimacy by the limitation of language for deity to abstract terms. Proposed, therefore, is the use of "Mother" as well as "Father," often with the accompanying uses of "she" and "he." Some scriptural bases are cited, as in the Wisdom traditions; but precedents, where drawn on, are more often from medieval piety or in broad Christian-related traditions — as explored in Caroline Walker Bynum's *Jesus As Mother* and found in the spirituality of Julian of Norwich) — or in the Mother-Father language of Mary Baker Eddy and early Gnostic spirituality at the edges of the tradition, as investigated in the studies of Elaine Pagels.

Usage of this sort may be confined to personal practice. It also can be found in corporate form, as in *An Inclusive Language Lectionary*, published by *the National Council of Churches*. The location of this position at a more advanced point on our scale is reflected in the amount of controversy within mainline churches surrounding the NCC lectionary, its critics including exponents of views 1 through 5 as well as those opposed to any changes.

7. Baptismal Language Revision

Because the Trinity is a basic Christian conviction and the traditional language for it — "Father, Son, and Holy Spirit" — is so universal, especially in the rite of Christian initiation, protagonists of view 7 hold the removal of this formula from worship and baptism to be at the heart of the struggle for inclusivity. While reinterpreters (view 2) may argue that the biblical "Father" has its own countercultural meaning, proponents here maintain that women with negative experiences of fatherhood are prevented from receiving the message of the divine love because of these human associations. The growing awareness of the extent of child abuse by fathers underscores for them the need to purge liturgical and sacramental language from any remnants of paternal imagery.

Regarding baptism, proposals by the lead-end-of-the-pencil advocates (view 3) that retain but enlarge the classical formula (such as "I baptize you in the name of the Father, the Son, and the Holy Spirit, Mother of all" or "I baptize you in the name of the Father of motherly love, the Son, the only child of God, and the Holy Spirit, our nurturer") are rejected as perpetuating offensive language. Alternative proposals range from the substitution of "Creator, Redeemer, and Sanctifier" or "God, Christ, and the Holy Spirit" to new question-and-answer liturgical formulations for the baptismal rite.

8. Doctrinal Revision

Linguistic change merges into doctrinal revision in the eighth view. Here inclusivity requires the elimination not just of language, but of classical symbols and teachings, ones that are seen to imply or sanction the abuse or subservience of women or other victims. The central Christian symbol of the cross, its associated theory of the atonement, and implied ethics of self-sacrifice are rejected on the following grounds:

- The revered status of the cross signals the legitimacy of victimhood and endorses violence and blood.
- The traditional teaching of the atonement is a case of divine "child abuse," in which an angry Father punishes an innocent Son. As such, it legitimates the practice of parental child abuse.
- The teaching that Jesus passively accepted suffering translates into an ethics of subservient self-sacrifice in which victims are told that it is a Christian virtue to accept without complaint their abusive circumstances.

In the place of the cross, its theology, and its ethics is substituted:
- Jesus the liberator of the oppressed.

- Emphasis on the resurrection understood as in human-scale terms, such as "radical courage": "Jesus climbed out of the grave in the Garden of Gethsemane when he refused to abandon his commitment to truth even though his enemies threatened him with death."

9. Goddess Partnership

Advocates of this view ask: How can language be truly inclusive and the equality of women asserted if the *masculine* term "God" is the central word for deity?

Various alternatives to the traditional name of the biblical deity have been proposed:
- Use alternately the terms/names "God" and "Goddess."
- Juxtapose, replace, or partner "Gaia," the Greek earth goddess, or immanent earth deity, with "God."
- Invent a neologism: "God/ess," "God/She."
- Find alternative language for deity, such as "Mother Spirit."
- Parallel to the renaming of deity proper, reidentify "Jesus Christ" in language and sculpture as "Jesa Christa."

10. Goddess Primacy

Advocates of this view hold that, on the basis of their harmful androcentric history, "God" and the belief structures associated with the name and word are intrinsically harmful to women and must be rejected. In their place a new language and spirituality are needed, which can be found in the ancient goddess traditions as they are appropriated and reconstrued in the context of today's struggle for the dignity of women.

11. Deconstructing Deity

Our final view holds that belief in a deity is, as such, an endorsement of an oppressive patriarchy and androcentric hierarchicalism. Further, it evacuates from human experience, especially the experience of women, the self-affirmations and dynamisms integral to a fulfilled life. The retrieval of goddess traditions, gnostic literature, or wicca practices may also be employed, although such appropriations as these are assigned metaphorical, not ontological, weight.

Observations

The Christian search for inclusivity is a theological quest as well as an ethical one, relating historic faith to our own context. The classical teaching about the Trinity and the Person of Christ can help us make our way through some of the issues of inclusivity. So, too, can learnings from churches in the African American tradition that have gone through their own struggles for justice and inclusivity. Reading these "minutes of the last meeting" prompts some concluding observations.

1. The Trinity

As noted, classical Christianity teaches that God is a triunity — three Persons in coequal and "coinherent" unity. This doctrine of coequal Life Together is a charter for equality in both the church and the wider society, challenging subordinationism and affirming inclusivity in human conduct.

As coequal and coinherent, the eternal second Person — Christ — is "of the same substance" *(homoousios)* as the first Person, and not a creature separated from, and subordinate to, "the Father" — the teaching of Arius rejected by the Council of Nicea in the fourth century. The proposal to substitute "Creator" for "Father" in such formulas for the Trinity as "Creator, Redeemer, and Sustainer" entails the very subordinationism that is challenged by the coequality asserted in the ancient teaching. (If the first Person is creator, then the second and third Persons are "creatures," the Arian view that legitimates subordination as well as denies the deity of Christ.) While off-putting to our modern pragmatic sensibilities, this technical language was developed to make clear fundamental Christian commitments in both theology and ethics, the implications of which often take centuries to come clear. The same kind of careful thought is needed today to avoid similar missteps.

2. Person of Christ

Along with the doctrine of the Trinity, the teaching about the Person of Christ as divine and human is shared by all Christian traditions. The naming of Christ as "Lord" is a standard way of expressing one dimension of the Person, the deity of Christ. As such, the christological employment of "Lord" is deeply imbedded in both Scripture and tradition, and reflected in the commonplace confession of "Jesus Christ as Lord and Savior" for church membership.

The cultural term "lord" in ancient context refers in dictionary definition to one who is "fully authorized and has the legal power of disposal." That this meant male authority is indisputable, an assumption carried into feudal society as descriptive of a "man of high rank," still the first dictionary usage. As applied to Jesus Christ in the New Testament, the word underwent two permutations. The first was its appropriation of Old Testament usage for deity. The second was its reconstrual of divine lordship from the cruciform center of the biblical story, with anticipations in the "long-suffering God" of Israel's covenant. Thus the lordship of Christ is the *counter*cultural assertion of the power of the "crucified God." As with "God" — with its own patriarchal origins — so with "Lord," the imperial invulnerabilities of the cultural deity are put radically in question. It is no accident that "Jesus is Lord" became the church's first confession, juxtaposed to the then-current demand for allegiance to "Caesar as lord." The counterconfession that "Christ is Lord" has since been a challenge to all human pretenders to sovereignty.

Situated in our own context, the historic understanding of Christ as Lord confronts all current claims to human hegemony. If Christ is Lord, no one else can occupy that place — no sex, class, race, nation. Classical Christology stands against every tyrant and victimizer.

3. Worship Patterns

The worship patterns of African American churches constitute a lesson in praxis that offers yet another assist in working through issues of inclusivity.

"Light" and "dark" are frequent terms in African American hymnody, prayer, preaching, and teaching. Are these traces of a self-demeaning racism yet to be extirpated from a retarded black consciousness? White inclusivists who make such arguments are innocent of the theological and linguistic subtleties of African American spirituality. In that tradition, "light" is not the equivalent of "white," nor "dark" the synonym for "black." These associations were made by an earlier white racism that labeled black Americans as "darkies" and identified its own color, "white," as "light."

Rather, as the writer learned from many African American students in the same systematics classes from which this inclusivity spectrum evolved, "light" is understood in the African American heritage as the full rainbow of color (positive), and "dark" is its absence (negative) — with black as a color in its own right: "black is beautiful." The censorship of "light/dark" imagery by well-intentioned whites, ironically, is a diminishment of historic black piety.

There are no "quick fixes" in the struggle for responsible inclusive language. As in all the notable disputes in church history, hard theological work is entailed. Without it, the best of intentions may produce proposals and practices that ill serve the very goals pursued. Let the conversation go forward.

1. Creation

The philosopher asks, "*Why* is there a world? Why is there something and not nothing?" The Bible gives no answer, nor does it ask the question.

How did the world come to be? *When* did it happen? *Where* were its origins? Scripture does have things to say about the world's origins, its times and circumstances: six "days" of creation's development, four thousand and four years before the birth of Christ by Bishop Ussher's famous calculations, a garden somewhere between the Tigris and Euphrates rivers by a popular topographer. Yet none of these "hows," "whens," and "wheres" appears in the ancient statements of belief of the universal Church, the Apostles' and Nicene creeds. Nor are they mentioned in the confessions, catechisms, and covenants of most of the branches of Christendom. Could it be that biblical dealings with these questions in the book of Genesis are the earthen vessels in which *other* treasure is to be found?

A study of Scripture that probes for its basic intentions — whether by today's critical scholar tracking the genre of writing in Genesis 1 and 2 or by the ancient creed-makers who sought for the centralities — finds answers to other questions of creation: not the "why," the "how," the "when," the "where," but the *who* and *what* of the matter. These are the fundamentals in the first chapter of the Story, the treasure in the earthen vessels of a prescientific worldview. Yes, the early writers spoke in the thought-forms of their day and age, but did so with a poetic grace meant to lead us past sight to insight. They used the cosmology of their time to express the truth opened to them by the Spirit about who God is and

63

what the world means. The cadences and figures of the Genesis accounts are theological poetry that lead us to the depths.

Who?

> In the beginning when God created the heavens and the earth
> . . . (Gen. 1:1 NRSV)

The very first line of the first chapter of our book tells us "who did it." Unlike the mystery tale that hides the secret until the end, this narrative tells all at the beginning. The implications are far-reaching.

The affirmation of God as Creator puts biblical faith on collision course with worldviews modern and ancient: protagonists of "chance" that hold our origins to be the roll of cosmic dice; confident agnostics who are sure they know that we do not know; believing gnostics whose deity is too far removed to dirty its hands with a second-rate creation, and sends a lieutenant god to do the work; disbelievers in beginnings who hold that the world always was; believers that God and the world came to be at the same time; and more.

The early Christians making their way in centuries awash with these kinds of doubt, belief, and disbelief made affirmations about Creator and creation in the very first article of belief:

> I believe in God the Father almighty, Creator of heaven and earth.
> (Apostles' Creed)

They did so because it makes a profound difference in how we think about this world and what we do in it and with it. If God made the world — not chance or fate or nothing or lesser deities or . . . — then the world is fundamentally *good*.

> God saw everything that he had made, and indeed it was very good.
> (Gen. 1:31 NRSV)

If it is "very good," that means it is not to be despised, fled from, abused, but is to be respected, entered into, and built up. Here is the germ of an ecological ethic, a social ethic, a vocational ethic about care for, and work in, the world.

64

The "Who" of creation, of course, is the God of the Story's prologue. The triune God brought the world to be. That has many implications for the "what" of the world. Already these two questions have been linked. We turn now more directly to the latter.

What?

Because God is Maker of heaven and earth, the world is good . . . but not God. Our first assertion about *what* the world is has to do with this "good, but not God" fundamental. It's been cast in the language of an age-old belief: *creatio ex nihilo,* "creation out of nothing." Based on a canonical reading of creation — the first chapters of Genesis in the light of the overall pattern of scriptural teaching — there was a time when the world was not. Therefore, the world is not eternal, not of a piece with God, not divine. It came to be, and thus appeared, by God's decision, from nothingness.

A world that is good but not God is to be honored, but not worshiped. Trees, sky and sea, sun and moon are to be treasured and investigated, but not deified. Human beings are of special delight to God, but are "creatures" not to be confused with their Creator.

Respect for this creature/Creator distinction separates the Story not only from animist religions but also from the romanticizing of any part of the created order. It denies the claims of some worldviews that humanity is at one with deity, that spirituality is getting in touch with our native divinity. Not so long ago, a "blood and soil" philosophy — in the interest of recovering the German nation's self-esteem after its time of troubles — erased the Creator-creature line with horrendous consequences for the Jews and ultimately for the world. *What* one perceives shapes what one does. Theology and ethics are inseparable. So the doctrine of creation by God of a world that is good but not God is a Christian basic.

The what-of-the-matter of creation entails a second affirmation: the world is a partner in God's plan. We have said that there is no biblical teaching of why the world was created. But given the nature of the triune God, the Story tells us what it is made *for.*

God is Community, a triune Life Together. Whatever God touches, so to speak, reflects that nature of ultimate Reality. Who God is, is what God wills. Thus the world is made for "life together."

A standard Christian view is that the Creator does not need the creation. God does not require the existence of another, in order to love, to have "community," being well supplied with it already in the trinitarian Society that God is (the divine "aseity"). But the world has come to be from a mysterious overflowing Love. God did not will to be God without the world (Karl Barth). What else can creation be for than to respond in kind to the overture of divine love? So the plot of the Story is conceived in eternity: God brings a world to be to reflect the kind of bonding that God is. Creation is a covenant the Creator makes to love and to be loved. We are its partners. Reciprocity is "what" is expected of us.

A third aspect of the *what* has to do with the composition of our end of the partnership. What is the nature of the world beckoned into reciprocal relationship? The world itself is a partnership called, in turn, to partnership with God. Its constituents are *nature, human nature,* and *supernature.*

Nature

At both the beginning and the end of the Bible, nature makes its presence felt.

> God called the light Day, and the darkness he called night . . . God called the dome Sky. . . . God called the dry land Earth, and the waters that were gathered together he called Seas. . . . And God said, "Let the waters bring forth swarms of living creatures, and let the birds fly above the earth and across the dome of the sky. . . ." (Gen. 1:5, 8, 10, 20 NRSV)

> Then I saw a new heaven and a new earth . . . the river of the water of life, bright as crystal . . . the tree of life with its twelve kinds of fruit, . . . (Rev. 21:1; 22:1, 2 NRSV)

From start to finish the Creator and Redeemer of the world includes the natural world in the divine plan and hope for life together. *Esse est bonum qua esse,* said St Augustine ("Being, as such, is good"). The being of the earth and sky, the birds, the rivers, the trees, the animals are brought to be by God and therefore

> God saw that it was good. (Gen. 1:25 NRSV)

Once again, the doctrine of creation has ethical import. Because the world of nature bears the stamp of God's approval, human carelessness about and perversity toward nature are a rebuke to the divine gift and blessing. The sky poisoned by our effluents, the acid rain that destroys both fish and water supplies, the chemical wastes that corrupt our soil and kill the creatures that depend upon it, the wanton decimation of our forests — all this disdains the Creator's gifts of sky, earth, rivers, trees, fruit, and the "swarms of living creatures." And, as we shall see in the chapter on the fall, we soon pay the consequences. Here is the creation before the fall. God gave us this *natural world* and declared it good. St Francis's love for the sun, the moon, the sky, and the earth puts us on the path toward reverence for life.

Who God is as "Free to be Together" tells us something about the design of nature. God leaves the divine impress — the "vestiges of the Trinity," as Augustine called it — on the natural world. The electron microscope, the Palomar telescope, the theories of the new physics, and the philosophical cosmologies that draw on these advances suggest both spontaneities and mutualities in nature that reflect the freedom and unity in its Maker. Does this shed light on the vision in the book of Revelation of nature itself freely praising God?

> I heard every creature in heaven and on earth and under the earth and in the sea, and all that is in them, singing, "To the one seated on the throne and to the Lamb be blessing and honor and glory and might forever and ever!" (Rev. 5:13 NRSV)

Even nature is designed to be freely together with its Creator, for a *Shalom* in which

> The wolf shall live with the lamb, the leopard shall lie down with the kid. (Isa. 11:6 NRSV)

Is this the time when the mysterious "withiness" of things (Teilhard de Chardin), the subatomic unpredictabilities (Heisenberg), the droplets of "feeling" that constitute the universe (Whitehead) finally conform to their proper end?

Nature is called to be God's partner, and ours.

Human Nature

With double meaning in mind, we move to another dimension of the created order, *human* nature. Sharing with other creatures the conditions of finitude — presently to be discussed — human beings are given by God a distinguishing gift: the *imago Dei*.

The Image of God: As Relationship

> God said, "Let us make humankind in our own image." (Gen. 1:26 NRSV)

What is this quality that confers on the creature with the human face its unique place in the scheme of things? Theories abound. Some say it is reason or will. Others hold that we are the only tool-making animals. Still others declare that we are the only creatures that can laugh. All these things are true, but the Story sets them in a larger frame of reference.

Humanity alone is set in special *relationship* with God. God enters into relations only with the human race that affect the very destiny of the world. At the center of these acts is Jesus Christ. God became a human being, not a stone or a star, an electron or an animal.

> The Word became flesh and dwelt among us. (John 1:14)

In the electing love of God that claimed Israel and was incarnate in Jesus Christ, the unique dignity of the human race is declared.

The unique bond God has with this creature entails both gift and demand. The gift is the worth conferred on the human person. As the "apple of God's eye," a human person — whatever state or stage — enjoys a dignity the violation of which is an assault on God's Purposes. The sanctity of persons does not reside in a quality that may or may not be present in them — a special race, class, sex, age, condition of body, mind, or spirit. Dignity is intrinsic to personhood by virtue of the *image of God* in which each is made. The "image" in this case is the *relationship* established by God's free decision.

Here, as with every Christian doctrine, are profound ethical consequences. All theories or practices that make human worth *conditional* are called into question. The Holocaust is the twentieth-century reminder of the horror of conditional dignity, denied by a blood-and-soil philosophy to Jewish flesh. Wherever qualifications of any kind are made to the honor due persons by God's electing and incarnate love, a biblical No! must be said. Such unconditionality as a warrant for human worth will take this generation of believers into complex areas of moral judgment at life's beginnings and endings. What are the implications of the *imago* for fetal dignity and the worth of the comatose? And in our times of ecological sensitivity, what is the relation of *nature's* goodness, established by the Creator, and *human nature's* worth, made as we are in the Creator's image? The section on ethics in the chapter on "salvation" will discuss a biblical framework for the church's struggle with these questions.

The word *soul* is very much part of the Christian code language. As with other terms, its meaning has often been influenced by the wider world, its philosophies, religions, and cultures. In some times and places, it has taken on a coloration from the ancient Greek world. "Soul" then became the spiritual segment of the self, to be contrasted with the lowly "body." As the latter has no lasting worth, it was said, death will dissolve it and the soul will separate itself in order to go to a higher plane. Such judgments denigrate the body. Biblical teaching has a higher regard for our destiny, declaring "the resurrection of the body." More about this in the last chapter of the Story.

"Soul" in its biblical sense has to do with the image of God we have, in all its specificity. To Gaius, the receiver of the epistle Third John, the writer says:

> Beloved, I pray that all may go well with you and that you may be in good health, just as it is well with your soul. (v. 2)

Soul is Gaius-in-relation-to-God. It is who you and I are in all our singularity before God. From our beginnings to our endings, from conception to death and beyond, that relationship exists. It can be in good or bad health, sick or "well," depending on how we live in that relationship. (The African American usage that speaks of *having* "soul" reflects this relational understanding.) 3 John's reference brings us to the reciprocal dimension of the image as relationship.

The other side of dignity is responsibility. To whom much is given, much will be required. To be made in the image of God means mirroring the Life Together that God is. Humans are *called to* "image" God's un-bounded love for all of creation. God makes humanity the *steward* of creation. Such stewardship includes the care of nature:

> The LORD God took the man and put him in the garden of Eden to till and keep it. (Gen. 2:15 NRSV)

Here the goodness of nature receives further confirmation by the mandate for humans to care for the earth.

While "stewardship" in popular usage tends to be about things, here expanded to the world of nature, its imaging responsibilities go further — to the world of human beings. To be made in the divine image means care for one another, as God cares for us. Already we have anticipated this dimension of the image of God. Integral to having the image as human is the imperative to honor it in others commensurate with the dignity so conferred on them.

> "You shall love your neighbor as yourself." (Matt. 22:39 NRSV)

And that love of others, our human neighbors, as well as our neighbor the good earth, cannot be separated from its foundations in the love of God. So its companion call:

> "You shall love the Lord your God with all your heart, and with all your soul, and with all your mind." (Matt. 22:37 NRSV)

In the New Testament, the references to the divine image pay special attention to this latter aspect: the living out of the singular relationship in which we stand with God, the love of God, neighbor, nature. In this sense, Jesus Christ has restored the image lost in the world's fall. He is what we are not, he did what we have failed to do. Christ *is*

> the image of God (2 Cor. 4:4 NRSV) . . . the image of the invisible God. (Col. 1:15 NRSV)

As the fulfillment "from our end," so to speak, of the relationship God has established, Jesus Christ is the *true* human being in the normative sense, the "proper human" as described in the Christian tradition. The implications of this for Christology will be explored subsequently.

The Image of God: As Capacity

To be in a relationship with high expectations — stewardship of creation, the love of God returned, and the love of neighbor displayed — presupposes the wherewithal to respond. The image in us entails *respondability* as well as responsibility, the latter because of the former. Here is the point at which various versions of respondability make their contribution to the understanding of the *imago Dei*. "Will," "spirit," "reason," "freedom" are ways of characterizing the unique *capacity* human beings are granted to respond, to enter from their end into the relationship with God — to say Yes! to God's invitation to life together.

As all of creation — nature, human nature, and supernature — is beckoned into harmony with God, "respondability" in some sense is not confined to human beings. From the most rudimentary spontaneities in nature to ranges of freedom granted to "powers and principalities," the world is accountable to its Maker. Yet the centerpiece of the Story is the use you and I are to make of the capacity to say to God, Yea or Nay.

"Spirit" is an encompassing term in Scripture and Christian tradition for the unique human capacity to live in relationship to God. It includes our reason, but transcends it. As imaging God, it is the spirit that reflects God *as* Spirit. As God is truly "free to be Together," so the human spirit is free — in order to be together with God and the world. Life together is born of love, indeed, *is* love. The image as capacity is what we are called to be when our spirits are in accord with the divine Spirit.

Creatureliness

Along with the rest of creation, human beings are creatures. We are finite, not infinite; temporal, not eternal. The mark of our finitude is the embodiment of the human spirit in the frailties of the natural world.

> The days of our life are seventy years, or perhaps eighty, if we are strong. (Ps. 90:10 NRSV)

While the psalmist was not privy to medical advances and biological research that now set the natural outer limits to one hundred and twenty years, the point is clear. We are of the earth, earthy; our bodies wear out and we die.

71

Creatureliness includes all the cares of the world and the ills of the flesh. We need food, clothing, and shelter to survive. We come to be and are shaped by genetic inheritances and environmental forces. We are set in a matrix of social, economic, and political institutions that leave their mark on us, for good or ill. Thus the capacity of spirit we have is enmeshed in "contingencies and necessities" not of our doing. While made in the soaring image of God, we are, at the same time, grounded in space and time — mortal and visible, not, as God is, "immortal and invisible."

Ethics again joins systematics. Because the Story tells us that human nature "lives at the juncture of nature and spirit" (Reinhold Niebuhr), the care for one another with which we are charged will take full account of this interrelationship. The life of the spirit, the capacity for freedom, is dragged down or lifted up by the earthy conditions in which it dwells. So the call for ministry to human need, the struggle for justice and peace for and with those overwhelmed by oppression and war. So, too, the ministries of bodily healing. We live with the imperative of Samaritan mercy.

Of course, the conjunction of nature and spirit means as well that the state of the spirit has its effects on the body. Spiritual healing will have its consequences in physical healing. But here we underscore the creatureliness too often ignored by the moralisms of the modern world, which are quick to make judgments about human responsibility divorced from human finitude, blaming the victims of untoward economic or social circumstance for failure to "pull themselves up by their own bootstraps." At the same time, the state of the spirit cannot be reduced to, or explained away by, our circumstances, for our freedom renders us accountable.

Ordering Our Body/Spirit

Our unique conjunction of flesh and spirit finds nourishment in institutional habitats, called in some traditions the "orders of creation." They include the need for social structures that make and keep human life human, such as the civilizing state and responsible economic order. The family is another ordering of body and spirit to which Scripture gives regular attention. Thus human sexuality finds fulfillment in a biological and spiritual partnership that provides an analogy for the divine Life itself:

72

So God created humankind in his image, / in the image of God he created them; / male and female he created them. . . . Therefore a man leaves his father and mother and clings to his wife, and they become one flesh. (Gen 1:27; 2:24 NRSV)

The one-flesh union with procreation as its issue both assures the existence of a next generation and provides an image in human form of God's own loving Life Together. So we conclude this reading of the Story's report on human creation by returning to the *imago Dei,* a relationship that mirrors the divine Community.

Supernature

"Supernature" refers to the dimension of the created order described in Scripture variously as "principalities and powers," "angels" (faithful and fallen), "thrones," "authorities," "world rulers." In a wider sense, it has to do with invisible realms as well as the powers within them — "heaven" in contrast to "earth" — including the realm of the dead.

Systematic theologies in modern dress often have little or nothing to say about supernature. (The earlier editions of *The Christian Story* were lacking in this respect.) Yet the world of the late twentieth century is not the recently trumpeted "secular society," but instead is preoccupied with "the supernatural." Angel books crowd the bestseller lists, and sightings of supernal beings are familiar fare on TV talk shows and in the checkout-counter press. Is there a word from the community of Christian faith about this realm beyond our conventional senses?

In the Christian Story, the world of supernature is a partner in creation.

In the beginning, God created the heavens and the earth. (Gen. 1:1)

While there is no account of the specific creation of powers and angels, a long tradition in theology holds that "the heavens" of Genesis 1 refer to the invisible world of supernature. What is clear from the rest of Scripture and the classical Christian tradition is the reality and activity of supernatural powers and principalities. Throughout the Bible, angels descend and ascend, sing from on high and rescue below, joyfully announce and sternly warn, ask and answer. They are "messengers of God" (Ps. 91:11; Matt. 28:5; Heb. 13:2).

How shall we interpret these appearances and actions? Are angels confined to biblical times, or are they among us today? Can we see them? Talk to them? Or, contrariwise, is modernity right that angelology is mythology?

Moderns in their own way acknowledge the reality of things unseen. Institutions, associations, organizations take on a life of their own; a whole proves to be more than the sum of its parts. A case can be made that biblical references to "principalities and powers" are related to these psychosocial phenomena — political, economic, and cultural forces that work ill or good among us, a "spirituality of institutions" as Walter Wink describes it.

The angelic and demonic so understood do enable us to grasp the significance of recalcitrant "thrones" and "authorities," which early Christians called to account under the lordship of Christ, and before which we still must bear witness. Indeed, a "theology of institutions" alert to the reality of these more-than-human powers among us is a vital concern for the ministry of today's laity, pushed and pulled as they are by angelic and demonic forces. But this empirical underside of the "heavenlies" does not exhaust their meaning, then or now. The biblical picture of reality is unfinished without its transcendent angelic edges, the Story incomplete without the more elusive presence of the "messengers of God."

We must speak of the mysteries of angel presence with a modesty appropriate to their marginal role in Scripture. John Calvin warns of the inordinate attention some give to them:

> Thus it happens that what belongs to God and Christ alone is transferred to them. . . . Even John in Revelation confesses that this happened to him, but at the same time he adds . . . , "You must not do that! . . . Worship God." (John Calvin, *Institutes of the Christian Religion*)

The most important word we have to speak to our contemporaries about all the powers that be is what the Story has to say about their origin and their own accountability. Supernature, like human nature and nature, is created and ruled by the triune God. Therefore, Jesus Christ, the eternal Word of God, participated in their creation and is their Lord:

> For in him all things in heaven and on earth were created, things visible and invisible, whether thrones or dominions, rulers or powers — all things were created through him and for him. (Col. 1:16 NRSV)

That means Christians today hold accountable to Christ all the political, economic, and social powers and principalities of this world. It means that all claims of angel visitation will show their authenticity by testimony to their Lord. (Biblical angels do not run our errands, but praise God and serve and witness to Jesus Christ.) And, because the Christ of resurrection morning has "disarmed the rulers and authorities" (Col. 2:15) inimical to God's Purposes, the Christian believer faces down the demonic in whatever form it takes among us. But that is to anticipate developments in the Story yet to come.

God wills into being a rich and varied world — nature, human nature, supernature — and calls it into partnership. In this first chapter of the Story, the Creator intends *Shalom* — life together — for the creation. But a more somber second chapter awaits us.

2. Fall

On the ceiling of the Sistine chapel the hand of God reaches out to bring humankind to be. In our storyline, Michelangelo's touch of creation can be seen as the divine invitation. Yet we need another panel for the next chapter. A fist made by Adam, shaken in the face of God. And then another — a shock, a shame, a stumble, and a *fall*.

God called the world into being, and graciously beckoned it into relationship. Our answer? No! We will have none of this "life together" — with God and with each other. In Christian theology, therefore, the chapter on the doctrine of creation is followed by the chapter on the doctrine of the fall.

As with creation, so with fall — the Genesis accounts of the world's beginnings play an important part in "hamartiology," the doctrine of the fall. Again, as with creation, so with the fall — the profundity of these early pages of Scripture is missed when we fix on our issues of "how," "when," and "where." Was there really a talking snake and a tempting fruit? How can we moderns believe such myths? Or, contrariwise, the pious defender of an oracular Scripture as encyclopedic history: "God said it. We believe it!"

To listen for the Word spoken to us in Scripture is to read the story of the snake, the tree, Adam, and Eve and cry, "God have mercy upon me, a sinner!" To hear the Word in Genesis 3 is to know that these words were written about us. They tell us *what* is universally so: the No! to God's invitation.

Human Nature

These chapters also tell us *who* we are, the human race, the chief of the Nay-sayers. Our stratagems to evade this searing Word are infinite. And one of them is the silencing of the theological intention of these passages by turning them into our scientific agendas, pro or con. The preoccupation of both "fundamentalists" and "modernists" with the hows, whens, and wheres misses the stinging whos and whats. We listen now for the Word spoken to us about the deep things of the human soul in the artistry of these early accounts.

Idolatry

The much-maligned primitivity of Genesis on the fall gives us a look into the character as well as the fact of our own universal No. Thus the serpent urges upon Adam and Eve the delights of forbidden fruit:

> "God knows that when you eat of it your eyes will be opened, and you will be like God, knowing good and evil." (Gen. 3:5 NRSV)

And eat it they did. From the beginning, we humans want to "be like God"; we are determined to *play God.* Here is a key theme in the Christian Story described by code word, *sin,* indeed, "original sin." And its essential meaning: *idolatry.* Sin is not what it is said to be in popular culture, breaking this or that rule. Far deeper, it has to do with our fundamental disorientation. We are not turned to God but instead do an about-face. We are turned away from the divine invitation, inward instead of outward, *incurved* (Martin Luther), *shutup* (Kierkegaard). Fixed upon ourselves, we displace our Maker. A new god has arrived on the scene. We are Number One. Sin, at bottom, is idolatry.

The Genesis story so read is done from within the whole Christian canon. The imperial "I" discerned in the grasp for godlike power is related to the history of the human race's rebellion chronicled in the two Testaments. Most of all, the depth of human sin is displayed in the reception given to God's own Son. We are finally exposed by the cross. The universality of sin in the Genesis tale is confirmed. Yes, we all *were there* "when they crucified my Lord," as much as we were in the adamic "I, me, and mine."

The primal No in the classical theological tradition is the "pride" that goes before the fall. In so describing it, we must keep in mind the context: the divine-human relationship. Sin is hauteur *coram Deo,* before God. Pride, as the deification of the self rather than God-centeredness, is our common condition. Pride in a *second* sense, as "lording it over others," is derivative from this basal egocentricity. Sometimes the two are confused, and "pride" dismissed as only the problem of the powerful. Not so. All of us, the strong and the weak, have our ways of playing God, which we might call "pride 1."

Why is there such a universal state of affairs? Why the resolute tendency in the human heart to think first of its own interests, to pursue its own agenda, to turn aside from the invitation to life together with God? Here, as in the doctrine of creation, the "why" is met with silence. Scripture and Christian tradition give us no more clear answer to "Why sin?" than "Why the world?" So the compelling response of Paul to our quandary is "the mystery of iniquity" (2 Thess. 2:7 KJV).

How far have we fallen? How deep has our willfulness penetrated our souls? The extent of human sin has been measured by its effects on the divine image, with special reference to its capacity for freedom and reason. Has the fall destroyed it? Shattered, but not destroyed, it? Cracked it? Only jarred it, but left it essentially intact?

An answer must distinguish between the *imago dei* as "relationship" and as "capacity." In our intrinsic relationship to God — as the creature with whom God has special business to do, as the one specially called and claimed, as in unique relationship — our image is intact. Humanity's dignity and responsibility remain unaffected. Matters are quite different with regard to the image as capacity.

The original capacity to say Yes to God, to be truly *free* to be together, is damaged beyond our repair. Our will to love God as God loves us, and thus our *theological* freedom, is "in bondage."

> I do not do the good I want, but the evil I do not want is what I do. Now if I do what I do not want, it is no longer I that do it, but sin that dwells within me. (Rom. 7:19-20 NRSV)

The human "spirit," as the capacity to answer aright the invitation of God, has run amok. Something in us — "sin" — unswervingly presses the self to serve only itself. Our reason, as a dimension of our spirit, is accordingly tainted by this implacable self-regard. In matters that touch our self-interest we rationalize rather than reason.

78

How Far the Fall?

Does the bondage of the human will, the breaking of its spirit and the distortion of its reason, mean that the image (as capacity) has been entirely lost? The answer here, as given canonically — reading the fact of our Genesis fall in the light of the entire Bible — is the Word of *damage,* not *destruction.* God "has not left himself without a witness. . . ." (Acts 14:17) in the human order. The echo of this despoiled but not destroyed image sounds throughout Scripture. In the rendering of the Story in this systematics, its defacing will be interpreted in the framework of the universal covenant with Noah. For now, we distinguish the damaged state from views of it as lost, on the one hand, and only cracked or even essentially sound, on the other.

Where a view resides on the continuum from loss to retention determines theological judgments about whether and to what extent our general human experience, as such, can give us access to truth about God, and whether God's special deeds and disclosures can or must be validated by our own human resources. Those trusting human capacities in their own right, or as aided by a universal grace, will have one conviction about the extent to which special revelation and redemption are required. Those less confident about the human state will have quite other emphases. This will affect our view of the revelatory and redemptive status of other religions and people of good conscience who have not been reached by the Gospel. We shall return to these questions in the chapter on covenant. Here, a broken image bespeaks sobriety about inordinate claims to universal human knowledge about ultimate matters or to virtue in the pursuit of them.

This "realism" about human nature, however, must be distinguished from a "cynicism" about the same. An example of that having to do with sin itself is the ability of human beings to know something of their own fallen state. Thus the famous "suspicionists" of modern times — Freud, Marx, Nietzsche — have relentlessly exposed human self-seeking and self-deception. However, secular hermeneuticians of suspicion are only provisionally realistic about our state, for they exempt themselves from their indictments.

Do fragmentary insights about the human condition come instead, circuitously, from the seepage of biblical teaching into Western soil? Advocates of a "social construction of reality" or the "cultural-linguistic" habitat of all thought might make such a case. However, where Scripture is acknowledged as theological source, its testimony of a flawed image sustained by the covenant with Noah is definitive, warranting as it does modest recognition of a broken but not destroyed *imago*.

Self-Righteousness

Sin smokescreens from others and ourselves our self-serving designs. We hide our lethal tendencies in the garments of righteousness. Our ideals, ideas, morality, and piety, our best institutions of law, education, and religion can cloak our power agenda and justify our self-aggrandizement. Thus the self-righteous pharisee rather than the penitent publican stands judged, and religious forces prove to be the predictable foes of Christ. Self-righteousness is sin in hiding, and therefore all the more dangerous. It is also one more indication that some fragment of the image is universally present, for one must have some discernment of the good and the true to claim it as cover for one's pretensions.

Penultimate Discernments

The universal darkening of the vision of God in the human mind and spirit, the bondage of the will, does not preclude the valid use of reason and freedom in *penultimate* matters. The fall has not damaged our ability to decide whether to make a left or right turn at a traffic light, to do arithmetic, to plan next week's food menu. When penultimate "when," "where," and "how" matters approach the ultimate whys and wherefores, whos and whats, then the bondage of will and the distortion of reason and spirit assert themselves.

Original Innocence

Was there a time in human history when there was no sin? The Genesis story certainly says so — a Paradise when all was well with the world. If there was no such "time," then the world would not have been created "good." Gnosticisms past and present hold the world to be so flawed, unworthy of a good God (so lieutenant deities are appointed to bring it to be . . . or it is said to be created by Evil itself . . . or is an illusion seen to be real by our faulty spiritual vision . . .). The consequences of such dualism play themselves out in invitations to escape from and denigrate the world of time and space.

As we have seen, the doctrine of creation puts Christians on a different course. The good God makes a good world. The doctrine of the fall continues that premise and therefore denies the existence of human sin coterminous with creation. Christian faith affirms its coming to be *in* time, thus entailing a prior untainted state. Looking for the *what* of the matter in the cosmology of the ancient Eden account requires discerning a meaning commensurate with our present knowledge of human beginnings. Does that mean belief in a period of sinlessness in the evolution of the race? Or perhaps the Genesis pre-fall and fall stories are only existential readings of everyperson's moments of temptation? But modern historicizing stretches credulity, and psychologizing still leaves the possibility of flawed creation.

Scripture's tale of human innocence before the fall can be understood instead as God's *intention* and our original *possibility*. The Garden is Scripture's vision of what might be, and its real temporal possibility, before the choices made by the human race. Prior to that historical moment of initial decision, we could have responded to the divine invitation. Human nature brought to be by the good God was yet innocent of its subsequent wrong turn. In the No we said (we "were there" in the race's rejection of the divine overture, as we "were there" in the crucifixion of Jesus), our human predisposition was disclosed, the "mystery of iniquity."

The forbidden fruit and its tree are not the knowledge of right and wrong as often described, for the prior commandment not to eat it declared by God to Adam and Eve is *already* such knowledge of good and evil (Gen. 3:2). Humanity had the awareness of what it was to do and not to do, a capacity given in the gift of the divine image. The "knowledge of good and evil" illicitly sought in our wrong turn refers to God's singular clarity and righteousness — to be "wise" (Gen. 3:6) as the divine Wisdom only can be wise. Primal sin is, accordingly, wanting to "be like God," to usurp the divine prerogative, to play at being God.

Arrogance

Original sin expresses itself in the plural — as "sin*s*." List making is a commonplace of Christian theology and piety, as in the "seven deadly sins." The seven, and other computations, sort out in two directions that follow the dimensions of the self: the image of God (in this case as "capacity"), and our creatureliness.

The capacity of freedom given to us in the *imago* is an expression of human power, power to rise above our creaturely rootage, power to know, to decide, to possess goods and shape society, to respond to the special relationship with God in which we stand. As this power grows — intellectual, moral, economic, social, political, spiritual — so grows the temptation to abuse it. Given our anterior state of idolatry, the acquisition of power entails its corruptibility: "power corrupts and absolute power tends to corrupt absolutely" (Lord Acton). Original sin therefore finds its way into a God-given capacity, turning it to its own ends.

The corruption associated with our gift of freedom is "pride," the will to power that lords it over others. This *second* meaning of the word, often confused with the first (pride as our universal, primal idolatry), has to do with our horizontal relationships — pride as the *arrogance* of the wielders of power. So the self that sees itself as the center of things (pride 1), given special economic, social, intellectual, spiritual powers, seeks to dominate and destroy (pride 2). Power over others so exercised may be over other human beings, or it may be over nature. Oppression of the weak is a widespread manifestation of the arrogance of the powerful. Human exploitation of nature is a pride that makes creation itself groan.

The abuse of power can take subtler forms that touch upon the best of the fruits of the mind and spirit. Those who grow in spiritual power, the "religious," are especially susceptible to the corruptions of power because their very piety obscures their willfulness. "Thank God I am not as others!" (Luke 18:11). So, too, the moralist, convinced of the righteousness of his or her own cause, divides the world up into the legions of light and the armies of night, the righteous "us" and the unrighteous "them." The history of failed movements of reform and revolution illustrates the arrogance that fails to see the sin in the champions of justice as well as in its foes. Similarly, the growth of intellectual power can court the illusion among the elite that human wisdom is the equivalent of human virtue.

The doctrine of the fall has its ethical and institutional implications.

Where there is sobriety about its temptations, absolute power will be challenged and social, economic, and political power dispersed. The American experiment, with all its shortcomings, draws on the doctrine of sin in its system of checks and balances — judicial, executive, and legislative — as well as its understanding of majority rule and minority rights. All pyramids of power are suspect.

Movements for social change, most recently of labor and liberation, have drawn on the wisdom that the agglomeration of power must be challenged by countermovements of the marginalized. At the same time, human effort in social change is itself susceptible to temptation as it gains a power that can corrupt the forces of "righteous" victims as well as it has their former victimizers.

Apathy

Idolatry works itself out in the *escape* from freedom as well as in its abuse. Apathy is the counterpart to arrogance. Apathy is the sin associated with creatureliness, as arrogance is with the divine image. We may be tempted to abdicate our power to choose, to act, and to think, as well as to corrupt it.

As we are creatures of the flesh, time, and space, our spirit is conditioned by our body, by the natural environment, by social networks and economic and political institutions. The stewardship of these involvements is a burden, as is the call to use our freedom responsibly. Flight from freedom is an ever-present temptation.

Escape can take the form of "sensuality," "concupiscence," the "sins of the flesh." We can use a created good — the body — as an avenue of retreat. The good gift of our sexuality becomes consuming, the god of our lives. Preoccupation becomes promiscuity. Freedom is also lost in a range of other all-too-familiar sensual captivities, from drug and alcohol abuse to the enticements of rich food, clothing, and shelter.

Escape has more artful and subtle ways than the manifest sins of sensuality. Apathy — also called in an ancient tradition *acedia* or *accidie* — includes the spiritual torpor that backs away from the moment of choice and retreats from the call of duty. Monks called it the "midday demon," the psalmist's "arrow that flieth at noonday," when chores seem too burdensome to execute and slumber beckons.

Apathy has its social expression when responsibility for change is abdicated, when the status quo goes unchallenged and the powers of evil remain unresisted. Escape, in this case, can entail the refusal to assert one's own dignity in the face of manifest oppression. God has given us the freedom of the divine image. When the powerful deny it, the powerless must resist. The sin that seduces the powerful is overlordship. The sin that beguiles the powerless is resignation. Christian resistance to oppressive power is not made on the basis of psychological and social theories of "self-esteem." These regularly obscure the sin in all human beings. The affirmation of one's own freedom from the world's enslavements is based on the innate dignity that the image of God confers.

Nature

The biblical story of the fall centers on the creature made in the divine image. Yet *all* creation shares in the state of alienation, even as all creation will participate in the final reconciliation. Nature, too, is promised a wholeness that it does not have. It, too, is destined for a new birth, and therefore in its present state "groans in travail" (Rom. 8:22).

Nature short of the reign of God gives evidence of its alienation, as "red in tooth and claw." The wolf and the lamb do not lie down together, and a child cannot without peril put its hand over the adder's den, all contradictions of Isaiah's portrayal of God's Purposes. The ravages of cancer and other diseases unnumbered, traceable not to our sin but to nature's chaos, are found throughout the created order. The devastations wrought in nature as well as on humanity by tornado, volcanic ash, earthquake, fire, and flood are much among us. Our own human pollutants wreak havoc on the environment. Yet much travail in nature is not of our making.

Are natural disasters part of God's design? Are they simply the way things are, scientific facts of life with which the good but not omnipotent God must learn to live? Or do they work out all right in the end, requirements of the cost/benefit necessitated by nature's laws? Such are some of the familiar justifications of nature's or God's ways, standard "theodicies" that attempt to explain nature's destructive tendencies. We shall return to this "problem of evil" in a later chapter.

In our narrative mode of interpreting Christian faith, natural disaster is part of the chapter on the fall. Nature, too, has refused the invitation to life together. How has this come to be? Once again, the "hows" must make way in Christian doctrine for the "whats." Has nature somehow fallen because of *human* sin, as in some readings of the Story? But then what do we make the devious serpent that preceded the fall? Does nature have a "freedom" that is subject to the same corruptibility as that capacity in humans? Indeed, a "how" explanation that points to the indeterminacies in the electron world or philosophy's speculations of rudimentary spontaneities and feelings could make a case for the same disorientation in nature as found at the level of human freedom. Finally, however, we do not know how nature's flaws came to be. While not the mystery of human iniquity, it is an inexplicable "surd" in existence. Nature, as well as human nature, has gone amok.

As there is a broken but not destroyed divine image in humans, so also a harmony is at work within the disharmonies of nature. Signs of the original vision are still discernible in the world of stones and stars, atoms and animals. God has not left us without a witness to the rhythms and beauties of natural and cosmic life together, a relic of what was, and by the promise of the Story a portent of what is yet to be.

Supernature

Dominions and powers, angels and archangels — messengers of God for the carrying out of the divine purposes. What is their part in the fall of creation?

The Christian tradition is replete with assertions and interpretations of the Devil and the demons. All point to the complicity in the fall of the supernatural world. From one end of the scale to the other — from the institutional authorities that show us their empirical face to more mysterious angelic powers — disobedience and disorientation are everywhere.

Reinhold Niebuhr, the twentieth-century theologian of Christian anthropology, has traced the effects of the fall on the social, economic, and political powers and principalities. In *Moral Man and Immoral Society* and beyond, he reminds us of the intransigence of corporate evil. Not amenable to either the moralisms of the pious or the arguments of the learned, oppressive power responds only to collective checks and commensurate corporate power. Later, Niebuhr acknowledged his too-simple distinctions between persons and institutions — "immoral man and even more immoral society" — and he also granted a modicum of common grace in institutions as well as persons. But his initial point holds true: the demonic has easy access to the orders of creation, the corruptibility of the state, the economy, and society large and small.

The distortions of supernature range, however, far beyond institutions and orders. An Evil exists that transcends corporate evil. Trans-empirical "powers of Evil" are as inextricable from the biblical story as angelic powers. In many harmful ways, they work against the purposes of God.

How, when, and where these malevolent powers came to be remains, yet again, an unanswered question in Scripture and classical teaching, although speculation about the "fall" of angels is not unknown. In dispute, as well, is the nature of these rebel powers. Do we not only capitalize the E, but also add a D? Are the ranks of Evil/the Devil made up of those who had a freedom comparable to ours to say an initial No to God? Are the spontaneities in nature and the freedom in humans matched by a willfulness in the ranks of the demonic? While the matter of a "who" can be debated, and too-quick anthropomorphisms challenged, the story of the fall is incomplete without the presence of a reality we can identify as supernatural Evil.

The muting of talk of the demonic and satanic in modern theology is surely influenced by Enlightenment dogmas about what can and cannot be believed. Here the Story must take precedence over secular ideology. But contemporary restraint also has to do with wariness about the inflated currency of apocalypticism. Fears of the Devil's control of this age and speculations about the demonic are popular in troubled times. These need to be challenged by the testimony to Christ's resurrection and present rule. That victory makes for courage in the struggle against the worldly under-side of the supernatural realm — rebel political, economic, and social power — because God has

> "brought down the powerful from their thrones, and lifted up the lowly."
> (Luke 1:52)

Easter faith also rejects apocalyptic claims of Satan's rule. And it fortifies us to resist the transcendent as well as the immanent powers of Evil. Let them be afraid of us, not vice versa, for Christ has already defeated these invisible powers and thrones, having disarmed the rulers and authorities and made a public example of them, triumphing over them in it. (Col. 2:15 NRSV)

While not to be muted, demonology, after the Christ who exorcised them and finally triumphed over them, is modest.

Death

In common parlance, "death" means biological termination. In Christian faith the meaning of death reaches further. It includes the culmination of history itself, a subject we shall deal with in the last chapter of the Story. And in its profoundest meaning death is separation from God. It is in this final sense that we deal with it here, for the wages of sin and evil are this kind of demise. The result of bondage is alienation.

Separation from God in our translation of the Story is estrangement from the Word, the death of the Dream of God. As such, it is severing all the ties that bind us. If life is the unity of humanity, nature, and God, then death is their fracture.

Death is the alienation of the self from God. It is turning away from the Light in pursuit of one's self-serving ends. Sin is the about-face that brings upon itself the stumble and fall into the darkness. What we choose is what we get: "sin pays a wage, and the wage is death" (Rom. 6:23).

Death is alienation *within* humanity as well as *between* humanity and God. As in Donald Baillie's suggestive figure of the circle of joyful dancers who choose to turn away from the Light and therefore must break their handclasps with companions (Appendix 1), so our alienation from God brings in its wake separation from the neighbor. The effect of our self-exaltation is the sundering of the bonds with fellow-humanity. And the unity within the self as well as the community among humans is destroyed as we experience inner discord together with outer strife.

Death is also alienation between humanity and nature. The arrogance of human sin is such that it carries out its designs against its neighbor, nature. Its attacks on the environment poison the atmosphere, contaminate the soil and waters, relentlessly consume its riches, and ravage the creatures with whom it shares this home.

Sin finds an ally in its destructive work in the powers of evil. These mysterious forces in both history and nature add their lethal impact. The fallen systems and structures of this world and the skewed processes of nature fashion pruning hooks into spears, make nature red in tooth and claw, and bring fire and flood, plague and pestilence (Rom. 8:22). And the demonic takes its mysterious toll.

Inseparable from this larger Death is mortality itself. As we are captive to the powers of sin and evil, our destiny in this world is not life, but death. God projected a larger Future for us, but we chose another path. The reminder of our wanderings in a far country is mortality and the sorrow that attends this end short of the Realm for which we have been made (Isa. 40:6-8). But the close of our odyssey on earth is not the End.

Death is the severed relationship between all the rest of creation and the realm of supernature. Angelic powers turn demonic. The orders of creation become the occasion for unfreedom and alienation; fallen systems and institutions fashion their pruning hooks into spears. The elusive More of powers and principalities turn against nature and human nature. Presumed "messengers of God" bring bad instead of good news. So the Devil is portrayed as tempter at the beginning of the Story and at its center in encounter with Christ, and as the emissary of ruin at the End.

3. Covenant

Not uncommon in traditional theology is the leap from the doctrines of creation and fall to the doctrine of Christ. While the biblical canon does not do this, the ancient creeds do. This move leaves out a chapter of the Story, underscoring the point made in the Introduction: even the best traditions are ministerial, not magisterial. They are a "resource" to faith, not its final "source," and therefore are subject to correction by a deeper reading of the Word. Thus the covenant with Israel is a not-to-be-forgotten chapter of the Christian Story.

"Covenant" includes more than the tale of God's bonding with a chosen people, Israel. God's Story is, throughout, covenantal: a covenant with creation itself, a covenant with Adam and Eve, the "new covenant in Christ." In this chapter the focus is on the election of Israel. But it also includes a prior bonding, a *universal* covenant that precedes this *particular* one with the Jewish people: the "covenant with Noah."

A covenant, *berith,* is a solemn promise to fulfill a declared purpose. Covenant is God's stubborn, unswerving commitment to the Shalom willed for the world. It is demand as well as gift. To whom much is given, much will be required. While no human act of obedience or disobedience can make or break covenants, consequences follow from our faithlessness — the judgment of God. Neither the rebellion of the world nor the disloyalty of a particular people can turn God aside from promises made. Yet imperatives come with the indicatives. Accountability to them takes place in the penultimate judgments of history and the ultimate reckonings of eternity.

The Covenant with Noah

We left the Story with the catastrophic word of judgment on the world's No to the divine overture. Alienation is the result of a refused invitation. In the generations succeeding Adam and Eve

> [T]he wickedness of humankind was great on the earth. (Gen. 6:5 NRSV)

Why not terminate this failed experiment in life together?

The story of the flood is testimony to the rigor of God's righteousness. But it is remembered as well, and more, as the first signal of the *patience* of God. The ark, as later New Testament writers viewed it, is a symbol of a grace that rescues, and thus a portent of a yet-to-be-baptized family of believers "saved through water" (1 Pet. 3:20). But the sign for which Noah is finally known is the "bow in the clouds" (Gen. 9:13). This "sign of the covenant" (Gen. 9:12) is a promise made that the Maker of heaven and earth will not abandon creation to its willful ways. God will not be put off the track toward the divine purpose by our waywardness. The Story will go forward.

In both Jewish and Christian theology, the "Noachic covenant" ("Noachite," "Noahic") has to do with the long-suffering God who will sustain creation even in its disobedience. Entailed in this gracious persistence is, as the sign of the rainbow suggests, the giving of just enough leading light for human beings to see their way into the future. Thus the covenant expectations regarding human behavior:

> "Whoever sheds the blood of a human, by a human shall that person's blood be shed; for in his own image God made humankind." (Gen. 9:6 NRSV)

To the human race comes the knowledge, after the fall, of life made sacrosanct by the *relationship* in which we are established by the divine image. Humans have everywhere intimations in "conscience" of this law of life together. The Noachic covenant, therefore, is God's promise to protect the remnant of the image of God as *capacity* after the fall. We have the ability to discern and to follow haltingly the elemental rules of life together. Without that universal glimpse of the good, the human race would destroy itself.

Does the rainbow sign illumine something of the source of these moral mandates? Exponents of "natural theology" do not hesitate to say Yes: our minds can know by rational argument the existence of God. They hold that the fall is not so shattering that reason cannot discern its Maker. More recently, other human capacities — moral, affective — are declared to be capable of discerning something of the reality of God, or ultimate reality.

Evidence for the extension of the Noachic covenant to include this (albeit limited) knowledge of God is ambiguous at best. The chapters in Genesis that follow the rainbow sign, and precede the next covenant act with Abraham, do suggest the human race's awareness of its existence before God (Gen. 9:18–11:32). At the same time, the tower of Babel thrusts skyward, revealing humanity's pretensions to divinity, "a tower with its top in the heavens . . ." (Gen. 11:4). And the sequel in which "the LORD confused the language of all the earth" (Gen. 11:9 NRSV) suggests the untrustworthiness of our claims to the natural knowledge of things divine or matters ultimate.

The Noachic covenant does carry with it promises of sustenance, with their corresponding modest sensibility of what we are made for, a "general (universal) revelation" of the elemental moral, intellectual, and spiritual conditions for human life. A *grace of preservation* enables the world to go forward toward its proper end, one that is destined to include the defining disclosures of "special revelation." In the time and space outside of God's particular deeds, a "common grace" is at work in both personal awarenesses and institutional regularities. In the latter instance, the structures of human life now, after the fall, become "orders of preservation" — the family, the state, the economic order that are necessary for sustaining human life. The rainbow sign of this preserving grace both illumines and embodies the beauty and order of the natural as well as the human world.

Providence

"Providence" is often the way Christians talk about the graces of the Noachic covenant. Providence, in this respect, is God's universal care of a fallen world. The Maker of heaven and earth is also its Sustainer.

Sustenance in a fallen world means support for the things that make for the continuation of the Story. In the most elementary terms, it is the conviction that "God takes care of God's own." God's own is first and foremost the divine Purpose. God takes care of Shalom, protecting it from its enemies and encouraging it in its friends. Thus Providence is the *power* of the Purpose that runs through the world, the Spirit that "in everything . . . works for good" (Rom. 8:28 RSV).

As history is the workshop for "perfectly wise and loving ends" (General Assembly, Church of Scotland), the belief in Providence is a way of viewing the entirety of the Christian narrative. Time is in holy keeping. Neither fate nor chance, neither the stars nor the cycles of nature and history, determine what shall be, but the implacable love of God moving toward its goal. Providence is not puppetry; we are free to be for that goal. But we are not free from its call and claim. As with creation and fall, so Providence rises out of the defining deeds of God, from the deliverance of Israel to the resurrection of Christ. Our understanding of divine governance comes out of Israel's history with God, our covenant chapter, and its fulfillment in the Person and Work of Jesus Christ. While we leap ahead of our Story for this direction, Providence at this point after the fall is witness to the power of God in the face of the most malignant of opposition. For the way in which a patient Providence establishes final dominion, we wait upon the climactic events of Easter and eschaton.

Providence can be seen in the processes of self and society, history and nature. It works to heal the scars of the destructive bolt of lightning that slashes a tree, it effects the same Shalom in the wounded body whose cells repair at the tender urging of this common grace, and its power is manifest in the mind cloven by hate that makes its way to health again. Providence can show a sterner face when a nature ravished by pollutants strikes back through the inversion layer over the city, the chemically eroded food and water sources, the infertile fields, and the desolated timber ranges. The work of judgment comes to the self that has failed to learn the lesson "love or perish," and to the society that has not listened to the prophetic call to let justice and righteousness reign and that therefore suffers from the "rod of my anger" (Isa. 10:5 RSV). In the history of nature and humanity there is a law of righteousness at work; when it is violated, the consequences are dire. We are met in judgment or buoyed up in grace by the Providence that "has brought down the monarchs from their thrones, but the humble have been lifted high" (Luke 1:52).

It is not only in the macrocosm of nature and history and in the boundaries set to the rebellion of the world that Providence does its work. There is also a tender and individuating care that numbers the hairs of our heads and marks the sparrow's fall (Matt. 10:29-31). The eye of faith sees the hand of God laboring to shape our personal lives toward "wise and loving ends." Indeed, the meanings to be found in this microcosm do not come easily. Providence struggles with "thrones and authorities" only too eager to fell the sparrow and bruise the head. Yet the light that comes from the central chapter of this Story, the knowledge that the powers of this fallen world do not have final charge of our destinies, illumines even those events whose darkness seems most impenetrable.

Toward the decisive act in this drama that gives us perspective on prologue, creation, and fall, we continue to move.

The Covenant with Israel

Covenant in biblical perspective is the stubborn, unswerving commitment to the Shalom God wills for the world. More than a general faithfulness to that purpose, it is a pledge to execute this intention through a particular people. We shall explore the living out of this compact in the deeds done, the word shared, and the vision disclosed in the life of a people and then in its chief prophet, priest, and king.

Why this people in this time and this place? We confront an enigma, the mystery of divine election, the sternest testing of the sturdiest. The fertile crescent is such a place to carry on an experiment in faithfulness, located in a Mediterranean land bridge for marching armies, a prey of imperialisms and the pawn of political machinations. If an act of loyal seeing and serving is to be authentic, it must weather the worst of the world's turmoil. And more than that, it must face the hatred evoked by that people's seeing and saying what the world is made for.

Why Israel as the chosen people? Finally our speculations fade into silence, replaced by our thanksgiving that God also is a stubborn God who will not give up on us, and therefore enters this covenant to keep the vision before us.

Exodus and Law

An event takes place that gives high visibility to the divine purpose. God does a deed among this people that enacts the dream of liberation and reconciliation. The chosen people are freed from slavery. God leads Israel out of Egypt and into a land flowing with milk and honey (Exod. 12:37–14:31). The people of God taste the fruit of the promised land of freedom. Exodus becomes the pivot on which their history turns, and the event that makes them a visionary people.

The deliverance from Egypt is followed by a rhythm of promise and fulfillment in the history of Israel. The God of the exodus displays a "mighty arm" preserving this people — goading them into loyalty, protecting them from the assaults of enemies, giving portents and signs of Shalom. In these events, Israel perceives and records the divine initiative and steadfastness of God.

This covenant cannot be understood without real hope for its embodiment in time and space, and belief in the God whose presence in history makes these promises possible. But this action of God comes in judgment as well as promise, for the One who liberates also rebukes (Exod. 32:30-35). Time after time God calls the people to account for breach of the covenant. Yet, especially in the early layers of covenant tradition, there is the assurance that the deliverance from Egypt represents a kind of relationship that the people of God can always expect from the One who has chosen them. Moreover, the covenant sealed by the exodus action of God points not only forward to fulfillment but also back to the covenant of creation. God does not will to be God without this world, and confirms the originating bond in the covenants with Noah and Abraham. Exodus and its antecedents and derivations, therefore, announce the action of God to pursue determinately the divine Purpose on the very terrain of its resistance, by way of enactment, disclosure, and support of a people.

As part of this covenanting action God sets forth the laws of the new land, the precepts of Shalom: a *decalogue* of imperatives of the love of God and the love of the neighbor (Exod. 20:1-12). Its recorder is given the eye to see clearly what our failed human vision only dimly perceives. This law is realistic, one that presupposes the already present fallenness of the world, couched as it is in its "thou shalt not's." Law is kept alive by priests who celebrate it and make atonement for those who break it and by sages who meditate on and expound it. Hence the ritual life of the temple that environs the Law, and the wisdom traditions of the people of God.

The Prophets

Most of all, the intended future, of which the promised land, its laws, rituals, and lore are at best foretastes, is given to certain *seers* of the ultimate Light. These *prophets* are forthtellers of the claims of God on the people. But they tell what they *see,* and are therefore fore*seers* as well. They perceive the future of God with their inner eye, and declare its meaning to the chosen people in both word and deed. The prophet portrays in the most vivid colors and sharpest outline the goal of God — a world in which nature, humanity, and God dwell in peace and freedom.

The life together to which the seer points reaches into the animal world. "The wolf shall live with the sheep, and the leopard lie down with the kid; the calf and the young lion shall grow up together . . . and the cow and the bear shall be friends, and their young shall lie down together" (Isa. 11:6, 7). From there it spreads throughout the realm of nature. "The wilderness will become grassland, and grassland will be cheap as scrub. Then justice shall make its home in the wilderness, and righteousness dwell in the grassland; when righteousness shall yield peace and its fruit be quietness and confidence forever" (Isa. 32:15-17). And this healed nature itself shall reunite with its Maker. "Mountains and hills shall break into cries of joy, and all the trees of the wild shall clap their hands, pine-trees shall shoot up in place of camel-thorn, myrtles instead of briars, all this shall win the LORD a great name, imperishable, a sign for all time" (Isa. 55:12-13). The restoration of nature from its tyrannies and alienations means that God shall "create new heavens and a new earth" (Isa. 65:17).

The new harmony reaches up to encompass humanity, reknitting the torn fabric of relationship between humanity and nature. "The infant shall play over the hole of the cobra, and the young child dance over the viper's nest" (Isa. 11:8). "Then my people shall live in a tranquil country. . . . [I]t will be cool on the slopes of the forest then, and cities shall lie peaceful on the plain. Happy shall you be, sowing every man by the waterside and letting ox and ass run free" (Isa. 32:18-20). "I will rid the land of wild beasts, and men shall live in peace of mind on the open pastures and sleep in the woods. I will settle them in the neighborhood of my hill and send them rain in due season, blessed rain. Trees in the countryside shall bear their fruit, and the land shall yield its produce, and men shall live in peace of mind on their own soil" (Ezek. 34:24-27).

To the healing of nature and the relationships between nature and humanity is added the healing of the nations. "They shall beat their swords into mattocks and their spears into pruning-knives; nation shall not lift sword against nation nor ever again be trained for war" (Isa. 2:4). And conjoined to this harmony will be freedom for the oppressed and justice for the downtrodden. "Listen to this, you cows of Bashan . . . you who oppress the poor, and crush the destitute" (Amos 4:1). "Shame on those who lie in bed planning evil and wicked deeds and then at daybreak they do them. . . . [T]hey covet the land and take it by force; if they want a house they seize it; they rob a man of his home and steal every man's inheritance" (Mic. 2:1-2).

The freedom and peace among people and nations becomes freedom and peace within persons as well. "Each man shall dwell under his own vine, under his own fig-tree, undisturbed" (Mic. 4:4).

The prophets gather the images of the future together under a common theme: "I will make with them a covenant of *shalom* . . . and they shall know that I am the LORD, when I break the bars of their yoke, and deliver them from the hand of those who enslave them. They shall no more be prey to the nations, nor shall the beasts of the land devour them; they shall dwell securely, and none shall make them afraid. And I will provide them plantations of *shalom* . . ." (Ezek. 34:25, 27-29). "Then justice and righteousness will dwell in the wilderness, and righteousness abide in the fruitful field. And the effect of righteousness will be *shalom,* and the result of righteousness, quietness and trust for ever" (Isa. 32:16-17 RSV). The chosen people have been stewards of Shalom since. They have seen the light and felt the heat of the rays of the Not Yet, and in turn share that pressure and pain with humanity. Through them we see what we were made for.

Being what we are, the response to that presence in our midst has been one of hostility. We do not like to be reminded of our Purpose. Its disclosure shames us. So the message is identified with a messenger. This people of the vision have had humanity's hate heaped upon them. The roots of anti-Semitism and anti-Judaism go deep into the soil of human sin. The resistance to the original Light finds yet another target in the holocaust history of the chosen people.

Where Does the Covenant Lead?

The clarity of Israel's vision of the purposes of God early posed certain enigmas to its people. If the Lord of history wills Shalom, then why do those who pursue it suffer and those who scorn it appear to prosper? The entreaties of the psalmist and the protests of Job combined with assurances and hopes of the same that this will not finally be so. Interlaced with the struggle over the disparity between the claims of Deity and deeds of the wicked, there was a sense that for those who breached the covenant there were ways of making amends. The priestly tradition's rituals of atonement were at first conceived in ceremonial, and later in moral, terms. Joined by penitence to the offering, the sinner made a sacrifice to God. Repentance so executed reestablished the broken bond.

As the prophet lived with the vision and read the calamities of Israel in the light of it, the earlier questions of the suffering of innocents and the sins of the wicked were seen in a deeper dimension. Now it was perceived that "the heart is the most deceitful of all things, desperately sick; who can fathom it?" (Jer. 17:9). The division between the righteous and the wicked is transcended by the division between God and humanity as such. Why are the good in fact sinful? And how can the Shalom of God exist when the chosen are faithless and the day of the Lord promises to be "darkness, not light" (Amos 5:20)? How will the steadfast God, who calls all wickedness to accountability, fulfill the promise to bring the kingdom, when all its hoped-for citizenry set their faces so resolutely against that purpose and deserve a rebuke commensurate with their rebellion?

Answers to those questions are advanced in various late traditions of the Old Testament. Their common features are:

1. God can be counted on to keep the divine promise. Wickedness will be punished, righteousness will prevail.
2. The future will be the time of fulfillment.
3. Consummation will be universal in scope, covering all history and nature.

Within the agreement that God shall vindicate the divine purposes exists a diversity of expectation. The late prophetic tradition suggests an intrahistorical consummation, in which the poor and oppressed will be vindicated and justice and peace will prevail. Yet the character of this fulfillment is so different from the way things now are, as for example in the transformation of nature ("the leopard shall lie down with the kid"), that it entails a qualitative rather than a quantitative leap, and thus a radical alternation of our world rather than a simple extension and perfection of what now is. Another strand of belief is much more stark in its declaration of discontinuity. For the apocalyptic tradition the world culminates in a catastrophe: a cleansed kingdom of righteousness replaces the old world.

In both the historical-transhistorical and the transcendent completions anticipated in the prophetic and apocalyptic traditions, there are the outlines for a figure who in some way facilitates the transformation. In the former case, a great prophet like Moses will lead the people out of slavery. In the latter, the hoped-for vindicator appears as the Son of Man, who will descend from heaven to settle accounts. A Messiah of mundane or supramundane qualities will fulfill God's purposes.

Another thread of Old Testament expectation appears: universal redemption must deal with the deeper problem of rebellion posed by the thwarting of God's intention by the "righteous" as well as the wicked. Universal fulfillment must take into account universal rebellion. A fundamental act of atonement will be part of consummation. Thus the messianic figure emerges as a "suffering servant." A rebellion so deep-going that the righteous and chosen *also* fall under judgment means that fulfillment must bear away radical sin. "On himself, he bore our suffering, our torments he carried, while we counted him smitten by God, struck down by disease and misery; but he was pierced for our transgressions, tortured for our iniquities; the chastisement he bore is health for us, and by his scourging we are healed. We are all strayed like sheep, each of us had his own way; but the LORD laid upon him the guilt of us all" (Isa. 53:4-6).

The dynamics within this chapter in the history of God's hope drive beyond themselves. The stage is set for the central act of the drama.[1]

---

1. For a discussion of whether the covenant with Israel *continues* after the coming of Christ — the issues of "supersessionism" and "antisupersessionism" — see the author's "The Place of Israel in Christian Faith," in *Ecumenical Faith in Evangelical Perspective* (Grand Rapids: William B. Eerdmans Publishing Company, 1993), 143-67.

4. Jesus Christ: Person and Work

W hat and who will it take to turn the world from night to Light? This narrative is the *Christian* Story because of the answer it gives to these questions. The *Person* of Jesus Christ is who it takes, and the *Work* of Jesus Christ is what is done. In this decisive chapter is an act of involvement with us that shows the *depths* and *lengths* to which God will go in the struggle with sin, evil, and death. The depth is the enfleshment of the eternal Purpose — the *Incarnation.* The length is seen in the life, suffering, death, and victory of the Vision — the *atonement.*

Although the Person and Work of Jesus Christ in the narrative itself are inseparable, for theological analysis it is necessary to treat them separately. The Person of Christ is explored in the doctrine of the Incarnation. The Work of Christ is investigated in the doctrine of the atonement.

The Person of Christ: Incarnation

Who is Jesus Christ? The clamor to answer is deafening:

- He is Jesus Christ Superstar, antihero of the counterculture.
- Not at all! He is the One who walks in the lush garden of Jesus People piety.
- By no means; Christ is no sentimental Savior of the lost soul, but the aggressive Liberator of the oppressed.

The air is filled with the claims and counterclaims of those who are quite sure they know him and walk with him — in the garden, or at the barricades.

In the current wave of interest in the figure of Jesus are two kinds of answers to the question of who he is, not unlike those that have recurred time and again in Christian history. One views him as someone much like us, the embodiment of our highest *values*. Jesus is what we are or aspire to be, writ large. Another view separates him from the ordinary lot and likes of humanity. He is what we are not and does what we cannot do, and thus is a fulfillment of our deepest *needs*. In the first case, Jesus is continuous with the world, in the second he is discontinuous; in one he is of a piece with us, albeit the brightest and best, in the other he is no part of us but comes from beyond. Which is he, Superstar or Superman?

This question also agitated theologians in the early centuries. Thus it was that the issue of the Person of Christ came to receive the greatest attention in this formative era. Just as in childhood we begin our own identity quest, so Christian theology was preoccupied with this quandary, Who is Jesus Christ? And as the maturation process in humans involves experimenting with different identities borrowed from others (playing the roles of a "significant other" — George Herbert Mead), so the Church's struggle with its identity is marked by a testing process in which some of its members tried on the hats, shoes, and clothing of contemporaries. Experimentation went on that reflected the same duality about Jesus we note today. The "spiritual" emphasis appeared in such points of view as Docetism, Apollinarianism, and Monophysitism. Beginning with the earlier forms and growing increasingly sophisticated variations on the same theme, each called into question the earthly reality and humanity of Christ. On the other hand, partisans of Christ's humanity reduced him to that single dimension, or so stressed it as to call into question its relationship to his unity with God. Hence, Ebionitism, Adoptionism, Arianism, and Nestorianism. As it happened, each of these particular options was finally deemed a "heresy," a partial truth that passed itself off as a full account of the Person of Christ. Their common shortcoming was their control by the values or needs of the interpreter. They did not do justice either to the record of Jesus in the Book of the Story or to the experience of and reflection about him in the life of the Christian community. Their account turned out to be more autobiography than the biography of God.

As it matured, the Church developed guidelines for its teaching about the Person of Christ. The heresies were clothing that had to be discarded, shoes that didn't fit, hats too garish, coats unsuitable for the climate. In the process the Christian community discovered some modest but basic things about who it really was as well as who it was not, having to do with the Person of its Lord. There affirmations have achieved universal recognition within the Church. They are related to the refrains we have seen expressed in both the current and ancient debates about the meaning of Christ. And as forceful as they are in both what they affirm and what they deny, the Church's theses are minimal, serving more as "no trespassing" signs, warnings of dangerous terrain, and signposts in the direction of promising exploration. Formulated in different stages at the councils of Nicea (325) and Chalcedon (451), these declarations still enjoy an ecumenical consensus. Who is Jesus Christ? He is *truly God, truly human, truly one.* This fundamental doctrine of the Incarnation — the deity, humanity, and unity of Jesus Christ — is the Church's effort to be faithful to the figure it met and meets in the pages of the Bible and in its own life with him. As we seek to say what these assertions mean to us today, we must go through that same discipline of understanding the biblical testimony and relating to the Christian community's experience, past and present.

The Biblical Witness

"Christology from below" is the cry today in some places. Theology is built on the Jesus who was once among us, sharing our common lot. This usually means developing a Christology from the earliest layers of Christian tradition, drawing a picture from those texts that can be established by critical scholarship to be closest to the words, deeds, and destiny of the Nazarene. This method draws heavily on the research of scholars engaged in "the new quest of the historical Jesus." They believe that the outlines of Jesus' teaching, behavior, self-understanding, and fate can be discerned in and through the overlay of the early Church's preaching, which another generation of scholars had deemed too thick to penetrate. Interest in this approach is also related to two other convictions. One is that the Church will receive a hearing from this secular generation only on the basis of well-founded historical claims. The other is that a religion rooted squarely in history needs the Jesus of *history.*

The quest from below is juxtaposed to Christology "from above." Here the stress is on the vertical incursion of God into our history, with little attention to the New Testament description of the actual career of Jesus. Assumed in this approach is the readiness to believe affirmations about transcendence in the culture and/or a knowledge from the larger habitat of Scripture and tradition of the God who comes among us at the Incarnation. In its traditional form, this method takes the New Testament texts at their face value, without the analysis of historical scholarship, and amasses them as evidence for demonstrating Christ's deity (for example, John 17:5; 12:45; 14:9-16; Matt. 3:17; 16:16; Mark 1:11; Luke 3:22; 22:69; Heb. 1:3; 7:3; Rev. 22:13) and humanity (for example, Matt. 1:1; 26:37-38; John 4:6; Luke 1:31; 4:2; 1 Tim. 2:5; 3:16; Gal. 4:4-5; Phil. 2:8; Rom. 8:3; Heb. 2:14; 1 John 4:2). In its critical form, the quest from above harnesses the results of historical scholarship (the study of the titles ascribed to Jesus, events in his career, homilies, liturgies, catechetical fragments, etc.), accepts the New Testament data as essentially the Church's proclamation, and develops its conception of the Person of Jesus from this testimony, disengaging it from ancient cosmology and sometimes reinterpreting it in existentialist categories.

The approach to Christology from below is a corrective to both the proof-text method of the tradition and the abstract tendencies of "kerygmatic" theology. However, in its present critical mode it gives imperial authority for interpreting the meaning of the central chapter of the Christian Story to a tiny segment of the Christian community, those with technical skills in historical scholarship. This expertise is a genuine gift to the Church and must be honored as a valuable perspective on the meaning of the Person of Christ. But it must also be demythologized, especially so when it reaches establishment status, with power commensurate thereto, for its offerings are themselves conditioned by the sin and finitude common to all. The statement of Christian doctrine is contoured by its learnings (the glass of vision shaped by the rings of Church and world), and the perception of the Gospel is influenced by its findings (the eye of faith peers through the rings of Church and world), but the light of truth is finally given by the Holy Spirit and passes through the biblical aperture open to all who choose to look through it. We shall make use of the findings "from below" as part, but only as part, of the larger effort to take into account the witness of the biblical seer to the meaning of the Person of Christ.

102

Our use here of key New Testament data about the Person of Christ is related to our narrative method of expounding Christian belief. As such it might be characterized as Christology "from before" rather than "from below" or "from above." We seek the meaning of Christ from within the unfolding Story. That plot is grounded in the primal Purpose of God and proceeds through the events of invitation, resistance, and overture: creation, fall, covenant. Our understanding of who Christ is must have an intrinsic relationship to the trajectory of this saga. We shall seek to interpret the doctrine of the Incarnation — the deity, humanity, and unity of Christ — against this background, drawing on the resources of Christian tradition and the setting of our contemporary world as well as the biblical source.

The Deity of Christ

Are there clues within the biblical record that connect the chapter on Incarnation with its antecedents? The fulfillment of messianic expectations constitutes one set of such clues. Christ's own self-interpretation, messianic or unitive with God in some way, is yet another, leaving aside the exegetical question of whether these passages are in fact the actual words of Christ or those of a later interpreter (for example, Christ's parable of the vine-dressers who refused the messengers, then killed the vineyard owner's emissary son, Luke 20:9-16). However, there is a commentary on the meaning of Jesus Christ that puts his coming into the longest possible perspective and makes daring connections between its ultimate origins and their sequel. The prologue of John is a classical locus of christological thought.

The author of this prologue sets the stage for the Incarnation in eternity. The "beginnings" of Jesus Christ lie in the Godhead, as its Logos — the eternal Word and Vision of God. Whatever Jesus is to the natural eye reviewing the events in Galilee, the eye of faith sees him in unity with the history of God's pursuit of the eternal Purpose. John traces that pilgrimage from the source — "In the beginning was the Word, and the Word was with God, and the Word was God" (John 1:1) — into the maelstrom of claim and rebuff. Thus comes creation, in which the Word marks all that is: "The Word, then, was with God at the beginning, and through him all things came to be; no single thing was created without him" (John 1:2-3). Also comes that special creature, humanity, called to

103

answer for the world God's invitation to Shalom: "All that came to be was alive with life, and that life was the light of men" (John 1:5). But darkness descended, the No said by the world to the offer of life and light. "But the darkness never mastered it" (John 1:5). The beckoning of God continues as the "law was given through Moses" (John 1:17). This new vision of the divine claim still does not turn the race away from its pursuit of darkness. Yet the last of the line of this people's visionaries, the prophet John, points to another horizon. For now what was far away, signaling to the world from a distance, has drawn near. This seer discerns in our midst the Light of the world. "This is the man I meant when I said, 'He came after me, but takes rank before me, for before I was born, he already was'" (John 1:15). In Jesus Christ "the Word became flesh; he came to dwell among us, and we saw his glory, such glory as befits the Father's only Son, full of grace and truth" (John 1:14).

The Incarnation is the arrival of the One whose previous invitations and entreaties have gone unheeded. Enfleshment means "Emmanuel," *God with us*. The coming of Jesus is the approach of God to the scene of rebellion. No more will messages and messengers do, the inner light of conscience, the rainbow over all creation, the pillar of fire that moves in history. These flashes have been obscured and avoided by the darkness of sin, evil, and death. Now no hiding is possible, for Light comes into our very midst (Luke 2:32; John 8:12; 9:5). "God was *in* Christ . . ." (2 Cor. 5:19).

The Journey of the Logos

The author uses the primarily personal or psychological metaphor of Logos, which allows distinctions to be made within Deity, carried through to God's singular presence in Jesus Christ.

Following the Logos distinctions made by Theophilus of Antioch, we might say that the narrative begins with the *Logos endiathetos,* the indwelling Logos, as the inner plan, purpose, reason, and vision of God. Thus God is conceived as *One with Logos,* in both senses of the phrase. There is no God without a Purpose, no designless, purposeless, planless, visionless God. Yet there is in this unity a distinction between Purpose and Purposer, Reason and Reasoner, Plan and Planner, Vision and Envisioner. Thus unity and duality are both honored by the metaphor: "The Logos was with God, and the Logos was God."

Since the writer's attention is fixed on the relation of God to Christ, there is no mention in the text of the third aspect of the Godhead, the Holy Spirit. But the narrative implies that the Holy Spirit is the Power to fulfill the Vision, an idea later made explicit as the Story in its fullness was unfolded.

The focus of the continuing narrative is on the Logos. This is the organ of divine activity, the way God reaches out. John switches to a secondary metaphor regularly associated with Logos, namely light. Reading it against its background meaning, the activity of the divine Light in creation is that of the *Logos prophorikos,* the outgoing of the indwelling Logos. Now inner reason becomes outer expression, or Word. In ancient thought, a word does what it says; it has effectual power. Hence, the Word is creative of the world. Brought to be is the covenant partner of God, the intended friend of God. By using this concept of Logos, the writer and his patristic interpreters were able to link their affirmations about Jesus and the God of Jesus with their cultural sensibilities. In this case it meant that he is of a piece with that design which shapes creation. And more: he is the key to knowing what it is.

At the peak of creation is humanity. Made in the image of God, granted the little light of reason and vision, human beings received the *Logos spermatikos.* This characterization from another ancient father, Justin Martyr, interprets John's references to the "light which enlightens" each person who comes into the world. Joining the metaphor of sowing to that of reasoning, Justin speaks of the seeds of divine wisdom scattered among all people and found in the spiritual and rational capacities of humans preserved in their brokenness by the covenant with Noah.

The climax of John's account takes us from an indwelling Logos through an outgoing and enlightening Logos enacted in the history of Israel to an *enfleshed* Logos. *Logos ensarkos* is the deep penetration of a recalcitrant world, God entering the arena of rebellion. Incarnation is the enfleshment of Shalom, God with us, God as the second Person of the eternal Trinity. In the familial imagery that grows out of the New Testament picture of Jesus' own intimacy with God, what took place at Bethlehem was the coming of the eternal Son of the Father. The trinitarian language of God as Father and Son expresses the duality in unity of enfleshed Logos. Jesus Christ is the singular and real Presence of God, a reach into history of the eternal Vision in the Godhead, the Logos that has been already in active and agonizing engagement with the world. Two wrongheaded conclusions can be drawn both from the kind of metaphor used to express the finally inexpressible mystery of the Incarnation and from our frail human attempts at clarification. The language of Word, Son, Vision suggests that Incarnation might not involve all of God, that the Envisioner or the Father is once removed from the encounter. Classical theology evolved the earlier-mentioned notion of "coinherence" of the Persons (mutual interpenetration) to fend off such misunderstanding. Incarnation means the enfleshment *of God as such,* not a feature or phase of Deity. The work to be accomplished in the Incarnation can only be efficacious if it is God in the fullness of Deity that enters the arena of rebellion. The interpenetration of the Persons of the Trinity means that all are present in the functions of each. Thus the Father and Spirit are present in the Person and Work of the Son. There is no Son without Father: the Logos is the "knowledge by which God knows himself" (Augustine); or the Vision by which God sees himself; Christ is the "effulgence of God's splendor, and the stamp of God's very being" (Heb. 1:3); God of God, Light of Light.

Another false path is to portray the Incarnation as the coming of either a supernatural man who lived with God from all eternity or the enfleshment of a second God called the Son, who sat in eternal council with Spirit and Father and left this region to be with us. The first idea is a denial of the Incarnation, postulating the preexistence of an eternal man and thus calling into question the uniqueness of the joining of Deity with real humanity in Christ. The second is "tritheism," which fractures the unity of God or becomes "bitheism" by the departure of the Son from heaven to earth.

The Miracle of Shalom

"Conceived by the Holy Spirit, and born of the virgin Mary." The ancient creed celebrates the historical reality of God's power. The descent of the Spirit, divine grace, is characterized always by *both* favor and power. Grace is *favor toward* and *power in.* The traditional debates about God's personal grace toward us have revolved around whether it is the declaration of pardon toward us or the activity of spiritual power in us. Exclusive emphasis on grace as power has fallen prey to the error of "salvation by works." Exclusive emphasis on grace as pardon has neglected the fact that we shall know the presence of grace by its fruits, its seeds springing up in good works. The foundation for the duality of favor and power is the Incarnation itself: "The girl's name was Mary. The angel went in and said to her, 'Greetings, most favored one! The Lord is with you'" (Luke 1:27-28). In the ancient world the conviction that the special favor of God had made its entrance into history at this point came to expression in the way divine intrusions were marked, by astounding nature miracles. Favor toward Jesus Christ meant power, and therefore power to make the ordinary extraordinary.

How can this authentic perception that grace is divine favor that manifests itself in divine power be expressed today? In our time it is not the astounding feat of nature but the miracle of history that commands attention. Rendered blasé by both the wonders of science and the constraints of its empirical worldview, the incarnational signal once given by the teaching of the virginal conception no longer is heard by the world. The premises of modernity by no means preclude it. In fact, a rigorous science will not declare impossible *a priori* a claim of this sort. However, in our era the sign of power is a changed life, the conviction carried by things seen. It is who Jesus was and what Jesus did in his day-to-day relationships that will be scrutinized for evidences of the power that authenticates.

Here a picture emerges from the work of contemporary biblical scholarship on the historical Jesus. The Incarnation of Shalom manifests itself in *miracles of Shalom.* In what Jesus Christ did in his life and ministry to liberate from the powers of darkness is attested the presence of the Power (Spirit) of the Light (Son). Where the sinner is forgiven and renewed, the arrogant and apathetic turned around, the principality of evil challenged or exorcised, the sick healed, the downtrodden lifted up, the dead raised, and the Good News preached, there the power of Shalom breaks into our history. The things that Jesus did were grounded in who he was. His life of selfless love and servanthood embodied the love and servanthood of God. His behavior gave evidence of a freedom from the dark powers and an unswerving commitment to the Light. The Incarnation as a theological affirmation was attested by the signs and wonders of his historical *being* and *doing.* In that twofold sense he is our Peace, our Liberator, our Reconciler.

The signs of divine power spill out from the being and doing into the teaching and preaching of Jesus. The human Jesus had the power to see the Vision of God. He pointed to and prayed for the onrushing Future. The reign of God was coming toward the world, the rule in which the pure in heart would see God, the peacemaker would be vindicated, the prisoner released, the lame walk, the dead be raised, and the Kingdom come. In political, personal, and natural idiom he portrayed Israel's ancient hope of Shalom. For him this New Age was at hand when nature, human nature, supernature, and God would be free and peaceful before and with each other.

107

This pointing was more than the future-orientation of the prophet. "At hand" meant *here,* as well as *near.* The power of evil was even now under attack and losing ground to the coming King. And this heavenly favor toward us manifests itself as the power of the Regent who even now casts out of the world the occupying armies of the Evil One. The sick are healed, sins are forgiven, demons exorcised, temptation overcome, and faith born! And we are called to pray that this Kingdom finally come on earth in the full glory of its Light.

The work of biblical scholars gives us a clue to Jesus' self-understanding. This "eschatological prophet" sees himself as the first wave of the inbreaking Future. Through him the powers of the New Age arrive. He has authority over the demonic and makes the wounded whole. He puts others in touch with the portents of freedom and reconciliation, the firstfruits of the coming Realm. The debate over the meaning and self-application of the titles of Jesus continues, but an impressive body of scholarship holds the view that Jesus saw himself to be one with the divine initiative being taken in the Kingdom's coming.

From Jesus' self-understanding, his embodiment of and teaching about the coming Reign of Shalom, it is not far to the Church's declaration that in Christ "dwells all the fulness of the Godhead bodily" (Col. 2:9 KJV). He is the Son of the Father, the second Adam, Lord, Logos. Here Light penetrated darkness.

The Humanity of Christ

Some accent "*God* with us" to the point of erasing "God with *us.*" This happened early in the history of Christian thought and practice, as in the Docetism of the second century, which turned the events in Jesus' life into phantom appearances. A highly spiritualized Jesus only *seemed* to have but did not in fact have a body that was born in the travail of childbirth, hungered when without food, and bled when pierced, or a spirit that doubted and suffered. And in subsequent times the same impulse to make Jesus more divine than God intended took subtler forms: as in Apollinarianism, which taught that the Logos preempted that all too fallible capacity in human beings called mind or spirit; or as in Monophysitism, in which the passion for divinizing Jesus acknowledged only in a formal way that the "two natures" of Christ — his full deity and full humanity — existed before the Incarnation, but so fused them after Bethlehem as to let the former annihilate the latter.

Subtler practices and beliefs of the Church of the early centuries pointed in the same direction but were never officially called to account. A favorite image, one used here, light, lent itself to the overdivinizing tendency, as the incandescent coal. The glowing coal ignited by the divine Fire suggests a transformation of the historical Jesus that does not comport with the formal declarations of these same writers of his real and persisting humanity. This view of Christ had its counterpart in both a portraiture of Jesus and a spirituality about him that was once removed from the moil and toil that God came to share and redeem. False spiritualizing of Christ continues as a tempting heresy to this day whenever the Christ who was born as we are, and suffered, struggled, and dies as we do, is censored from the Story.

Docetism and its heirs are a wrong reading because the picture they paint of Christ bears no resemblance to the figure described in the Bible. Further, as the Church soon declared, the Incarnation of the Word means divine *solidarity* with us. The battle for Shalom must be fought out on this plane. If the enemy are to be met, they must be confronted in the arena in which they are to be found. Sin, evil, and death do their business here.

The way of solidarity is to respect the integrity of the created order. As Irenaeus put it, God plays fair, engaging the foe by the "persuasion" that befits the divine nature, not by the tyranny of brute force. Incarnation happens in our own homeland, for the divine vulnerability wills to encounter the foe on its own terrain rather than rule by fiat.

Not only must the struggle be *waged* here, but it must be *won* in and through a human being. To this end God takes our flesh. The Work of salvation is to be done by a "truly human" Person, and can be accomplished only by a divine Person. The creature with the human face is at the heart of the problem, and only God can solve it. Jesus Christ — the God who is truly human.

Sharing Our Common Lot

True humanity, in the sense that we mean it here (it can also mean truly human in a *normative* sense as well as in this *descriptive* sense — as what persons ought to be at their best, not only what they most essentially are in their common humanity), true humanity in Jesus covers each dimension of our ordinariness. In its most elemental aspect, Jesus' humanity is his *bodily* humanity. From the genuine pangs of his birth, through his suckling at Mary's breast and "diapering" at her hand, to the stomach hungers and aching arms at noonday in Joseph's carpenter shop, the dusty and dirty feet and sweaty limbs in his Galilean pilgrimages, and finally the hemorrhaging side and parched lips and agonizing physical pains of his death, he truly shared our common lot. Identification with us is participation in all the ills to which mortal flesh is heir.

Sharing our common lot also means having a truly human *mind*. (We are using the familiar tripartite distinction of body, mind, and spirit as a way of expressing the dimensions of our humanity, understanding that these are not separate segments of our being as in the older "faculty psychology" but inseparable activities within a psychosomatic unity.) Jesus thought the way we think. To take this affirmation of a truly human mind as seriously as we take the equivalent declaration about Jesus' truly human body does not come easily. Many of us draw back from its implications and at this point become practicing Docetists. For to believe that Jesus Christ is truly human in his intellectual powers means that he simply does not know everything. He is no creature whose X-ray eyes can penetrate objects and even know the thoughts of others, a superhuman view of Jesus that has had a long history in popular Christianity. His mind is formed by the times and teaching to which he was exposed, evolving as it does for everyone else in natural fashion: he "grew in wisdom and stature" (Luke 2:52). This means that Jesus thought in the categories provided for him by the period in which he lived, a time of late Jewish Messianism, a period of outward struggle with Rome and inward struggle marked by the religious and political factions of the day. His teaching took these contemporary thought-forms and modeled them according to his unique vision. Marked as this teaching is by the transient movements and perceptions of time, it carries all their limitations, including the expectation of the end of the world in the years immediately ahead of him. When God chose solidarity with us, the divine Self-limitation risked that kind of finitude.

He is "one who in every respect has been tempted as we are . . ." (Heb. 4:15 RSV). Participation in the depths of human existence means acceptance of *all* its vulnerability. As the writer of Hebrews is at pains to point out, this entails vulnerability of *spirit* as well as mind and body. Christ did not have cast-iron protection against the cares and allurements of this world any more than against the ills of this mortal flesh. He could hear the beguiling voices of temptation to arrogance at the beginning of his ministry and despair at its close, the invitations of sensual satisfaction and the easy out. Dare we imagine Christ was subject to the same onslaughts of spiritual incitement or malaise as we are? Yet how could we not believe this to be so if he is to be the one who rescues us? "He can help those who are tempted because he has been tempted and suffered" (Heb. 2:18). He speaks and acts with the authority of one who has been there too.

The more forthrightly we attend to the human qualities of Christ, the more insistently comes the question: If Jesus is the enfleshment of the Almighty God, how can this kind of frailty and finitude be ascribed to him? Must not the God-human by definition be "above it all," sharing in the divine omnipotence? While this quandary belongs to our exploration of the unity of the Person to be discussed next, we examine it here at this special pressure point.

The uneasiness about a full-blooded affirmation of Christ's humanity is invariably associated with a false conception of divine presence and power with which we have to contend throughout the Christian narrative. It is a notion that conceives of God's almightiness according to our own norms of absolute power as instant control everywhere. But in the trinitarian origins of the Christian Story the Power of God is the Holy Spirit, the Spirit of the Son and Word of God. The Spirit that brings freedom and peace acts in a fashion commensurate with that end, not by despotic overlordship but by a liberating and reconciling love. To forswear machismo means that in all the deeds of God from creation to consummation, we have to do not with "sultanic" power but with "He who lets us be" (Geddes MacGregor). In the Incarnation this vulnerable Love manifests its omnipotence precisely in its capacity to let Jesus be fully human, in withholding the impulse to dominate. Ultimately that omnipotence is exercised in both the Person and Work of Christ when the power of powerlessness, the lure of the Vision of suffering Love, brings to be in the Nazarene the "first of a new race" destined to live in unity with God. "God's weakness is stronger than human strength" (1 Cor. 1:25 RSV).

The Sinlessness of Jesus

He was "tempted as we are, yet without sinning" (Heb. 4:15 RSV). What is this? An intrusion on the unfolding logic of Jesus' real humanity? A perverse change in the thrust of the text by forces bent on defending Docetism at one last barricade? Modern humanizers of Jesus dismiss not

111

only this text, but the long tradition declaring the sinlessness of Jesus as just that kind of timidity unwilling to acknowledge the radical identification with the human condition, which is sin itself. And is there not a Pauline assertion that for us he was in fact "made sin" (2 Cor. 5:21)? Out of such reasoning comes the lush growth of contemporary speculation on this or that sin to which Jesus gave either tacit assent or active expression.

Clarity on this aspect of the Person of Christ requires that we ask whether the insistence on the sinlessness of Christ in Christian tradition is accounted for only by a latent Docetism. Also, we must be clear about the meaning of the term as it applies to Jesus.

We interpret the sinlessness of Jesus in the Christian Story in terms of one of our translation keys, vision. Sin is blindness to the Light, turning away from the Vision of God in pursuit of our own dreams. Sinlessness is unswerving sight of the divine Light, undeviating obedience to the divine Vision. The sinlessness of Jesus is "unclouded vision" (Herbert Farmer) of the Kingdom of God and the "set of the will" (C. F. D. Moule) commensurate thereto. Here is the purity of heart that wills one thing. When the Kingdom comes, "the pure in heart shall see God" (Matt. 5:8 KJV). But this Realm has entered our history in Jesus, the sight of God has been given, and this One who sees *is* pure in heart. The power of the divine Light has pierced the darkness of this world, drawing Jesus toward its Source. Christ as the seer and server of the Vision of God has unclouded sight; he is "of purer eyes than to behold iniquity" (Hab. 1:13 KJV). The firmness of this perceptual bond as it is attested to in the New Testament record is such as to prompt the traditional formulations of Christ as *non posse peccare:* Jesus was not able to sin. He so lived out of this Vision that he could not be other than what he was. In spite of the tempting bypaths, it was impossible for him to be out of character.

Clarity of vision, steadiness of intent, and purity of heart do not exhaust the meaning of sinlessness. Implied in these things is Jesus' public expression of the divine Purpose. By whatever measure we have, be it the outlines of his behavior perceived through historical analysis of the most primitive layers of New Testament tradition, the testimony of the Gospels, or the absence of any tradition outside the corpus of Christian writings that questions its character, a life emerges whose conduct conforms to the ways of righteousness and truth. Jesus of Nazareth liberated us from the bondages of sin, evil, and death and made possible a reconciliation between humanity, nature, and God.

The Church came to assert the sinlessness of Jesus not only from its confrontation with the New Testament portrait but also from what appeared to be the logic of the atonement. If redemption of the world from sin, evil, and death happened here, then the person who did the work had to have certain characteristics. Satisfaction, substitutionary, and sacrificial theories required a guileless Jesus who deserved no punishment and therefore was free to offer his innocent life in propitiation for our sins. Even if these understandings of the atonement are less than adequate, they do demonstrate the inseparability of Person and Work and illustrate the importance of the teaching of Jesus' sinlessness. Can we restate their intention in our own framework?

As we shall see in our subsequent examination of the Work of Christ, the role of Jesus as Prophet, the seer and exemplar of the Realm of God, is one of the aspects of his Work. Here the Purpose of God is displayed in human history, one that discloses who God is and exposes who we are. If this Work is to be done, then the life of Christ must be transparent to the divine Light. We must be able to see in and through him the unstinting Love that bears the world toward freedom and peace. What adds further to this role is the interpretation we have given here of the power of God that gives visibility to the favor of God declared to be present in the Incarnation. For the Work of Christ as revealer of Shalom there must be a clear glass of vision, and for the reality of Christ as the Person of Shalom, there must be the evidence of miracles of Love. Sinlessness means that in and through the attitude and action of Jesus of Nazareth we have an unobstructed view of ultimate Reality. This has nothing to do with speculations about the ambiguity of moral decisions of one who lived and worked in the real world of a carpenter's shop (that Jesus could have used products that might have been looted from some passing camel train), or legalistic observations (that the breaking of the alabaster vase and the cleansing of the temple, although intended to witness to his messianic role, were short of his own concern for the poor and his cheek-turning counsels), or theories that interpret temptation as itself already sin. The sinlessness of Jesus is not a pedantic tabulation. Rather, it is the capacity of this figure in its firmness of intent and constancy of character to direct the eye of faith to the Vision of God.

The atoning work is not exhausted by the Prophet of Galilee, but moves toward the suffering Priest of Calvary and the risen King of Easter morning. The earlier-mentioned theories of atonement have rightly seen that the sinlessness of Christ is a necessary assumption of the priestly office of Christ. But its integral relation to the crucifixion does not consist of a need for an innocent sacrifice slaughtered in our place in order to appease an angry Deity. (An alternative understanding of the act of substitution will be explored in our subsequent inquiry concerning the work accomplished on Golgotha.) Rather, it is the necessity of finding in this human being the kind of undeviating commitment and radical obedience that constitutes the requisite organ of atonement. Jesus' sinlessness in passion and crucifixion consisted of that set of the will and unswerving pursuit of the Light that beckoned him forward to his destiny. His perfection consisted in his "obedience unto death" (Phil 2:8). He was the fit instrument for the work of suffering that was to defeat sin and evil, a hard-won faithfulness that passed through the fires of temptation to deviate from the course, one that persisted to the very end. That is the consummate nobility of purpose and action that draws from the faith community the testimony that there is one who has conquered where we have experienced defeat: "true humanity" in the *normative* sense. Here is the one who is "tempted as we are, yet without sinning."

Believing in the sinlessness of Christ is no guarantee that the Incarnation will be given its full due. In fact those who have spoken most enthusiastically about the character of Jesus, as have his nineteenth-century biographers, may say nothing about the "*God* with us" aspect of this chapter of the Story. In this respect it is analogous to insistence on the virgin birth. Belief in the virginal conception is no guarantee of a high doctrine of Christ, for among its most vigorous defenders were the second-century "Adoptionists," who asserted that Christ acquired divinity at his baptism or his resurrection.

As the first centuries of church history were characterized by the overdivinizing tendencies noted earlier, so this same time of experimentation produced other kinds of overhumanization like that of the Adoptionists. The earliest wave was represented by Ebionites, for whom Jesus was the greatest in the line of Israel's patriarchs and prophets. As the councils and creeds of the Church became more explicit in declaring off-limits the cruder forms of overhumanizing, this anthropocentrism took subtler forms, as in the famous Arian view that the Son was divine but created in time, falling short of participation in the eternal being of the Father. And in the still hotly debated position of Nestorianism, the humanity was so accented as to call into question its genuine unity with God in the

Person of Jesus, the two natures being joined in popular Nestorianism like glued pieces of wood.

The uneasy peace between affirmations of both the deity and the humanity of Christ leads us to the climactic assertion in the early debates about the Person of Christ, and the third element of what has come to be an ecumenical consensus on the Incarnation: the unity of Christ. To this we now turn.

The Unity of Christ

The formal declaration of the unity of Jesus Christ's Person was made by the ancient Church-in-council at Chalcedon in A.D. 451. In him is to be found *one Person* in *two natures*. And these natures are "without confusion, without change, without division, without separation; the distinction of the natures being in no wise done away by the union. . . ."

The assertion of oneness of Person was made against the immediate background of the Nestorians' seeming inability to get the two natures together, ending up with what looked like a concept that turned Christ into two persons. On the other hand, the Monophysites, pressing for the deity of Christ and pursuing relentlessly a simplistic unity, ended by turning the unity of the Person into a oneness of nature, the divine nature. How are we to walk this tightrope, falling off neither on the side of two persons nor on the side of one nature?

Some things came clear in the early debates about what ought to be and ought not to be asserted in this critical balance. We get a clue from the struggle with the Apollinarians mentioned earlier. In this exchange the right of Jesus to his own human ego was won. It is strange indeed that this had to be defended, but such is the imperialistic inclination of the partisans of Christ's divinity. The integrity of Jesus' self was reiterated in the sixth century in the Dyothelete controversy, when Monothelitism was rejected and the reality of Christ's own human *will* was affirmed. Thus two natures means that two centers of choosing, two egos, have to be taken into account in any statement of the unity of Christ.

But does not this violate the oneness of Person? Is this not a Christ with a double personality? To find a way of saying No to this while saying Yes to the two natures is difficult indeed. Another blind alley was marked out in the debates around the word *anhypostasia,* which is translated as impersonal human nature. The ancient Church opted for this in some of its formulas because it seems to guard the unity of Christ. It declares that there can be only one Person in Christ, and that is the second Person of the Trinity, the Logos, the Son of the Father. Thus the unity of the Person of Christ is assured by the integrating role of the divine Person. What happens to the humanity of Jesus then? It must be asserted, but interpreted as *impersonal* humanity. Here we run into translation problems because the Greek word *hypostasis,* which we translate "person," does not necessarily nor originally mean self-consciousness as it does in modern parlance, but *subsistence* or *continuing identity.* Hence what is being said in the notion of anhypostasia is that the fundamental defining identity of Christ is given by the "Godness" of Christ, that without it there would be no uniqueness. However, our translation of this as impersonal human nature is an awkward one, as it seems to suggest a cold, abstract, and non-self-conscious quality. But the rejection of Apollinarianism and Monothelitism argues otherwise; it does not mean non-personness in the sense of non-ego, or non-self-conscious willing. What we can learn from this debate is that (1) unity must be maintained whatever the duality of selves and (2) the unity is finally grounded in God.

Can we go beyond saying what this unity is not, avoiding the temptations to fall off on either side and having only the barest of guidelines (one Person, two natures)? Some say this is as far as we can go in making sense out of this classic teaching. Or as it is sometimes put, we have to do here with a "paradox." A paradox or antinomy is the bold assertion of mutually contradictory statements. Those who defend this characterization of the Incarnation are at pains to distinguish paradox from a straightforward contradiction. A paradox is something made necessary by our experience. The experience cited may be the commitment one has to the Scriptures or to the traditions of the Church. Here the belief in Jesus Christ as both God and human is assumed or asserted, and we bow before this authority. Or experience may be understood as our own personal religious experience, in which we come to know Christ personally in this mysterious duality-in-unity. Or, as in Donald Baillie's famous discussion of paradox, our *experience of grace* as captured in Paul's declaration "I . . . yet not I" (1 Cor. 15:10) may be used as an analogy for understanding the Incarnation. Yet again, we may demonstrate that paradoxes are necessary for the grasping of many general human experiences, as for example the complementarity of wave and particle theories of light.

116

However used, the idea of paradox seeks to maintain the modesty that is appropriate to the mystery of the Incarnation.

The option of paradox seems particularly inviting when the efforts to go beyond it in the history of Christian thought are canvassed. Their zeal to explain the mystery drives them regularly off one side of the tightrope or the other. Here is the key, says a popular modern option: the unity lies in the fact that the humanity of Jesus maximized is what the deity of Jesus means: human love reaching its zenith is God's love. However elaborated (as for example by making Jesus' love light-years away from our puny efforts), this scenario cannot intrinsically recognize the radical new-ness, the overagainstness, the action of God toward us, that the Incarnation of deity is meant to announce, for it is trapped in a distinction of degree. But *here* is the key, says another: the unity of Christ consists in the manifest power of God in the extraordinary not the ordinary, the superhuman not the human, the miraculous not the natural. But if deity so construed is seen in the wonder-worker or in the moral and spiritual paragon, where then is the ordinary, the human, the natural that the doctrine of Incarna-tion honors? So Christ becomes God walking around in the disguise of a human being, and once again Docetism beckons. The sacrifice of either true deity in the first instance or true humanity in the second is too high a price to pay for a neatly drawn formula of unity.

A Shared Vision

The philosophical or religious reductionisms that erode the affirmation of one Person and two natures do not exhaust the options. The paradox cannot be *explained,* but it can be *explored.* While the final mystery of the Incarnation cannot be penetrated, we do not have to settle for a simple assertion of paradoxical unity-in-duality. A metaphor-motif in our trans-lation process sheds a small glimmer of light on what the paradox might mean for us and our contemporaries.

The visionary movements and persons of our time have given us some experience of the process of envisioning. Whether it be a Martin Luther King, Jr., who holds up a brilliant dream of liberation from op-pression, or a modern astrophysicist who dreams of the exploring of outer space, we know something about lifting the sights of vision to view what these seers project. It is *their* vision. If it were not for them our sight would be dimmed, but the fires of their perception kindle ours. And we come to see something of what they point to. In fact, where this enabling of widespread dreaming does not happen, a culture is seriously impoverished. "Where there is no vision, the people perish" (Prov. 29:18 KJV). Visions are made to be shared.

The unity of Jesus with God is to be found in their common Vision. What God projects on the screen of the future, the man of Galilee sees. This is the eternal Logos, the Son of the Father. Jesus is one with the eternal Logos. His Vision of the Kingdom is God's Vision. The nature of Jesus' seeing is his own, as is also the nature of the projecting God. Yet they coalesce in the unity of the Sight seen. The seeing by the inner eye of the human Jesus is not possible except by the prevenient action of deity. The Vision of God goes before the Vision of Jesus. Thus the identity of the Person of Christ is taken from deity, as the awkward language of anhypostasia sought to say, but it in no way eliminates the genuine human process in which Jesus "catches sight of" the Glory of God.

While this metaphor gives some meaning to the paradox of unity in Christ, it cannot be pushed to its limits without doing violence to that same unity. Thus it assumes a psychological setting, the development of Jesus to the place where he points to and announces the Kingdom of God, and does not cover that time from conception to the launching of this ministry. Driven to its logical extreme, it would express a form of Adoptionism and foreshorten the Incarnation. But Shalom is in unity with Jesus not only when he perceives it, but throughout his life. He lives and moves and has his being in the Light, envisioned or otherwise. Thus it is but a modest metaphor that yields up some insight but does not give a God's-eye view. It is an explored but not an explained paradox, and therefore remains a paradox, meaningful but not metaphysically encompassed.

Jesus Christ, truly human, truly God, truly one, the Word made flesh, the Light of God in the face of Jesus (2 Cor. 4:6). "And we saw his glory, such glory as befits the Father's only Son, full of grace and truth" (John 1:14).

The Work of Christ: Atonement

We come now to the fundamental action of the Christian drama. The chief protagonist confronts the antagonists on their own ground. The incarnate Light meets the armies of night. Here, Christians believe, deliverance happens, Jesus Christ liberates from sin, evil, and death, and makes possible the reconciliation, the *at-one-ment* of a broken creation.

As this is the turning point in the epic of redemption, so its report and interpretation are central to the life of faith and theology. The Work of Christ is Christian faith in microcosm. What we have to say about this teaching is the key to how we read the whole Christian Story.

A strange irony attends this centrality. We have an ecumenical consensus about the Person of Christ — Jesus Christ, truly God, truly human, truly one. There is no equivalent agreement in Christian history on the Work of Christ. We may have to qualify this by an "as yet." Just as it took four hundred years in the childhood of the Christian community to establish its most elementary self-concept, the Person of Christ, so the search for an understanding of the Work may be an adolescent identity quest. Indeed, some of the tumultuous struggles from the high Middle Ages through the Reformation and Enlightenment to the erratic pendulum swings of contemporary theology (from the death of God to the new surge of piety) seem to suggest just that kind of puberty. Be that as it may, there is no comparable framework for examining Christian belief about this crucial affirmation. And it may be because of its fundamental nature that the faith community must work that much harder and longer on its definition, living through the high passions and partisanships surrounding the search. Clarity of conviction also waits on the coming of a life together within the Christian community. Catholicity of belief rises out of universality of corporate existence, a common life we have not had since the first major cleavage of the eleventh century. Perhaps the growing informal unity of common mission and theological work portends that community of life and thought.

While there are no ecumenical assertions about the atonement, there is a rich vein of material that is mined by various theological working parties. This ore is shared by all and suggests a unity of direction that the specific differences of formula may conceal. Let us examine this common lode.

A. Biblical Data

1. Old Testament Trajectories

Included here are the sacrificial-priestly, visionary-prophetic, and political-kingly traditions in a messianic framework.

2. Contemporary Jesus Research

In the discussion of the Person of Christ, we traced the outlines of the figure of Jesus of Nazareth as these are discerned by contemporary historical scholarship. That material is important also for our understanding of the atonement. The glimpse we have of the Galilean includes his proclamation of the coming Kingdom of God, its presence as well as its futurity, its powerful signs to be seen wherever liberation and reconciliation happen in our midst, Jesus' own profound sense of unity with this Kingdom and its God and the authority this unity gave him to call to account and to forgive sin, and his power to embody an extravagant freedom and love.

3. Critical Events or Life Segments

Birth, Galilean ministry, crucifixion, and resurrection are the focal points.

4. Titles Ascribed to Jesus

While these are often examined with a view to his Person, they also have strong implications for his Work. They include Messiah, Lord, Son of God, Son of Man, Master, Teacher, Servant, Logos, Shepherd, Lamb of God, Prophet, Priest, King.

5. Metaphors of Work Accomplished

The Work of Christ receives its earliest formulations by way of a cascade of rich images drawn from the world of the first century. Dominant metaphors are taken from (a) the temple: atonement itself, purification, offering, cultic and priestly practice (John 1:29; 1 John 1:7; 3:5; Titus 2:14; Heb. 9:28; Rev. 7:14); (b) law court: judgment, punishment, forensic framework (Acts 10:42; 17:31; Rom. 3:20; 8:32-34; 2 Cor. 5:10; 2 Tim.

4:1; 1 Pet. 3:18); (c) the marketplace: debt, purchase, payment, redemption, commerce (Acts 20:28; Rom. 3:24; Gal. 3:13; 4:5; Titus 2:14; 1 Pet. 1:18); (d) pedagogy: teaching, learning, exemplifying, revealing (Matt. 20:26-28; Matt. 5–7; Mark 4:1-34; John 3:2); (e) battle: captivity, liberation, ransom, peace, victory (Mark 3:27; 10:45; Eph. 2:14-16; 6:14; Phil. 2:9-10; Col. 2:15); (f) presence: transfiguration, life, light (John 1:4; 5:26, 40; 8:12; 10:10; 11:25; 14:6).

B. Tradition

1. Theories

The complexity of the data and the need to bring the Christian message to bear on the problems the Church faced as it confronted changing circumstances combined to generate a number of theories of atonement. The process usually involved the elaboration of a particular metaphor. Thus the cultic imagery is developed into one or another form of sacrificial theory; the image of the law court is drawn out in terms of a penal substitutionary theory; a commercial theory emerges out of the marketplace metaphor; a conflict and victory or liberation theory extends the battlefield metaphor; a moral influence theory expands the pedagogical image; and beyond these constructs are exemplarist, incarnational, ransom, rectoral, satisfaction, penitential, representative, and other theories. In an attempt to do justice to other New Testament metaphors as well as to the richness of biblical data in general, each theory uses other imagery and themes as well. So in practice, the distinctions are never quite as sharp as the labels suggest. But one metaphor does tend to be the organizing center for the others and provide its dominant language.

2. Issues

Contributing to the choice of metaphor and the line of thought developed in connection with it is the question posed by the culture out of which the theory grows, or the issue felt to be most compelling by the theory maker. Thus a principle of selection is introduced into the biblical text by the problem faced by the Church in a given time and place. If transiency and mortality press the Church for some word, then the interpretation of the Work of Christ is predisposed to think in terms of immortality made possible by the Eternal entering time, and hence a focus on the Incarnation. If ignorance is viewed as the issue, then the understanding of Christ as the revealer comes to be stressed. If the perils of nature or history are to the fore, then it is the liberating Work of Christ that takes on significance. And if sin and guilt grip a culture, or ought to, then judgment and mercy are decisive themes. In this way, questions and issues in a given milieu make their presence felt on a doctrine of the atonement. And further, answers developed within the culture in the form of philosophical, social, or political systems and patterns also congregate around the question posed, influencing its understanding of the Work of Christ.

3. Segments of Christ's Career

Another factor that shapes Christian thinking about the atonement is the attraction of the events on one or another leg of Christ's own journey. In fact, there is a strong correlation between the issue felt to be decisive for the Work of Christ and the stage on Christ's way. Thus the problem of the passingness of things, as in ancient Greek culture and philosophy, draws from the Church the incarnational themes of patristic thought, focusing, therefore, on Bethlehem. The questions of knowledge and power have a way of fixing attention on the life and ministry of Jesus, with Galilee seen as the locus of Christ's work. Sin and guilt as issues give rise to metaphors and meanings that gather around the cross, hence Calvary. Questions of evil and hopelessness about the future, penultimate and ultimate, prompt attention to the resurrection, with Easter becoming central.

C. Role Models

Discernible within the theories and the biblical data in general are the outlines of four ways of understanding the Work of Christ, four recurring "role models" of Jesus' atoning action. They tend to take shape around the issues and segments noted and are also influenced by one or another target. In considering each role model, attention will be given to the *issue* it addresses, the segment of Christ's life to which it gives attention as its *locus,* the target of Jesus' Work as its *focus,* the *action* involved in the Work, and the *outcome* of the action. Assessments will be made along the way looking toward the description later of an encompassing and ecumenical fifth model.

1. Jesus as Example and Teacher

The problem faced, the *issue* confronted in this first model, is the lack of knowledge of the truth and the absence of commitment to what little we do know. The bane of the race is its ignorance and apathy, our darkened minds and hearts.

Where do we go for deliverance from error and torpor? The *locus* of salvation is the Christ of Galilee. He is the Teacher of the truth and the inspiring Example of its practice. His ministry is the articulation and exemplification of a compelling way of life. The *action* is the disclosure of who God is and what we must do. In Jesus' words and deeds we learn that God is love and that we are called to be loving. This gift and claim, expressed in another day as "the Fatherhood of God and the brotherhood of man," is the sum and substance of Christian religion. The *focus* of this Example and Teacher is you and me. Atonement means changing the hearts and minds of human beings so that they may love God and love their neighbors. The *outcome* of the action is the illumination of our darkened minds and the inspiration of our apathetic hearts so that human beings may be at one with God and with each other.

The strengths of this model? It takes seriously the life and ministry of Jesus of Nazareth. His earthly career does reveal the Purpose of God. It understands a crucial feature of his ministry to be proclamation of the Kingdom of God. It gives forceful attention to the love of God, underscoring the Agape so central to the Christian faith. It is committed to an understanding of Christianity that expects the change of hearts and minds, especially reckoning with the ethical imperatives of biblical faith. We do need illumination and inspiration, insight and empowerment.

This model's weaknesses? One is suggested by a comment of one who tried it: "We need more than good advice. We need Good News." The issue we confront is far more lethal than this model understands, and therefore the Work of Christ must be more radical than that of an example and teacher. At three points is this true: (a) Human sin is titanic. The apathy and arrogance of the human race do not yield to insistences to love God and love the neighbor. "The good that I would I cannot . . . the evil that I would not, that I do." Paul's honest admission says volumes about the incurred self, the bondage of the human will to its own self-serving agendas. (b) The problem of evil is far more intractable than this model grasps. The historical holocausts and the vast natural disasters point to the presence of demonic principalities and powers in our midst. It is not enough to speak about the loving Father in heaven or the need to love others in the face of these horrors and our helplessness before them. There is no Good News if there is no word to be said about the outcome of our struggle and destiny with the demonic. (c) Inseparable from the problem of sin and evil is their result, death, both the mortality that we face individually and the larger meaning of death, the death of the Hope of God, the hopelessness that shatters the future of this great experiment in Shalom. When these preceptions about the depth and pervasiveness of sin, evil, in death are weak or absent, there is a commensurate neglect of the acts in the drama of Jesus addressed to these agonies — the cross and resurrection, Good Friday and Easter. Often absent as well is the deepest meaning of Incarnation, God with us in Jesus. For when the depth of the world's plight is not adequately measured, the radical cure by the enfleshment, struggle, and victory of God is not understood.

Standing alone, the Work of the Example and Teacher leaves us with unanswered questions. Indeed, if Jesus of Nazareth is taken with absolute seriousness, just those questions are radicalized. As Luther found in his spiritual pilgrimage, the more one strives to be obedient to the imperative of good works, the more apparent our shortcomings and self-will. The kindly face of Christ the Example and Teacher becomes the stern face of Christ the Judge. We do not love God or our neighbor as we ought. The revelation of the Law of this love drives us to despair or to clever evasions. *Disclosure* becomes *exposure*. In the face of this exposure something more is needed for atonement than illumination and inspiration. The ambiguities in the first model have given rise to a second one.

2. Jesus as Substitute and Savior

In this second model the meaning of the Work of Christ consists not in what Christ *shows to us,* but in what Christ *does for us.* We require drastic action because we are in deep trouble. Our sin has evoked the wrath and judgment of God. We stand guilty before the divine righteousness, deserving death and damnation. The *issue,* therefore, is sin and guilt. Because we are trapped in our sin, we cannot do what the Example and Teacher says we must do; we need a Savior. We need one who steps in to do what we cannot do, who represents us before the judgment bar, who stands in our place to deal with the well-deserved and terrible punishment. The *focus* of this model is not, first and foremost, the change of human attitudes and behavior, but the change of God's relationship to us, his severe judgment on us.

The eye of faith that sees Christ as Substitute and Savior turns to the cross. Here is a *locus* with passion and depth that suggest the scale of agony and punishment appropriate to sin and guilt. And here, most essentially, is the *action* of the only One who can deal with their deadly consequences. The death of Christ on the cross meets the divine severity and turns aside the wrath of God. Just how judgment is transformed into mercy depends on the particular theory that expresses this model of Substitute and Savior. In one case, Anselm's "satisfaction" theory, couched in the language of medieval serf-lord relationships and the penance system of the Middle Ages, the death of Christ is a beyond-the-call-of-duty act, much like the extraordinary sacrifices of saint and monk, whose consequent store of heavenly merits was thought to be transferable to sinners. Thus the favor won from the Father by the merits of Christ's supererogatory sacrifice on the cross satisfies the offended honor of the Lord. In another case, that of the penal substitutionary theory of Reformation orthodoxy, influenced by the judicial codes and penal practices of the emerging nation state (including a practice in which a friend could stand as surety for bail), the death of Christ was the endurance of the punishment for sin, now understood as the breach of divine law. By a passive receiving of the sentence rendered, in contrast to the active offering of death in the satisfaction theory, atonement is made. And in yet another instance of this model, the sacrificial theory, developed in conjunction with the temple ritual metaphors of the Old Testament, the death of Christ is viewed as an offering well pleasing to God. (In modern versions, the absence of ideas of legalistic equivalency of punishment are stressed, and also our own act of sorrowful and faithful coparticipation.) In all forms of this model, the *outcome* of the action is the reconciliation of God and human beings. The obstruction is removed, whether it be offended honor, deserved punishment, or propitiatory condition. Jesus' intervention makes possible our acceptance.

Models characteristically attempt to include metaphors and meanings not directly related to their own construct. Thus this one seeks to do justice to the Galilean ministry of Jesus. The moral and spiritual perfections of Example and Teacher constitute the purity that gives efficacy to the death of Christ. In the satisfaction theory, only a perfect Jesus who did not have to die as punishment for sin could use his death as a merit transferable to sinners. In the penal theory, only a perfect Jesus who did not have to be punished by death for his own sin could offer his death as a substitute for others. And in the sacrificial theory, only the purity of an innocent Lamb would be pleasing to God.

We have spent longer on the exposition of this model because the idea of atonement is associated in popular Christianity with one or another form of it. And indeed the notion of atonement itself comes originally from the sacrificial metaphor expanded by one version of this model. In taking sin more seriously than the first mode, it is profounder in its understanding of both human perversity and divine judgment. It sees more clearly the gravity of human sin and our accountability before the righteous God who does not lightly indulge our assault on the divine purposes. Its strength also includes the importance given to the cross, the central symbol of the Christian faith, and the sign of the agonizing cost, suffering and death, of any at-one-ment worth having. Further, its emphasis on the passion and crucifixion is faithful to the stress on these in the Gospels, in the redemption scenarios of Paul, and in the proclamations of the early Church. Again, in this model the humanity of Jesus, the real choices and actions of one who faces toward God, is not lost from view.

The weakness of the second model lies in its reductionism. Its tunnel vision of the Work of Christ does not allow Galilee or Easter or finally Bethlehem to enlarge the significance of atonement and even deepen the meaning of the cross itself.

A fundamental effect of a reductionism that eliminates a critical aspect of "Bethlehem" — the doctrine of the Incarnation that is the premise of any sound understanding of atonement — has to do with the relation of Jesus to God on the cross. The logic of this model was expressed by the story of a convert won to the Church by its preaching (as described by William Wolf). Seeing the picture painted of the sacrificial Jesus appeasing the wrath of God by his suffering and death, the convert declared, "I love Jesus, but I hate God." In the conventional forms of this model, God is portrayed as a distant figure calling judgment down on us. This wrathful Father is over against the "friend we have in Jesus." Jesus takes the punishment meted out by God. But the doctrine of the Incarnation shows that something is missing here. "God was *in* Christ reconciling the world to himself . . ."(2 Cor. 5:19 RSV). To believe in the Incarnation is to close the gap between God and Jesus, to see the cross as the *Work of God*, not the appeasement of God by the human Jesus.

A variation on this theme of cleavage is to be found in a view that acknowledges the presence of God in Jesus, but describes the act of propitiation as done by the Second Person of the Trinity to the First Person, by the Son to the Father. Here we find another polarization, this time between God the Father and God the Son, violating the divine unity expressed in the ancient teaching that "all the works of the Trinity are one."

The rift between Jesus and God, or Father and Son, is the result also of a single motif model that gives no vital place to the Galilean ministry. In Jesus' life and teaching, God the Father is revealed as unconditional love, an Agape that is poured out on all, regardless of payments or deserts. The Substitute and Savior model carries with it a worldly conception of mercy that has not been transfigured by this disclosure of unmerited acceptance. The continuity of the metaphor of judgment between its secular meaning and its description of the cross is that the crime of human sin cannot go unpunished in the Kingdom of a righteous God. The Judge shall execute the judgment. But the metaphor is transmuted by the New Testament vision of unconditional love and Incarnational action. The worldly assumption that the only way to avoid the penalty is to have the judgment evaded by its transfer to another, the Judge being "bought off" or his anger appeased by a satisfactory alternative, is transfigured into the affirmation that the Judge steps down before the bar and is meted out the very punishment that fits the crime. The Judge receives the judgment. God's suffering Agape takes into itself at Calvary the judgment on human sin.

The second model needs to be challenged and enlarged by the first on yet another count: the ethical mandate intrinsic to any full understanding of the Work of Christ. Preoccupation with the cleansing of personal sin effected by the cross tends to eliminate the Vision of Shalom to which the Galilean Christ beckons us. The imperative of earth disappears from view as we either become numbed by the sense of our own incapacity to respond to these mandates or become caught up in the excitement of discovery of the expiation wrought on Calvary. But a full understanding of atonement will make a place for the imperatives of the Shalom disclosed in the life, teaching, and ministry of Christ, as well as in his judgment on us and restoration of us enacted at Golgotha.

As the Galilee before Calvary does not receive its fullest due in this model, neither does the Easter event after it. While resurrection is always affirmed in the expiatory view, it receives attention more as an appendage to its central idea — as the overcoming of our mortality — than as integral to its own understanding of the Work of Christ. This is because of the exclusive focus on the problem of personal sin, and thus the reduced interest in the world's bondage to the powers of evil and death in their profoundest sense. The foes that Jesus Christ engages in his atoning Work include *all* the principalities ranged against the divine intent: those in history and the cosmos as well as in the self. Easter announces this victory, and with it is proclaimed the overcoming of that final death that is eternal separation of God and the world. The conquest of the powers of evil and the call to participate in the present struggle against them, and the joining of hope for the future with faith in the forgiveness of sins, are also key aspects of the atonement.

3. Jesus as Conqueror and Lord

In times marked by numbing historical crisis or natural cataclysm, the picture of Christ the Conqueror emerges with power in the Church. During the rise of totalitarian movements in the Europe of the 1930s, the Swedish theologian Gustaf Aulén sketched in *Christus Victor* the outlines of this model. He declared that a too simple typology of subjective and objective theories of atonement (corresponding to Example and Teacher and Substitute and Savior) ignored a third view, one that he asserted to be that of the New Testament itself and of such interpreters as Irenaeus and Luther.

In this model the *issue* is evil and death in their various expressions. In the ancient world the struggle took the form of conflict with demons attacking as sea monster, madness of mind, malady of body, the day-to-day perils of life, the whispers of temptation. In more secular times the enemy stalks in the random terror of natural disaster and the perennial sorrows and enigmas of disease, tragedy, old age. To the groaning of creation is added the agonized cries of history, the poverty, hunger, and tyranny over body, mind, and spirit caused by political, economic, and social principalities and powers. And over all hangs the pall of death, both the fact of our mortality and the fear that evil will triumph, the suspicion that not only our life but the life of the world will end as "a tale told by an idiot, full of sound and fury, signifying nothing."

The *action* of Christ in this understanding of atonement is to meet and defeat the foes of God. And it is not our behavior or God's relationship to us but the enemy powers that are the *focus* of the Work. The beginnings of the battle are traced to the Galilean ministry of Jesus. Here Christ confronts the Devil and the demonic hordes in the encounters of temptation, the infestation of the sick and troubled by the powers of darkness, and the resistance to his ministry. Christ is empowered to deal effectively with the enemy as the Kingdom he embodies and points to is at work healing torn bodies, minds, and spirits and exorcising and fending off the armies of night. Yet a final assault is launched against the inbreaking Kingdom and its King, and victory of the foe seems assured as death overwhelms this Pretender to the throne of the Kingdoms of this world ruled by the powers of darkness.

What gives meaning to the life and death of Christ shadowed by these powers of darkness is the light of Easter morning. In the resurrection of Jesus Christ from the dead, the *locus* of saving action, the question mark is removed. The defeat of the Purposes of God in the death of Jesus is not what it appeared to be. Rather, the cross was the weapon of suffering Love, persuasion not coercion, that befits the God who will not act contrary to the divine nature. The sign that this weapon *does* defeat the dark powers is the resurrection. That God raised Jesus Christ from the dead signifies the victory over the powers of evil, and finally also victory over death in its deepest meaning, the death of hope for the world. Thus fear of the powers of this world and hopelessness about the future of the world are overcome by Christ the Conqueror of evil and death. Liberation from these powers, and life together with God, is the *outcome* of the atoning Work.

The belief in powers of evil is not the assertion of a raw "dualism," the notion that there are forces alongside of Deity in eternal conflict with God. The powers are themselves part of the good creation brought to be by God. But as humanity fell, so the powers, too, have become corrupted and now exist in opposition to the intention of God. The conquest of these authorities, viewed eschatologically as beginning at Easter and culminating at the Last Day, further underscores the nondualistic character of the powers of evil. For all that, there is a genuine intermediate conflict, and thus in Aulén's words a "provisional dualism."

The assumption about the nature of God has to do with the relation of Incarnation to atonement. In an effort to affirm Bethlehem as the premise of Easter, and also its presence in Galilee and Calvary, the Conqueror model views the Work of Jesus "through and through" as the Work of God. Deity wages war with the powers of evil and death in the Person of Jesus Christ. Hence this dramatic view of the atonement is one that portrays salvation as the contest of God with the enemy forces, carried out on earth in the life, death, and resurrection of the man Jesus Christ.

This model gives rightful attention to the resurrection of Christ. As in no other view, Easter plays a key role in the Work of Christ. Here the wretched of the earth, felled by the powers of evil and death, hear a Word that speaks to their condition. In our own time, the liberation theologies strike this note, seeking to understand Christ against the background of the struggle against oppression. And as their strange ally, those less politically oriented interpretations of Christian faith that address themselves to the problem of evil and death, ones that may engage in exorcism and esoterica on the one hand, or view faith as a way of dealing with death and dying, on the other, represent a version of this model. Whatever their strategies and programs, their antennae are tuned to modern questions of theodicy — the "problem of evil" — and they offer in turn some understanding of Christ as Lord and Conqueror.

A further strength of this model is its recognition that the structures of nature and history are part and parcel of the arena in which the atonement takes place. Christ is Lord over natural and supernatural powers as well as persons; his Kingdom is cosmic in scope. Tendencies to narrow the range of atonement to the inner life or to personal and interpersonal relationships are here challenged. And not only are historical structures given their due, but also in this time of ecological sensibility the lordship of Christ over the environment and ultimately over the heights and depths of the whole universe is affirmed.

When the human problem is seen to consist of the evil and death "out there" in nature and history, then the corruption "in here," the self and its sin, can be overlooked in all its horror and depth. This is a basic weakness of the Conqueror model in both ancient and contemporary thought. The focus is so relentlessly on the struggle with the powers external to the self that the "enemy within" gets short shrift. Where attempts are made to include the presence of sin as a foe, the sin tends to be so objectified as a power that the aspect of personal culpability is not given its due. Paul's own use of the term "sin" gives it this role of over-againstness, one followed by Luther, but the way the word operates in both is as a relationship of the self to God, rather than simply as an objective power over against both humanity and God, as with evil and death. Thus wherever the model achieves prominence, from ancient thought to current versions of liberation theology, the persistence and universality of sin in the self are not given their due.

A related weakness has to do with expectations about history that accompany the Conqueror model, particularly as its commitments are politicized. Where sin is not seen as a fundamental foe, its corrupting effects, especially when they work on the righteous (as is recognized in the realism of the New Testament about self-righteousness and in the classic Christian understanding of pride as the basic sin), are not assessed profoundly enough. This means that too sanguine hopes for history are cultivated by those who see Christ as the Conqueror of the powers of evil and Liberator of the oppressed. This utopianism, as Reinhold Niebuhr has helped us to see, eventuates in either despair at the frustration of inordinate historical expectations or fanaticism in the claims of those who believe they march in the legions of the conquering Lord. The fanatic fails to see the omnipresence of sin, especially as it grafts itself onto power, and most of all righteous power, and therefore has no principle of criticism by which to call to account, and expose the perversities of, the most just and virtuous movements. A fuller understanding of the Conqueror and Lord motif must include liberation from the sin of the self as well as from the powers and principalities of evil.

The use of the military metaphor that is integral to this model opens it up to yet another criticism. While the previous weaknesses are related to the missing expiation motif, this one is connected with the relative absence of the Galilean accent. The compassionate Christ who moves in selfless love throughout the pages of the New Testament does not sit well with the warlike metaphor. The tenderness of the Galilean Christ and the suffering of the Savior need to take their place alongside the ringing commands and shouts of conquest of a Lord and Liberator.

A final weakness has to do with this model's attempt to relate Incarnation to atonement. Its stress on atonement as a thoroughly divine action tends to reduce the significance of the human nature of Jesus. Jesus' actions are so suffused with deity that the hard and vital choices that constitute his ministry fade from view. While those choices are maintained in the second model at the price of distancing the reconciling God from the action, in this model the overwhelming Presence of the God who was in Christ erodes the human action, however formally insisted on (while conquest is done *by* God, it must be done *in* and *through* a human).

4. Jesus as Presence

The Incarnation makes a significant impact on the previous model. But there is a fourth type of atonement thought, in which the Incarnation is virtually identical with the atonement. Such a view is related to the definition of the world's problem in terms of carnality itself. The *issue* in our fourth perspective is transiency and mortality. Decay and death are all around us. Who will bring life and light?

The *locus* of atonement here is the moment of at-one-ment between time and eternity, the enfleshment of God at Bethlehem. The *focus* of the Work embodied in the very being of the Person is not the change of our hearts and minds, nor alteration of the divine attitude and behavior toward us, nor defeat of the powers ranged against the Purposes of God, but the transformation of time and space. This happens in the very union of Deity and humanity. For in the *action* of Incarnation the whole universe is taken up into a new reality. As a drop of dye colors a glass of water, so the presence of Deity at Bethlehem and beyond transfigures the cosmos. The *outcome* of this incarnate action is deification, the taking *in principle* of the world into the divine life, and *in fact* of those so joined to the Person by faith.

To see the presence of God as the Work of Christ makes it utterly clear that atonement is through and through a divine action. In so stressing God's enfleshment, this model underscores the fact that Incarnation is the presupposition of atonement, that Bethlehem is the framework for Galilee, Calvary, and Easter. Futhermore, the ambiguities of life in this world, its passingness and mortality, are not ignored; we are destined for something more than decay and death.

Yet, as in the other models, reductionism so scissors the fullness of the biblical witness that critical sections of the Christian Story are left out. The Galilean ministry and mandates do not receive the attention they deserve; the preoccupation with one's own finitude, while helping us to come to terms with things that cannot be changed, does not make sufficient room for life and living and the imperatives to serve the neighbor in need, things that can be changed. Further, the exclusive focus on temporality obscures the anterior problem of human sin, our culpability and need for divine mercy. And the struggle against the historical powers and principalities in the battle for historical hope in the face of hopelessness gets less than its due. Thus Jesus the Example and Teacher, Sufferer and Savior, Lord and Conqueror, has something to teach the exponents of this incarnational view.

The four models of the Work of Christ may be portrayed in this way:

Model	Issue	Locus	Focus	Action	Outcome
Example and Teacher	ignorance and apathy	Galilee	Human attitudes and behavior	disclosure by word and deed of love of God and neighbor	illumination and inspiration
Substitute and Savior	sin and guilt	Calvary	relationship of God to humanity	vicarious suffering and death	judgment turned to mercy
Conqueror and Lord	evil and death	Easter	powers and principalities	resurrection victory	defeat of powers of evil and death
Presence	transiency and mortality	Bethlehem	temporality	incarnation	life and immortality

The Threefold Work of Jesus Christ

Our typology of role models suggests that a process is going on in the Church's exploration of the Work of Christ not unlike that to be found in the development of the doctrine of the Person of Christ. There is focus on one or another important motif, elaboration of it, and a tendency to reduce the multifaceted richness of the meaning of Christ to that one theme. Whereas the reductionisms associated with the Person have to do with either the humanity or the deity of Christ, those that attend the Work gather around one or another of the stages on Christ's way: Bethlehem, Galilee, Calvary, Easter.

While there is no ecumenical consensus about the Work, juxtaposed to the reductionist models, as there is in the Person (holding together humanity, deity, and unity), there is an ecumenical tradition that has sought to honor the pluriform Work of Christ. It has been called the *munus triplex,* the threefold office of Christ. The insights to be found in the models of Example and Teacher, Substitute and Savior, Conqueror and Lord are captured in the terminology of *Prophet, Priest,* and *King.* And when these roles are seen to be executed by the God-human, and therefore the Presence enfleshed, then Bethlehem is viewed as the presupposition of Galilee, Calvary, and Easter. Some version of this imagery and conceptuality appears as far back as Eusebius, continues in Jerome, Augustine, Aquinas, and Schleiermacher, and appears in such recent thinkers as Bulgakov, Visser 't Hooft, and Barth. John Calvin has given it extended treatment in *The Institutes of the Christian Religion.* There is by no means universal agreement about this way of affirming and organizing the various atonement themes, but it has proved to be of value in catechisms and statements of faith throughout the Church as well as in the theology of specific thinkers. Thus it constitutes a developing fifth and ecumenical model of the Work of Christ.

Its interpreters have noted that as the three offices in the Old Testament were set apart by the act of anointing, so in the threefold Work of Christ, the "anointed one," we have the fulfillment of the covenant promise. While the continuity with the Old Testament is an important value in this formulation, both the specifics and the semantics of anointing are not solidly grounded by historical research. The threefold office must be rooted more fundamentally in the legitimacy of Prophet, Priest, and King as ways of expressing the themes in the Work of Christ and their interrelationships. We shall attempt to describe the fullness of Christ's Work in a way that incorporates the various motifs and resists the attendant reductionisms.

The Christian Story tells us that Jesus Christ is our liberator and reconciler. He works to defeat the powers of sin, evil, and death, and brings us together with nature, humanity, and God. He does this Work as Prophet, Priest, and King. In language closer to our contemporary idiom, he is Seer, Sufferer, and Liberator. And the One who accomplishes this Work is the Person of Jesus Christ, truly human, truly God, fully one.

Prophet and Seer

The Old Testament prophet is a seer of the Vision of God. He is the forthteller who *makes it plain.* Jesus of Nazareth stands deeply in this tradition (Matt. 21:11; Luke 4:24; 7:16; 24:19). He caught sight of and pointed toward the coming Kingdom, in which the will of God would be done on earth as well as it is in Heaven. He is the revealer of the Future of God. In this New Time the mourners will be comforted; those who hunger, and those who hunger for righteousness, will be filled; the merciful will obtain mercy; the peacemakers and persecuted shall be vindicated; the poor, and the poor in spirit, shall be satisfied; and the meek shall inherit the earth (Matt. 5:3; Luke 6:17, 20-23). All human bondages shall be broken and the oppressed liberated (Luke 4:18-19). This deliverance is extended to all the alienations and disharmonies of nature as well, for Jesus preached and practiced the healing of the body and the restoration of a fallen creation (Matt. 4:24; Mark 4:39-41). The Kingdom of Shalom is more than horizontal, for it is marked by a freedom from the powers that separate humanity from God, as well as from neighbor and nature, and the overcoming of blindness to the covenant partner: the arrival of Shalom means that "those whose hearts are pure . . . shall see God" (Matt. 5:8).

The coming of Shalom means judgment as well as fulfillment, justice executed against oppression, and estrangement as part of the Vision of redemption. "Alas for you who are rich . . . alas for you who are well-fed now . . . alas for you who laugh . . . alas for you when all speak well of you; just so did their fathers treat the false prophets" (Luke 6:24-26).

The unmistakable sights of foreseeing and the notes of foretelling and forewarning that identify the prophet are to be found in Jesus' preaching and teaching about the Kingdom of God.

But this prophet penetrates more deeply into the Vision of God. In his description of the coming Realm is portrayed the *ground* as well as the *goal* of our pilgrimage. The characterizations of the future speak of the wellsprings of Shalom: *Agape.* Jesus points to the boundless unconditional Love that makes possible the final liberation and reconciliation of all things.

What is the nature of this Love that lies behind the ultimate freedom and peace? (1) It is *neighbor* love (Luke 10:25-37). Its focus is the one in need, the victim on the Jericho road unseen by those who pass by. Agape is the sight to see and serve the invisible, those who do not come in range of the fallen world's vision. It includes all the helpless and hurt: the poor, the hungry, the sick, the oppressed, the stranger, the prisoner. It encompasses those of lesser estate and second-class citizenship: the widow, the orphan, women, children, the aged. In Jesus' teaching and in his conduct toward the debilitated and the dysfunctional, he healed the sick, treated women and children, the weak, the old, and the outcast with dignity and compassion, fed the hungry, and preached good news to the poor and those in bondage (Matt. 25:31-46; 15:22-28; 18:2-6; Mark 12:42-43). (2) Agape is a love that goes deeper than the care for the physically, mentally, and socially afflicted. It reaches out to the *lawless* as well as to the loveless. While Jesus did not scorn the law, he had compassion for those who breached it. In fact, he kept company with "sinners." The tax collectors, against whom a case could be made for both conniving and collusion with tyranny, harlot and adulteress, those considered immoral and impious were the ones whom he sought out and with whom he associated (Matt. 9:11; Luke 5:27; John 8:3-11). Why so? The unmerited love of the God to whom he bore witness and the Kingdom toward which the world moves also reach toward such people. "Your heavenly Father . . . makes his sun rise on good and bad alike, and sends the rain on the honest and the dishonest. If you love only those who love you, what reward can you expect? . . . There must be no limits to your goodness, as your Heavenly Father's goodness knows no bounds" (Matt. 5:45-46, 48). (3) The radical nature of Agape is demonstrated by its final reaches. It extends not only to the victim and to the unjust, but to the *enemy.* There is nothing that can turn aside the open arms of an unconditional Agape. It pushes past the resistance of those who hate it, and rushes toward those who despitefully use it (Luke 15:20). And when assaulted directly, it turns the other cheek and goes the second mile (Matt. 5:38-44). This capacity to accept the unacceptable and love the unloving is forgiveness. Forgiveness is fore-giving, readiness to give and go before without promise of reciprocity and in the face of rebuff. It is the always-open channel of communication, the in-spite-of care that persists no matter how deep the hurt or painful the wound. This is the quality that makes reconciliation possible. And we are enjoined to pursue it relentlessly (Matt. 18:21-22). (4) No radical love of the neighbor in need, the reprobate, and the enemy is possible if it is not ultimately rooted in selflessness. The self that is not prepared to abandon itself is not capable of dealing with this agenda. The cost-benefit analysis of Agape shows a preposterous balance sheet; its bottom line is written in the red of crucifixion. Agape is spendthrift, an uncalculating love that is the opposite of self-preservation, other-directed rather than self-directed. This is the unstinting servanthood that Jesus taught and was. "Whoever wants to be great among you must be your servant, and whoever wants to be first must be the willing slave of all. For even the Son of Man did not come to be served but to serve, and to give up his life as a ransom for many" (Mark 10:44-45).

Jesus was as good as his word. As a prophet sets forth the message in deed as well as in word, so Jesus enacted the Vision of Agape-Shalom that he preached. He did what he said, giving himself in abandonment to the needs of the unloved and unlovable. The issue of this Agape was the liberation of the enslaved and the reconciliation of the estranged. And as there is "no greater love than this, that a man should lay down his life for his friends" (John 15:13), he climaxed this Galilean ministry on Calvary.

Indeed, Jesus did seal his prophetic office with his own blood. As it was the fate of the ancient prophet to be despised and rejected, so Christ evoked the wrath of those he called to account. As he disclosed the contours of Shalom, an angry world thrust this embarrassing specter from its sight. In the destruction of Jesus on the cross the depth of the world's hate was manifest. Thus the Work of the Prophet is both the disclosure of the ultimate reaches of the Vision and also the *exposure* of the depths of resistance to it by the powers of sin and evil. That a larger meaning is to be found here we shall explore presently, when we look at the Work of Priest joined to the Work of Prophet on Golgotha.

The Agape that suffuses Shalom is the love we are to have in the Realm that is coming and to which we are called right now. But it is this kind of love because it is the mirror of God's own love. The outcast, the oppressed, the malefactor, and the adversary are to be the object of our giving and forgiving because they are the object of God's giving and forgiving. The final ground of Shalom, therefore, is the *divine Agape,* the unmerited, spontaneous, uncalculating compassion of God's own heart. We are invited to participate in the liberation and reconciliation that God brings, and we are called to keep company with the wretched of the earth, to forgive the sinner seventy times seven because the God to whom Jesus points is present with and ministers to the neighbor in need, the sinner, and the enemy.

This prophet not only points to this God, but understands himself to be in unique relationship to the divine Agape. Jesus addresses God in terms of special intimacy, "Abba" (Mark 14:36). In fact he calls people to relate to him as to the inbreaking Kingdom, and commands an authority that sets him apart from former models of teacher and preacher (Matt. 7:29). He pictures the Kingdom not just as near but also as here. It bursts into the present, and signs of its arrival are everywhere. The sight of the Future is caught in the deeds that are done in the midst of the words that are said. The healing of the sick and the exorcism of demonic powers are the foretastes of Shalom that confirm the report that the Kingdom is coming. Misery and death are contested and ignorance is overcome, happenings in which the enemies of darkness begin to feel the light and heat of the new Day arriving. The most startling claim of the special bond with God is Jesus' assumption of the power to pardon sin (Matt. 9:2, 5; Luke 7:48). And it was this offer of forgiveness, the prerogative of God alone, that brought down upon him the wrath of the pious.

Jesus' self-understanding is confirmed to the Church in his resurrection, and proclaimed as a central article of its faith. The Prophet is not only the man of God but the God-Man; the Incarnation underlies all the atonement offices. God was in the Christ of Galilee (2 Cor. 5:19). Jesus not only sees the Vision but *is* the Vision. The light of God shines in the face of Jesus as well as toward the eye of this seer. Not only is he the prophet of Shalom, but he "is our Shalom" (Eph. 2:14).

Conceived by the Holy Spirit, the Power of the Vision makes this Light shine in and through him. The capacity to see the length and breadth of the Kingdom and finally to see into the depths of Agape and to enact as well as to portray the ground and goal of all things is by the Love and Hope of God made flesh in the Person of the carpenter of Nazareth. Jesus Christ: divine and human; Prophet and Seer of liberation and reconciliation.

Priest and Sufferer

As the prophets of Israel do not stand alone in the formation of a covenant that had the priestly tradition as partner, so the Work of Christ brings together priestly and prophetic offices. While the prophet casts up on the screen of the future the Purpose of God and calls people toward it, the priest deals with the gap between the Vision and the reality of where the people are in their listless and rebellious journey toward the future. So the central act of the priest is to deal with the fact of sin — to make a sacrifice for the offense of the people against the Purpose of God (Heb. 9:12). Jesus Christ takes this ancient office, presses it against the radical imperatives of his own prophetic Work, and transforms it by the unique character of his sacrificial act. It is to Calvary that our attention is turned, for here the ultimate sacrifice is made.

Why the determined attack on Christ by both the power structure and the people to whom he came to show Light and share Vision? Paul tells us that love has a way of pouring hot coals on its enemies (Rom. 12:20). It burns into us an awareness of what we are called to be. And we seek to put the hot brand away from our too tender skins. We are judged by Christ's life, and therefore we put him to death. We cannot stand the sight of our image as it was meant to be. Jesus Christ is the victim of the sinful humanity common to us and to our first-century counterparts. We were all there when they crucified our Lord.

That attack reveals who we really are, creatures prepared to go to any lengths to remove from our sight the embarrassing Presence of what we are called to be. Human nature demonstrates the depth to which it can descend, as Christ evokes the hatred of which we are capable. Jesus Christ's purity beings out the worst in us. We are ready with the nails and armed with the spear. This prophetic exposure of what we are is also the beginning of the priestly act of dealing with it. Effective engagement requires the full visibility of the enemy.

The exposure of the depths of the world's animosity is understood when Jesus of Nazareth is seen as an event in the history of God as well as in our own history, the Presence incarnate. Here is the Shalom of God in our midst. What is done to Jesus of Nazareth on Calvary is done also *to God* (Col. 1:19-20). The nails that pierced his hands are driven into Deity itself. The blood of Jesus is the "blood of God." The sacrificial victim is the Lamb of God. One gasps at the horror of this happening. Our assaults reach into the Godhead itself. This is the measure of our sin.

When we try to describe the cross in the language we have been using to tell the Christian Story, we must speak of this profound wounding as an attack on the Vision and Word of God (Col. 2:9). The crucifixion of Jesus, the incarnate God, is an enemy sally against the innermost

139

sanctuary of the divine hope. The death of Jesus is the passing away of Shalom, the demise of the Dream of God. This is not the death *of* God, but death *in* God (Jürgen Moltmann). There is "a cross in the heart of God" (Charles Dinsmore). Here on Calvary God died a little death. As the life of Christ discloses the Intention of God, the death of Christ exposes the depth of our sin.

But Jesus Christ not only suffers *from* but suffers *for* his assailants. Here is the Lamb of God who takes away the sins of the world. Atonement is expiation (Eph. 2:13-16).

Jesus Christ is the suffering Savior who redeems from sin and guilt. We have seen how our second model of the Work of Christ seeks to do justice to this crucial New Testament affirmation. Yet how easy it is to take the world's own understanding of expiation, the mollifying of God or the gods by altar sacrifice, as the key to Christ's Work, and thus the rupturing of the unity of Jesus and God. Because God was *in* Christ on the cross reconciling the world, the priestly office is an act done *by* Deity, not the appeasement *of* Deity. The Incarnation is the presupposition of the atonement. Just as it was God's own heart that was broken by our sin, so it is God's own heart that takes into itself the consequences of that sin. The consequences, the wages, of sin are death. In the righteousness of God there is no possible evasion of the scales of this justice. Death follows sin as night follows day. The aggression of the human race against the Purpose of God is not indulged, overlooked, waved aside, or winked at. But the miracle of Calvary is that God the Judge goes into the dock for the sentencing. It is on Deity that the consequences fall. It is in Deity that the price is paid. Here the judgment that befits our crime was meted out, received, absorbed. Here in the heart of God is where death descended and a cross formed.

In our metaphor-motif, the Vision of God was darkened on Calvary. Its Light was put out by human sin. Yet in this death a *suffering* Love bore our guilt. As the heart of God was broken, the profoundest depths in the divine life were reached. The suffering Love to be found there was drawn on to deal with God's judgment. The pain experienced by God in those depths, the anguished receiving by God of God's own No to sin we can only dimly guess. In these inner regions of the divine life Shalom was borne up by Agape, the unconditional love that does not return in kind but accepts the unacceptable and loves the unlovable. Acceptance of the sinner is no cheap grace. It costs God to accept what righteousness must rebuke. The cost is the pain of judgment turned in on God rather than out toward us. That is the suffering Agape that bears Shalom. Agape is the ground and Shalom is the goal of the history of God.

Jesus' story of the love of the parent for the prodigal son gives us a clue to the stirrings in the divine depths (Luke 15:11-32). It is a tale of the suffering father whose son is what we also are. We can see in that figure of wasted gifts and violated hopes something of our own flight into a far country. And we can also see something of the anguished love in a parent who swallows his pride and hurt, who absorbs his own righteous anger and, more terribly, the sorrow of defeated expectations, receiving back the one who caused that hurt, yes, running toward him! So the broken heart of God mends itself with suffering Love. And the future comes to live again, now on new terms. Here is offered a *new covenant* based on mercy, one that does not depend on our response, but one that goes before us as the father rushed to meet his son. The wrath and righteousness of the parent have been met and absorbed by the pathos of the parent. What we do toward the turned figure and outreached arms is a question of our own turning and running, a matter with which we must deal in succeeding chapters, when God's Story becomes our story.

The vulnerability of the Father that this narrative assumes and the Christian Story proclaims is a fundamental part of the priestly action, but one often slighted by the conventional wisdom of expiation. It is not only the tit-for-tat premises of ordinary experience that obscure this perception, but also secular notions of power transferred into Christian context. Thus the Oriental potentate of ancient politics and the aloof philosopher who is truest when devoid of pathos exemplified qualities attributed to God. With this conceptuality it was unthinkable that Deity would participate in the moil and toil of passion and crucifixion. At best it would be the human nature of Jesus to which suffering might be attributed, but never to God. This worldly wisdom about Deity has helped turn the crucial expiatory motif into the reductionist second model, polarizing Jesus with God. In fact, the Christian Story of atonement as the action of an Incarnate Deity cannot be read aright without perceiving the passion of God in the crucifixion of Christ. Here is no anger of one bought off by the sacrifice of another, but the divine Wrath overcome by the divine Love, the "curse" absorbed by the "blessing" (Luther).

While the second model settles too quickly for the world's wisdom on sacrifice — done by humanity toward God — and does not grasp the vulnerable love of God in this event, it has held us firmly to history. Against any tendency to vaporize the event of Calvary, to project it so deeply into the transcendent Realm that the human Jesus does not figure in the action, it has stressed the blood and tears of a real Savior. Calvary happened not only in the history of God but in our history as well. Without this tree and the person who hung upon it, without recognition of the choices of this figure, there is no sound biblical interpretation of the cross. Jesus is not a robot acting out in our midst something that really occurred only in the heart of God. Suffering took place on earth by the hard choices made there by the historical Jesus (Mark 14:32-36 RSV). Without the real choices of the historical Jesus, in this case the decision to go to the cross, there would have been no enactment of the drama within the Godhead in the drama on Golgotha — and therefore no communication to us of the mercy of God for us. And more, Jesus represented the whole human race when he looked into the abyss and cried, "My God, my God, why hast thou forsaken me?" (Matt. 27:46). He saw the death in God of the Hope of Shalom. He watched the Dream die. He experienced the sorrow of the broken heart of God. Jesus the Seer of the Galilean Vision also saw its suffering and passing on Calvary. In this sense, too, the judgment of God fell on the cross of Christ.

But why should the crucified humanity of Jesus be of such consequence? The answer is obvious if the suffering of human innocence is necessary to mollify an angry God. But if the pain of judgment is taken up into the Godhead itself rather than executed on a third party, how can any meaning be given to the claim that *Jesus* died for our sins? And if the dubious notion of one guileless human being's death providing an equivalent punishment of the race's guilt is also rejected (the strength of this assertion was always the incarnational premise that only God had the power to deal with the debt incurred, the conviction implicit in our understanding here that equivalency of judgment means that only the pain of God can take away the sins of the world), how again can it be said that redemption from sin happened on the cross of Golgotha? If it is the suffering of God that accomplishes salvation from sin and guilt, what is the need and significance of the suffering of Jesus of Nazareth?

The answer to this question, given or implied, by many of those who have spoken about the passion of God is that the cross *shows* us what goes on in the divine depths. If it were not for this window into ultimate Reality we would not know of the suffering Love of God. This is, as far

142

as it goes, an important meaning of the crucifixion. But it cannot be the last word on its significance. Standing alone, it represents a version, albeit a more profound version, of the exemplarist model of the atonement. In it Jesus exists to disclose what God is like in order that we might be changed in heart and mind. But the Work of priest not only reveals information and gives inspiration, but also participates in the very action that effects the new relationship between God and humanity. Without the deed of Jesus not only would we be ignorant of the forgiveness of sin, but there would be no forgiveness of sin. This is the astounding claim made over and over again in the New Testament, one that the Substitute and Savior model has sought to explain. Is there any other way to honor that claim without making the mistake of polarizing God and Jesus or bifurcating Father and Son as is done by this model?

A much scorned patristic tradition gives us a clue to such a way. Many of the Fathers spoke of redemption as the deceit of the devil, using the fishhook-bait metaphor to render it meaningful to ancient society. Jesus was portrayed as a tempting morsel presented to Satan in order to lure him from his hiding place in the undersea world. The bait that was dangled before him was too much to resist and he struck at the target. But in seizing Jesus, the Evil One was hooked. Thus the sinless Jesus served to conquer the enemy.

Embedded in this picturesque imagery is another way of conceiving the role of the human Jesus as Savior. For God to deal with the militancy of the world against the divine purpose, it was necessary to engage the enemy in its fullest manifestation. Incarnation means encounter with the total depth of bondage and alienation. Sin, evil, and death must show their truest and ugliest face. It is the presence of Purity that enrages the powers and principalities, evoking their true being. As in the patristic imagery, the innocence of Jesus draws from the depths the ultimate assaults of sin, evil, and death. Only by such a human being living on the plane of history where sin and evil make their home, and where death can do its most demonic work — the destruction of hope itself — can the enemy be induced from its lair and be what it is. Thus the very Purpose of God turns on the obedience of Jesus, an obedience in life and obedience "unto death" in willingness to draw from the powers of darkness their mightiest effort. Jesus' steadfast loyalty brought the monsters of the deep into engagement not only with human innocence, but in and with it the power of the enfleshed God, whose very suffering Love proved to be the weapon able to deal with our enmity. Here on the cross is the Lamb of God that takes away the sin of the world.

Jesus Christ is suffering Priest. He offers himself as victim of the world's knife thrust through to the heart of Shalom. In the shed blood he is the God who suffers in our place, and the human who chooses that agony as the agent of our reconciliation with God and our liberation from sin and guilt.

King and Liberator

Sin and guilt meet their match in the priestly Work of Christ. But the powers of evil remain to be finally dealt with. So does the last enemy, death. In the royal Work of Christ these foes are met and overcome. This contest takes us out of the cavernous underground land of the spirit, where sin dwells, and onto the broad ranges of history and nature, where evil and death roam. And it takes us also from the cross to the resurrection, where this final engagement is decisively fought and won.

The Work of Christ the Conqueror does not wait on the Easter event but begins at Bethlehem. At Incarnation the battle is joined. Here the Word of God enters the land to which the powers of evil and death lay claim and where they have had their way. It is into the flesh of humanity that sickness, sorrow, and mortality have driven their spears. It is on the plane of history that the thrones and authorities, the structures of power, have strutted and tyrannized. And it is among the birds of the air and the flowers of the field that the groans of nature can be heard. It is with this reality that the Vision of God comes to grips, and into this arena that it plunges. Here night meets Light.

The battle with the powers of this world rages in Galilee. Christ reports the Vision that empowers his struggle: "I watched how Satan fell, like lightning out of the sky" (Luke 10:18). Out of this perception of a foe already on the run, he meets the Tempter at the opening of his ministry, pursues him at every turn, and wrestles with him at the climax in Gethsemane. The work of evil in temptation is matched by its work in agonies of the body and mind. Again Christ confronts and ousts the enemy in healing and in exorcising the demonic powers (Matt. 10:1). The engagement with evil extends into the arena of political, social, and economic power structures that he meets at each turn of his ministry, from the Sanhedrin to imperial Rome (Matt. 26:59-68; 27:11-14).

But does this last encounter not tell another story? In the confrontation with the might of the power structures, all seems to be lost. For in the final assault by an alliance of political, military, economic, and ecclesiastical principalities, sin conspires with evil to bring death. In the crucifixion of Jesus Christ, it is not only a human that is destroyed, but also a Dream. Here is the last best Hope of the world, and it is gone.

If the narrative ended here, hope would be dead. In fact, the life, teachings, and cross would themselves tell a different tale. It is only the next event in the unfolding drama, Easter, that transforms the meaning of Galilee and Calvary. This sequel is the Work of Christ as Liberator from the powers of evil and death (Col. 2:15). On resurrection morning, Christ beats down Satan and all his hosts and destroys death. The very worst that the world can do cannot finally extinguish the Light of God (Col. 1:13). The resurrection of Jesus Christ means that evil in all its forms — the ills of the flesh, the disasters of nature, the holocausts of history — does not have the last word. The enemy does not control the future. The intention of God to bring the Kingdom cannot be turned aside; Shalom will be! And as doom is spelled for the powers of evil, and sin is overcome by the divine mercy, so, too, *death* meets its match. When Christ rose from the grave, he signaled the death of death and the coming of life. Easter means that the Vision is victorious. The reconciliation of all things is the destiny of the Great Experiment of creation. "Courage! The victory is mine; I have conquered the world" (John 16:33).

What really happened in first-century Jerusalem to warrant these astounding claims? Something took place among a dispirited band of disciples that gave rise to this Easter faith and its dramatic consequences. These are the logical possibilities:

1. The physical body of Jesus was resuscitated.
2. A "spiritual body" was raised.
3. The physical body of Jesus was raised and transfigured into a "spiritual body."

(In the case of 1, 2, and 3, the event may have been perceived through either the eyes of faith or the eyes of sight.)

4. The Easter experiences were psychic events in the lives of the seers.
5. The Easter experiences were a resurgence of faith in the hearts of the early Christians.

145

A case could be made that all of these views of Easter can be combined with a theological affirmation of the resurrection, in the sense that Jesus is alive now with God, and that the Easter experience marked that passage. Thus some would argue that the fact that "Jesus was raised up by God" (Acts 2:32) is what is important, not the way it was done, including the possibility that a spiritual experience of the resurrection was a *veridical* vision and not a hallucination, or that the resurgence of faith among the apostles was a sign given by God that Jesus is alive with God. Yet the nature of the apostolic testimony (Matt. 28; Mark 16; Luke 24; John 20–21; Acts 9:3-6; 1 Cor. 15:3-8) and the implication of this event for other chapters in the Christian Story point to option 3: the empty tomb and transfigured body. (The significance of history and the dignity of things physical in the Christian faith, and the clue in Christ's resurrection to our own eschatological hope, underscore this interpretation.) In and through this testimony, Easter faith declares the victory of Jesus Christ over sin, evil, and death, as seen by the apostles in the resurrection appearances. These are resurrection appearances in both meanings of the term: genuine experiences of real people and an authentic arrival of the Future of God, Jesus Christ, in and through these experiences.

The light of Easter dawn is shed back on the crucifixion, disclosing it as the way of conquest over evil and death, and the weapon of victory over sin. The sword of the Liberator is the cross. Suffering Love is the way in which not only forgiveness of sin is made possible, but also the defeat of evil and death. God in Christ works to conquer all the enemy in a fashion commensurate with the divine nature: not by force but by "persuasion." The might of the Lord is suffering Love (Eph. 2:16). Agape is the road God takes toward Shalom.

As our understanding of how suffering Love conquers sin is helped by the parable of a grieving and forgiving father, so there are New Testament clues and human analogs that hint at the finally imponderable conquest of evil and death by the Agape of God. Thus the compassion of Jesus that conquers illness is portrayed in the anthropomorphisms of an exorcised demon (Mark 1:34), or the repentance of a symbol of the power structure, Nicodemus (John 7:50), or the raising of a Lazarus (John 12:17).

And from that elusive event in our own history when a soft answer turns away wrath, a power structure is humbled, and systemic change occurs by the life and witness of a Martin Luther King, healing happens, or the sting of death is removed through the agency of suffering Love. But these are just clues, for until the final reckoning with evil and death in that eschatological goal toward which history now drives, suffering Love continues as crucified love, and the Kingdom comes as portent and first-fruit and not fulfillment. Evil does not recognize its defeat, and our mortality is a sign of its refusal to acknowledge its Lord. Therefore, in the half-light of the Already–Not Yet of Christ's resurrection victory, it is not given to us to see *how* suffering Love achieves its end. We live by the eyes of faith, not empirical sight.

Easter is the liberation from evil and death in portent and principle, pressing toward the liberation in fulfillment and fact in the consummation of all things. Christ's conquest in the resurrection is a *finished* Work in that the rule of the powers of darkness is over at this Dawn. But it is a *continuing* Work, in that the acknowledgment and completion of this lordship await the End. In the time between Easter and Eschaton we contest the forces that continue to militate against Christ the King. About the continuing and final Work of the Liberator in our age, and his call to keep step with him in the Work of liberation today, we shall speak in our exploration of the present and future Work of Christ.

Christ and King achieves the Work of reconciliation in and through the Work of liberation. As the conquest of sin is the reconciliation of humanity with God, so the victory over evil and death is the reconciliation of nature and history with God, within themselves, and with each other. Won in portent and principle by Calvary and Easter, this coming together is looked for at the End, when the wolf will lie down with the lamb, the child will put its hand over the viper's den, swords shall be beaten into plowshares, the creation will no longer groan, the New Jerusalem will descend, and the Kingdom come. It is looked for as well in the firstfruits of this Finale in the healings in, and hopes for, nature and history in this time between the Times. Thus the continuing Work of reconciliation in this world is one in which Christ saves from evil and death and brings wholeness to the fractures of this world.

Theodicy

The age-old problem of evil is an agony to be wrestled with in the Christian understanding of Christ the King, and so we deal with theodicy: the "justification of God," the defense of divine goodness and omnipotence despite the presence of evil. While theodicy draws its most profound resources from eschatology, the atonement speaks the first word of faith about the engagement with the powers of evil.

The Incarnation and atonement affect the issue of theodicy by changing the usual terms in which the question is posed. Thus the three ingredients in the problem of evil — the power of God, the goodness of God, and the presence of evil — are defined with reference to the Good Friday–Easter events rather than given content by cultural assumptions.

Traditional theodicies frequently accept uncritically a conception of power inherent in the original pre-Christian formulation of the problem. Regularly the premises of Greek philosophy, Oriental statecraft, and patriarchal society intrude. How can a loving God, who is also all-powerful, countenance the presence of evil in the world? Traditional answers assume "power" to mean the instant and omnipresent control of an Oriental potentate with the traits of a dominating masculinity and a timeless Greek form — an "in charge" Deity. To interpret theodicy from the atoning center of Christian faith, and thus to wrest it from these cultural assumptions, is to reject machismo and despotic notions of power. Power is reconceived as the Holy Spirit of suffering Shalom, not invincible autocracy. Power is power *enough* to fulfill the Vision of God, not totalitarian hegemony. Power also expresses itself along the time line of the Christian Story, not as instant fiat.

Reconstruing power from the point of view of the atonement illumines the problem of evil in this way: God overcomes evil in the crucifixion and resurrection by a vulnerable but victorious Shalom. The outcome will be that "He will wipe away every tear from their eyes; there shall be an end to death, and to mourning and crying and pain; for the old order has passed away" (Rev. 21:4). The sufferings of persons, history, and nature will be redeemed. Evil has been defeated, and therefore its work will be undone. The Deity who achieves this Purpose is no monarch who rules with the iron hand that requires instant obeisance, but one who rules in a fashion commensurate with long-suffering love. God opens up maneuvering room for response to the divine beckoning, a vista of time from Easter to Eschaton. Here is a dawn in which shadows still persist, the ambiguity of an Already–Not Yet that continues until the high noon when God is "all in all." The evil at work in this span of time is absolutely real, a night that stands against the Light. Yet it is "pro-visional," going before the Vision that is to be. It is the perversion of the freedom God grants a good creation, endemic to history but overcome in eternity. The Power of

148

God, the Holy Spirit, secures the goodness of God in a world still afflicted by evil but moving toward redemption. The crucial distinctions introduced by a christocentric definition of power make the difference between a triumphalist deity and a triumphant God.

The sensitive humanists or morally outraged atheists who deny God because they grasp the horror of evil (though not sin) more than most, and the defensive theists who attempt to justify the ways of a Deity believed to be in some sense the cause of the world's misery, are at one in their misunderstanding. The atoning Power wages a victorious battle against the principalities of this world — on their terrain, but on God's terms. And the aesthetic and pedagogical traditions in theodicy fail at another point, for they do not probe deeply enough the depths of evil in their attempt to protect the goodness and power of God. The defenders of a finite God fall into a dualism that grants the Devil more than his due and/or denies the omnipotence of God. When omnipotence is viewed from the perspective of Good Friday and Easter, "all-powerful" becomes a "narrative" potency on its way to the divine end.

The Shared Work of Prophet, Priest, and King

As the humanity and deity of Christ are in unity in the Person of Christ, and as the three Persons of the Godhead coinhere, so the offices in the Work of Christ mutually interpenetrate. The one Christ accomplishes the Work of atonement. Each office represents a distinguishable role of Christ, but the exercise of each role merges with the others.

Christ as Prophet discloses by word and deed the Purposes of God. But this Work of revelation is also a Work of conquest, and thus a royal action. Ignorance of the Light afflicts a world turned in and away from its horizon. In the Work of disclosure Christ liberates from the power of darkness, thus anticipating the resurrection victory. The powers of evil and death have already begun to meet their master in those same Galilean events. Here, too, is the anticipation of the cross and the Work of Christ the Priest, for the ground of Shalom as well as its goal is revealed in the life and teachings of Jesus, the depths of suffering Love reached on the cross. In the ministry of the Prophet the forgiveness of sins is proclaimed and shared, a forgiveness whose final foundation is built on Golgotha. Thus the Galilean Prophet portends and embodies the Work of Priest and King.

149

Christ as Priest is continuous with the Galilean ministry. The cross is the crown and completion of the suffering Love manifest in the life, healings, and teachings of the Prophet. As such, Calvary in its darkest hour is also disclosure of the invisible light of God. And the disclosure of the Prophet becomes exposure of the hostility of the world in the act of crucifixion. King as well as Prophet makes his presence known on the cross, for here royalty is at work conquering sin in the sacrifice made. And evil and death are being confronted as well, for it is by the sword of the cross that they are finally felled. Thus Prophet and King enter the Work of Priest.

Christ the King is in unity with Christ the Prophet, for the resurrection discloses the victory to which the Prophet points and authenticates the claims of Jesus the Example and Teacher of Shalom. Here also the way of the Prophet, Agape, is the way of conquest by the royal office, and that way embodied in the Galilean Christ is the same suffering Love wielded by the King on the cross. There, too, is the Liberator from sin, as well as the way of the Liberator from evil and death. A royal Work is inextricable from prophetic and priestly ministries.

The Deed of Christ

What did Christ do? He brought us at-one-ment, liberation from sin, evil, and death, and reconciliation with God, neighbor, and nature. As the divine-human Person who does this prophetic, priestly, and royal Work, Jesus Christ is the central chapter in the developing narrative. This being and action constitute the Christian claim to uniqueness. At this one place in the history of God with the world, something happens that changes the relationship of the partners in the covenant. Herein lies the "scandal of particularity."

The deed of Christ begins in his prophetic Work. He saw and shared the Vision of God. He was the Prophet who perceived and pointed to the horizon Light of God's Shalom — a Prophet but more than a Prophet, for the Light that shone toward him also shone *in* him. The Vision became flesh and manifested itself in deeds of liberation and reconciliation.

He was a Seer but also a Sufferer, a Priest as well as a Prophet. He suffered for the Vision of God, exposing the hate of the world as it sought to extinguish the Light of God. And so, too, he suffered the sight of the eclipse of the sun of Shalom, obedient unto death. And he *was* the embodied Vision of God that suffered that death, and in that suffering took into the divine life our punishment, releasing the mercy that covers our sin.

He was the Seer and Sufferer, but also the Liberator and Lord. The sword of the cross pierced the armor of the powers and principalities. The risen Christ is the Conqueror who opens the Future and assures the coming of the Realm of God. No more do we fear the thrones and authorities that rattle their swords in this world, for they have met their match. We are empowered to resist them in the liberation and reconciliation struggles of our time, even as we meet the last enemy, death, in hope.

"Thanks be to God, who has given us the victory through our Lord Jesus Christ."

5. Church: Nature and Mission

Nature

Divine grace is power as well as favor. The grace of God in Jesus Christ that offers the world liberation and reconciliation makes its presence felt in the liberating and reconciling power released into the world. And so we come to that chapter in the Christian Story that has to do with the pouring out of the Holy Spirit, the coming of the Power of God on the day of Pentecost. Our exploration of the doctrine of the Church, ecclesiology, will begin with the original record of this event. The early chapters of Acts provide the biblical framework for understanding what the Church is and does, its nature and mission.

The Ascended Lord

The account of the ascension in the first chapter of Acts builds a bridge from the Person and Work of Christ to the nature and mission of the Church. "As they watched, he was lifted up, and a cloud removed him from their sight" (Acts 1:9). In this striking visual imagery the risen Lord mounts to the "right hand of God." As with other chapters in the Christian Story, debate about the cosmology of the biblical narrator can deflect us from the Word to be heard and the Vision to be seen in and through the text. Attention to the *that* and *what* of the matter here, rather than the *how* and *when* of changing scientific worldviews, discloses a crucial act in the drama of redemption.

152

In traditional language the ascension declares the glorification of Christ and, more specifically, the glorified humanity of Christ. The world in which we live is one in which Jesus Christ actively exercises his kingly rule. This same Jesus — truly human, truly God, truly one — now is the world's indisputable Lord; the world is "Christic." Indeed, he reigns by the power of suffering Love, not by the instruments of the rulers of this world. The exaltation of Christ is the active regency of Shalom. "He's got the whole world in his hands."

The time of rulership is the occasion for "the continuing Work of Christ." Things happen on earth as well as in heaven. The *ascent* of the Son means the *descent* of the Spirit.

The Descended Spirit

The second chapter of the book of Acts reports the evidence of the sovereign power of the exalted Christ. The radiance of the Light that bathes the world comes as fire in the midst of it. "While the day of Pentecost was running its course, they were all together in one place, when suddenly there came from the sky a noise like that of a strong driving wind, which filled the whole house where they were sitting. And there appeared to them tongues like flames of fire, dispersed among them and resting on each one. And they were filled with the Holy Spirit and began to talk in other tongues, as the Spirit gave them power of utterance" (Acts 2:1-4). The power of the divine Light, the Holy Spirit, descends on a people, enflaming them with the language of another land and sights of the Vision of God. The exalted humanity of Christ lets its glory shine in the world, taking form as the Body of Christ on earth. At Pentecost the Holy Spirit brings the Church to birth (cf. Eph. 4:7-16).

This happening occurs among the most ordinary of mortals. Those who see with the natural eyes ask, "Why, they are all Galileans, are they not, the men who are speaking?" (Acts 2:7). In the same way the Church's later antagonists, seeing Peter and John, "perceived that they were uneducated, common men . . ." (Acts 4:13 RSV). Thus in a different frame of reference the antinomies of Incarnation are repeated as the *Body* of Christ is paradoxically seen to be at the same time a *body* of ordinary people.

What are these fires of Pentecost? Those today with the "gift of tongues" trace their lineage to this event. Yet others distinguish the articulate languages described here from the glossolalia of the Corinthian congregation, finding in this Acts text the missionary call to reach the nations. Our guideline to the meaning of the text's "flames of fire" is their significance relative to the birthday of the Church. The language of Heaven and the sights of new Vision portray a new outpouring of the Spirit and its empowerment of a new People as the Body of the glorified Lord.

The illumination of the pentecostal birthday comes from within the event itself. Peter declares, "This is what the prophet spoke of: God says, 'This will happen in the last days. I will pour out on everyone a portion of my spirit; and your sons and daughters shall prophesy; your young men shall see visions, and your old men shall dream dreams. Yet, I will endue even my slaves, both men and women, with a portion of my spirit, and they shall prophesy'" (Acts 2:17-18). The work of the Spirit is the bringing to be of the Vision of God. At Pentecost the empowerment of Shalom takes place as the capacitating of persons to "see visions and dream dreams." It is the fulfillment of the Old Testament hope that there be a people of Christ who will see and serve the Future of God. This new perception is an eschatological event: "In the last days. . . ." The birth of the Church is the beginning of the End. The Kingdom of God as the miracle of ocular newness creates a new *visionary community.* The scales fall from the eyes of these seers who discern the risen and ascended Lord and experience the power of his coming Kingdom. The sign that they have been invaded from the future is their report of "the mighty works of God" (Acts 2:11) in eschatological language. Whether those tongues that burst forth be interpreted as intelligible — "how is it that each of us hears in our own language?" (Acts 2:6) — or as a rush of unintelligible glossolalia — "Others mocking said, 'They are filled with new wine'" (Acts 2:13) — it is the language of the world to come, a universal Shalom that is not confined to the particularities of our finitude, nor does it settle into our neat and manageable coherencies. Therefore in this birth of the Church, the risen and ascended Lord takes to himself a Body on earth with eyes opened by the Spirit to see the future. These are the Dawn People, the children of Light empowered to see the Purposes of God.

People who have had visions of the end for which we have been made, who have seen the Future, are restless with anything short of that destination. The Church's foretaste of the fruits of the new Realm creates a dissatisfaction with present reality. Its eschatological pereption makes the

Christian community a stranger and pilgrim in this world. Herein lies its radical leverage. Because it knows how the world should be, it sets up signs in the Now pointing to the Not Yet. By the power of the Spirit that opened this new horizon, it seeks to orient reality to the Vision.

The effects of this Future shock are to be seen in the events that take place within the Christian community, which we shall presently explore, ones that show its struggle to be a colony of the Future. And subsequently, as described in Acts 3 and 4 and beyond, this revolution within pushes its perimeters further and further into the world without.

The Acts report focuses on the corporate nature of envisioning; it is about a new people. Yet the miracle of new sight is also an individual matter, as the text soon enough suggests: "Whoever calls on the name of the Lord shall be saved" (Acts 2:21 ASV). We shall explore this individuating aspect of the Church's creation, personal salvation, in our next chapter. Here we are concerned to understand Pentecost as a deed of God that brings a singular community into existence.

A return to the original record in Acts of the Church's creation helps to root the doctrine of the Church in the inner ring of authority and also to draw on its rich visual and visionary imagery. In the more conventional language of traditional theology, our exegesis has sought to express the dual nature of Church as a divine-human institution. It is an "earthen vessel" subject to the frailties of its membership and to the play of sociological forces. Yet it carries treasure. God is in the midst of this sinful and finite people. Jesus Christ is truly present by the Spirit that gives this Body life. The uniqueness of the Church consists in this special bond with its Lord. We have spoken of it as the empowerment of the people by the Spirit that abides in its midst to see the Vision of God. As such, the Church is an eschatological community. The Future penetrates the present; the rays of its Light are seen by the opened eyes of faith. Indeed, we do not see "face to face" the coming God. The Church can make no pretense of *being* the Kingdom. It is portent and firstfruit of what is yet to come, unfulfilled, broken, subject to error and ambiguity. But in our present period of ecclesiastical self-criticism, we cannot forget the Church's fundamental identity. A covenant bond has been forged by the Spirit with this people, in all its frailty. While there is no transparency of the future here, we do "see through a glass darkly." In this community we are offered communion with the coming God.

155

The Gifts of the Spirit and Marks of the Church

The Spirit strengthens the ties to the Future with special gifts given to the people of God. The outpouring of the Spirit on the day of Pentecost manifests itself in the appearance of the "marks of the Church." We use this identification (*notae ecclesiae*), usually associated with either the four defining features mentioned in the Apostles' Creed — one, holy, catholic, and apostolic — or the two of traditional Protestantism — Word and Sacraments — to show their relationship to events in the narrative itself. This procedure also sheds light on some of the traditional disputes regarding the number and nature of the marks, a subject to which we shall return after reviewing the New Testament emergence of these gifts of the Spirit.

Kerygma

The presence of the Spirit fires the people of God to say what it sees. The first act of the empowered people is *kerygma*, the report of the Good News, the proclamation of the Gospel. Thus Peter announces to the onlookers, "Men of Israel, listen to me: I speak of Jesus of Nazareth, a man singled out by God . . ." (Acts 2:22). So the Christian Story is told. And it is told against the background and in the idiom of the people of the Covenant, out of whose history this new Word and Vision comes. Peter presses the narrative back into the Prologue, the "plan and foreknowledge of God" (Acts 2:23 RSV), and forward from that to crucifixion, resurrection, and ascension, and thence to the call to participate in the unfolding drama. As the message has an audience in mind, it is addressed here to the "house of Israel." The narration of the Tale of the deeds of God, the *telling* of the Story, is a sign of the presence of the Spirit, and a tool the Spirit uses to build the Church. The kerygma, therefore, is a constitutive factor of the Christian community. Where the Word is preached, the Body of Christ takes form in the world.

Leitourgia

The stirrings of the Spirit continue. "Those who received his word were baptized, and there were added that day about three thousand souls. And they devoted themselves to the apostles' teaching and fellowship, to the breaking of bread and the prayers. . . . And day by day, attending the temple together and breaking bread in their homes, they partook of food with glad and generous hearts, praising God . . ." (Acts 2:41-42, 46-47 RSV). Prayer and praise, the waters of baptism and the bread of the supper, these gifts of the Spirit and worship acts of the people appear in the midst of the aborning congregation. *Leitourgia* joins kerygma as a mark of the Church. The Church *celebrates* as well as tells the Story. In the sacramental form of baptism and eucharist an "outward and visible sign" of the Spirit complements the verbal one of proclamation. Word and Sacrament keep company in sustaining the life of the Church. Yet the sacramental signs do not exhaust the liturgical life of the Body. Corporate prayer and praise in its multifarious expressions, meditative and celebrative, are vehicles of the Spirit in maintaining and strengthening the Body of Christ. The prayers and songs of the Church keep the people of God in communion with the Purposes of God. In worship the Spirit keeps the Body moving by the eye of faithful prayer and praise turned toward the Horizon.

The life of prayer is at the center of worship, communal or personal. Prayer, mental or verbal, is conscious communication with God. Here an I meets a Thou, the human person encounters the divine Self. Prayer in Christian idiom is offered "though Jesus Christ our Lord." Christ is the reference point for our supplication and adoration.

In the acts of prayer, praise, confession, thanksgiving, intercession, petition, and commitment we are catapulted forward to meet the coming Lord. Prayer therefore frees us from bondage to the present moment, gives perspective on it and leverage in dealing with it. But it is not these pragmatic benefits of "spirituality" that justify prayer. In fact they can only be had when they are not sought. "Seek first his kingdom and his righteousness, and all these things shall be yours as well" (Matt. 6:33 RSV). Rather, it is the love of God "for his own sake," the company kept with the One who comes, that is the ultimate warrant for what we do on our knees before our Maker and Redeemer.

Diakonia

"All those whose faith had drawn them together held everything in common; they would sell their property and possessions and make a general distribution as the need of each required" (Acts 2:44-45). As the Spirit opens the eye of faith to see the Light, so it empowers the visionary community as well to see *in* the Light the brother and sister in Christ.

Illumination by the divine Light means in this instance a *diakonia*, a serving of the neighbor in need within the Christian community. This meant a very radical act of physical support in the primitive Church, a pooling of property and possessions and redistribution on the principle "to each according to his need." As this commitment worked itself out in the ensuing life of the community, it took the form of care for, and the honoring of the dignity of, the dysfunctional within ancient society, the "nobodies" of that culture: the widow, orphan, prisoner, slave, and poor. The Church demonstrated the meaning of Agape in its internal life, *doing* the Story, loving the unloved, and thus intuitively modeling the quality of life in the Realm to come. Servanthood comes naturally to be a gift of the Spirit of a Shalom in which the bondages of deprivation and indignity are challenged, and the broken *bodies* of human beings are made whole by bread and wine and water as well as broken *spirits* healed by participation in the sacramental life.

How diakonia is enacted changes with each new occasion. The form of servanthood may be the communitarian caring of the earliest Christians or the mercy and justice ministries of later ones. And its neighbor may be the slave and orphan of the first century or the aged and poor of the twentieth century. But the fact of diakonia continues in each new setting to be a mark of an authentic Church. The care in body as well as spirit for the brothers and sisters in Christ is a constitutive factor of the Christian community.

Koinonia

"They met constantly . . . to share the common life. . . . With one mind they kept up their daily attendance at the temple, and, breaking bread in private houses, shared their meals with unaffected joy . . ." (Acts 2:42, 46). Sharing the common life and meals was more than a ministry of material benevolence. In and through the diakonia was to be seen and felt the throb of *koinonia*. The Spirit gives the gift of *being* as well as doing: being together. Koinonia is the life together of sister and brother in Christ, *being* the Story. Luther, identifying it as a mark of the Church, calls it the "mutual conversation and consolation" of the brothers and sisters. A sign of the Church, therefore, is its reality as a "support system." Here joys are shared and burdens are borne. The tepid word *fellowship* does not convey the deep sharing that koinonia implies as it was lived out by the Acts community and is relived by people of God wherever the Spirit is at work. Koinonia happens when there is an authentic "common life," a sharing and caring life together in which the people of God dwell in the joyful unity of the Spirit.

What happened at Pentecost? The Body of Christ was born on earth, formed by and filled with the Holy Spirit and living under the known sovereignty of its exalted Lord. The sign of the birth of the Body and the presence of the Spirit is the seeing of visions and the dreaming of dreams by sons and daughters, young and old. The people of God catch sight of the Vision of God. The rays of the Future draw from them words and deeds through which the Spirit keeps the Vision alive and compelling. These are the organs in the Body of Christ, by which the Spirit keeps it alive and alert.

The nature of the Church, therefore, is its existence as a divine human organism, the Body of Christ manifest in a body of people, empowered by the Holy Spirit, to know who is Lord, and to tell, celebrate, do, and be the Story. The gifts of the Spirit that keep the Body alive and alert, the marks of the Church, are kerygma, diakonia, koinonia, and leitourgia.

Marks and Models

The four dynamisms of corporate life in the first Christian community correspond to four of the "models of the Church" identified by Avery Dulles in his formative work of that name. For some *kerygma* becomes definitive in "the Church as Herald"; for others, *leitourgia* in "the Church as Sacrament"; for others, *koinonia* in "the Church as Community"; for others, *diakonia* in "the Church as Servant." In our view here, Dulles's fifth model, "the Church as Institution," is the routinization of charisma, the institutionalism of these dynamisms, rather than a separate mark or model.

In the living out of ecclesial existence the gifts given tend to be stewarded by one or another subcommunity of Christians. Such concentration gives each gift high visibility in the continuing life of the Church. On the other hand, when a mark becomes the defining characteristic of a group, reductionism and polarization often result. The fullness of the gifts requires the wholeness of the Body (1 Cor. 12:4-30).

The necessity of this fullness and wholeness with its four constituents

159

is seen in the classic marks of the Church found in the Apostles' Creed: unity, holiness, catholicity, and apostolicity. What these terms mean has been the subject of unending discussion, and the warrant put forward for the way boundaries are drawn in the Church. Lines of definition there must be; but what they are and how they are drawn must accord with the unfolding narrative and its christological norm. We therefore view the ancient landmarks in the light of the four gifts of the Spirit given at Pentecost.

The oneness of the Church is its life together. The Spirit is at work in the community when separation is overcome and brothers and sisters dwell in unity. Oneness is this fellowship in Christ, *koinonia*. The holiness of the Church is its manifest bonding with God. The Spirit gives power to the Church, making it righteous as well as declaring it elect. This sanctification is the gift of service from the One who is the Servant, *diakonia*. The catholicity of the Church is its common worship. Sacramental life in baptism and supper, prayer and praise, is universal. The Church is never without this gift of the Spirit and work of the people, *leitourgia*. The apostolicity of the Church is its link to its origins. Born in the Spirit's fires of apostolic testimony, the Church exists where this Word is heard and Vision seen. Continuity with its genesis is faithful proclamation, *kerygma*.

The right preaching of the Word and the proper administration of the sacraments are often identified by traditions stemming from Luther and Calvin as the constitutive marks of the Church. What is the relation of these two definitive characteristics to the four creedal marks and the four New Testament gifts? The proclamation of the Word and the celebration of the sacraments correspond to two of the Spirit's gifts and two of the classical marks. Kerygma and leitourgia, apostolicity and catholicity, are the "objective" marks of the Church. They are indisputably there, visible and audible to anyone who chooses to look and listen. Their empirical reality is of a piece with the historical nature of the Incarnation, the presence of God in discernible things of the earth. As "objective," they do not depend on the unpredictability of human attitudes or behavior, or the uncertainty and invisibility of our subjective responses. The Reformers were trying to maintain the objective pole of the Church's life, but doing it in a manner befitting their commitment to the primacy of Scripture, the centrality of preaching, and the large place they made for baptism and supper, as well as the challenge they made to definitions of apostolicity and catholicity as ministerial lineage and obedience to the see of Peter. Since the Reformers did place such stress on the response of personal faith and the vitality of the Christian community, one would expect these might have found their way into their understanding of the marks of the Church, parallel as they are to the subjective features, koinonia and diakonia. Indeed, that was sometimes the case, as when church discipline was understood to be a third mark, or the *hearing* and *doing* of the Word and sacraments were added. The left wing of the Reformation moved toward the subjective marks, even to the weakening or exclusion of the objective ones. By and large, the mainstream Reformers did not follow this way because of their strong belief in human sin, and thus their reluctance to build the meaning of the Church on our subjective responses, frail and ambiguous as they are.

The biblical narrative of the giving of primal gifts makes it clear, however, that the Church is not fully what it is called to be without all four of its defining features. Following the ancient tradition, therefore, we speak of four instead of two marks, staying as close to their functioning in the original narrative as possible. Yet, acknowledging the insight of the Reformers, we shall recognize the distinction between the objective and subjective marks, and go with them (and with the ancient tradition, which also stressed objectivity but tended to view all four of the credal themes in the objective sense) in this way: the *validity* of the Church is guaranteed by kerygmatic and liturgical graces, the right preaching of the Word and the celebration of the sacraments, the apostolic and catholic gifts. Christ keeps his promise to be present where two or three are gathered around the Word and in worship. Even the most lackluster and rebellious Christian community cannot prevent the entrance of Christ, who comes among us in spite of who we are, not because of who we are. Yet a valid Church is not yet a *faithful* Church.

The fullness of the Church's being takes place only where the subjective marks are also present, diakonia and koinonia. This is the Church of the New Testament, and thus the faithful Bride of Christ. Because it is not so easy to discern the subjective gifts, the distinction sometimes is made between the visible church, in which the true offer of Christ is made, and the invisible church, where there is a response of heart and life. The purifiers of the Church are impatient with these distinctions, insisting that the church of subjective commitment *is* the only true Church, while those inordinately impressed by the presence of sin virtually identify loyalty to the objective marks with faithfulness. While the word "invisible" does not take into account sufficiently the significance of subjective conduct that is discernible, the visible-invisible distinction does honor the objective dimension manifest in the ordinary means of grace. Christ is so present not because of what we do, but in spite of it, loving us in all our unlovability.

The distinction between validity and faithfulness, or, as we shall identify it, identity and vitality, will reappear in our discussion of the nature of ministry.

Our narrative approach to systematic theology has taken us to the pentecostal chapter. Here we learn the "nature" of the Church, with its four marks. Its nature is also its *nurture*. The pentecostal event brings the Church to be and nourishes its very existence. As such, it focuses on the inner life of the people of God, hence *inreach*. But the work of the Church is mission as well as nurture, *outreach* joined to inreach. In the chronology of the primitive Church, this explosion outward comes in the wake of the pentecostal implosion. Thus Acts 3 and 4 report the movement of the Church beyond the boundaries of the community that has just been created and described in Acts 2 — its mission.

Mission

Reaching out is intrinsic to the saga of God. The Christian Story is about the *Missio Dei,* the mission of God in the pursuit of the divine Purpose. The ancient Church interpreted the "economic Trinity" in terms of this going forth. The plan of God was played out in the "missions" of the Trinity as the Father acted in creation, the Son in reconciliation, and the Spirit in redemption.

The mission of the Church grows out of the mission of God, by way of participation in the mission of the Spirit. The Spirit does not cease its ecclesial work by creating a community that tells and does the Story to itself, and celebrates and is the Story within itself. The Spirit nurtures this community with these gifts in order that it may be in *mission*. Light and fire are for warmth and power. Inreach is fulfilled in outreach. Indeed, this is how the drama of the Church's beginnings unfolds. The ascent of Christ, descent of the Spirit, and birth of the Body of Christ described in Acts 1 and 2 are followed by the movement outward in mission narrated in Acts

3 and 4. The Vision seen and Word heard by this community at Pentecost lead it beyond its own life to share the Light and serve in it. The very gifts of kerygma, diakonia, koinonia, and leitóurgia are honored, paradoxically, to the extent that they are given away to others. We follow the path of mission as it is charted in the texts.

Deed

"One day at three in the afternoon, the hour of prayer, Peter and John were on their way up to the temple. Now a man who had been a cripple from birth used to be carried there and laid every day by the gate of the temple, called, 'Beautiful Gate,' to beg from people as they went in. When he saw Peter and John on their way into the temple, he asked for charity. But Peter fixed his eyes on him, as John did also, and said, 'Look at us.' Expecting a gift from them, the man was all attention. And Peter said, 'I have no silver or gold; but what I have I will give you; in the name of Jesus Christ of Nazareth, walk'" (Acts 3:1-7). As in the Samaritan story (Luke 10:29-37), the eye of love was opened while others passed by on the other side. And the Spirit enabled the disciples to do a deed of Shalom. Mission is *diakonia,* the empowerment of the Church to see *in* the Light the victim "by the gate of the temple." The Spirit opens the eyes of the Christian community to see and serve the invisible of the world.

Servanthood is not doing the conventional but the unconventional, the unthinkable, the miracle. How that miracle is performed depends on the resources the Spirit provides. Again, it is the *fact,* not the *form,* of grace that is integral to the Story. The heart of the miracle at the gate is not the divine methods in the narrative but the God of surprise, who moves the Church to think the unthinkable and do the undoable. The Spirit uses a variety of means to liberate from the bondage of the powers of pain and hurt when the rest of the world accepts these circumstances as unalterable.

Word

In the midst of the deed comes a word. The same Peter whose proclamation was an instrument of the Spirit's pentecostal gathering of the Christian community again tells the Story. This time it is kerygma "outside the gate."

"Men of Israel, why be surprised at this? Why stare at us as if we had made this man walk by some power or godliness of our own? The God of Abraham, Isaac, and Jacob, the God of our fathers, has given the highest honor to his servant Jesus . . ."(Acts 3:12-13). The Word is preached, the Story told. And it is told in translation, in the context of the language and history of its hearers. Mission, therefore, does not stop with the act of mercy and justice but brings the word into companionship with the deed. Evangelism in its broadest sense is the task of getting the Story out, flinging the Christian faith in the air. Evangelism in its apostolic sense as practiced by Peter and John, *Acts evangelism,* is the conjoining of word and deed. It is neither a deedless word nor a wordless deed but word *in* deed, in the context of the deed. The signature of the Spirit is seen where evangelists give visibility to the Vision by a miracle of Shalom done to wounded bodies, and audibility to the Word by a bold witness to broken spirits.

Call

Missionary kerygma is no academic exercise. The telling of the Story is a call to consider our own personal tale. So Peter's narrative concludes, "Repent then and turn to God, so that your sins may be wiped out" (Acts 3:19). Do you want to see the Light? If so, wrench loose from the powers of darkness! Do an about-face (*metanoia*). The teller of the Story comes with a call to decision.

That invitation is corporate as well as individual. It beckons one into the Christian community. Orientation to this Horizon is pilgrimage with the children of Light. Where the Spirit undergirds the deed and word yet another miracle takes place: "Many of those who heard the word believed; and they numbered about five thousand" (Acts 4:4 NRSV). When the seed of the Story is planted in fertile soil it springs up. "Church growth" is an expectation of mission. The debate on the character of this growth is a vigorous one. But the rightness of this hope cannot be disputed. Mission includes the welcome of the five thousand into the Body of Christ, and the expectation that "God gives the growth" (1 Cor. 3:7 KJV).

Confrontation

Sowing in mission goes on among the brambles and rocky soil as well as in fertile soil. In the Acts narrative resistance to both word and deed comes from those who have the most to lose from this outreach: the powers and principalities of the dying Age. The structures of power that took offense at the Good News, in this case, are made up of a military-political-ecclesiastical complex that felt its hegemony threatened by the visual and verbal signs of the New Age. "They were still addressing the people when the chief priests came on them, together with the Controller of the Temple and the Sadducees, exasperated at their teaching the people and proclaiming the resurrection from the dead — the resurrection of Jesus. They were arrested and put in prison for the night . . ." (Acts 4:1-3). Later the occasion for the attack is described by Peter this way: "Rulers of the people and elders . . . the question put to us today is about help given to a sick man . . ." (Acts 4:8-9). Testimony to the risen and ascended Lord whose sovereign power now rules the rulers, testimony given in both word and deed, evoked the anger of the powers that be. Confrontation with authorities and principalities is a mark of mission. Because this aspect so easily gets lost from view in conventional understanding of mission, we give it added attention here.

Early in the career of the Church its mission found itself in controversy with the authorities and rulers. Whether we interpret these powers in ancient idiom as cosmic forces or personal beings or in modern perspective as institutions and systems, the common feature is the presence of social, economic, and political power organized into entities that are more than the sum of the individuals they comprise. Peter and John confronted the same kind of power structure that Martin Luther faced at Worms, that Martin Luther King, Jr., met in the Birmingham jail, and that Christ encountered in Pilate. And as is regularly the case, the powers of this world are hostile to the witness of word and deed.

Mission in and to the structures of power has included from the beginning at least two characteristics: (1) the readiness to confront the thrones and authorities, and (2) the calling to accountability of these structures of authority. To them must be said, "We must obey God rather than any human authority" (Acts 5:29 NRSV). They do not control the world but are subject to the lordship of Christ.

As the eschatological expectations of the early Church lengthened,

165

and no imminent cosmic finale was any longer anticipated (one that would render superfluous any effort to change the structures of power, an effort also made improbable by the relative powerlessness of the Christian community itself), the sense of responsibility for the secular systems and processes increased. That expanded purview has led at worst to the captivity of the Church by the authorities and powers in its attempt to penetrate them, and at best to the prophetic challenge to and change of these structures. The involvement of the Church in this mission has proceeded in a fashion not unlike that described in the Acts texts: the ministry to individual human needs is the entry point, one that leads ultimately to systemic confrontation, or in the current language, a movement from social service to social action.

To resist the powers is to court the enmity of this world. If we are to love our enemies we must make some. So we are called to participate in "the sufferings of God in the world" (Bonhoeffer).

Life and Worship Together

In the early chapters of Acts, mission has a rhythm. Outreach is followed by inreach, which in turn is succeeded by outreach. Thus Peter and John return for renewal to the life together of prayer, praise, preaching. "After they were released, they went to their friends and reported what the chief priests and the elders had said to them. When they heard it they raised their voices together to God. . . . When they had prayed, the place in which they had gathered together was shaken, and they were all filled with the Holy Spirit and spoke the word of God with boldness" (Acts 4:23-24, 31 NRSV). Mission without is rooted in the nurture of the inner life of the Church.

Suggested as well in this account is the missionary dimension of inreach itself. "Raised voices" and a "place . . . shaken" were unlikely to have been ignored by the world outside! While leitourgia and koinonia in their outreach form are not specifically mentioned in our narrative, their missionary function is certainly implied.

The defining marks of the Church/gifts of the Spirit have their reaches in nurture and mission in the first Christian community. A congregation or larger expression of church life today faithful to its apostolic origins will manifest the same richness of telling, doing, being, and celebrating in its life within and without. A way to test that faithfulness in contemporary terms is represented in the following chart:

Nurture (Inreach)	Gifts of the Spirit and Marks of the Church	Mission (Outreach)
Preaching and teaching	*Kerygma* (Telling)	Evangelism
Servanthood within (Care for brothers and sisters)	*Diakonia* (Doing)	Servanthood without (Social service and social action)
Life together within	*Koinonia* (Being)	Life together without
Worship	*Leitourgia* (Celebrating)	Festival

Sect and Church

To interpret the meaning of the Church in an eschatological framework tends to move it in the direction of the "sect-type" view (Troeltsch) of ecclesiology. If the Church is to be what it is called to be, it must emphasize radical obedience to God's will. The pressure of the final Vision makes for a "company of the committed" separated out from fallen humanity. Somewhere these demands of the *sect principle* must be honored in ecclesiology, or else the Church is tempted to settle comfortably into its environment. Such visionless accommodation is the hazard of the "church-type" ecclesiology, with its loose membership requirements and flirtation with "culture-Christianity."

While the sect principle must make its contribution, the *church principle* has an important witness as well. In contrast to the exclusivist view of the former, which limits the Christian community to the "pure" or "saints," the latter is inclusive, letting the "wheat and tares grow up together" (Matt. 13:30), making room for both saints and sinners. It views the being of the Church as an objective status conferred by the Spirit on

167

a company of sinners, not as a state of moral and spiritual attainment subjectively demonstrable by a company of saints.

To honor the validity of both principles means that we conceive the Church as an eschatological community, but one living under the conditions of this present age. It is the *ecclesia,* those called out of the present and toward the Future, but not yet living there. As it is Dawn and not High Noon, the shadows permeate this colony as well as its worldly environment. In its common life Shalom is present as *foretaste* and not as fulfillment. The reality of Christ in the midst of sinful people establishes the Church's singular being and constitutes its call. The church principle witnesses to this with its insistence on a catholicity and inclusiveness of the last and the least, and its stress on the divine objectivity and initiative. The gifts of kerygma and leitourgia assured the real Presence of Christ in and through Word and Sacrament.

But where there is Light there is also Fire, and where there is Fire something happens as it did on the day of Pentecost. The Power of God accompanies the Word of God. The Spirit bringing Christ to this community bears the fruit of Shalom. The sect principle testifies to the efficacy of the Spirit in spiritual. and moral vitality that makes the authentic Church. Where the Spirit is, there is life and light struggling against death and night. The Church always lives under both the imperative and the expectation of radical obedience, even as it lives out of its existence as an inclusive company of forgiven sinners.

The partnership of exclusion and inclusion, commitment and catholicity, can be embodied institutionally in terms of the ancient notion of "ecclesiola in ecclesia," the little church within the Church. That is, within the broad institutional life of the Christian community there is a place for a subcommunity of special visionaries. Just as the body part of glossolalia serves the function of keeping the Corinthian church off balance, so the Church in every period needs those who talk the strange language of the Not Yet, those who peer further into the Future and strain toward that goal in their attitude and behavior. These visionaries are not necessarily more advanced in their spiritual and moral life, for the sin of pride and self-righteousness visits them more habitually and intensely than most, precisely because of their intensity of purpose, thus keeping them also in the company of sinners. Rather, their role calls the Church away from its easygoing accommodation to the world. The "orders" within the ancient Church and the renewal movements of the present Christian community (including the charismatic movement itself when it has learned to relativize its role and is open to other gifts given to the Body, 1 Cor. 12–14) serve this purpose. This visionary role is always exercised as part of the Body and is not to be mistaken for the whole, as in the case of the sect type, whose reductionism excludes those with other gifts and ministries. The visionary is part of an inclusive community of those who see and serve the light that shines on them. "The eye cannot say to the the hand, 'I do not need you . . .' "(1 Cor. 12:21).

Church, World, and God

Related to this question of the purity of commitment within the Christian community is the recent debate on the interrelationship of "God, Church, and world." Some portray their connections in this fashion: God → Church → World. In its most stringent form, this view is expressed as "no salvation outside the Church." God, so understood, is to be encountered redemptively by passage out of the world and into the Church. Against this "ecclesiocentric" view of grace and salvation others argue that the proper relationship is: God → World → Church. Here, God works first and foremost through worldly action. The Church must gravitate to the world's places and processes of healing and hope. Thus the Church is a "postscript" to the world, relinquishing the claims made by the church-centered view, and existing only by a secular grace.

As a corrective to the ecclesiocentricism of the first position, the second perception must be affirmed. However, this view cannot stand alone as a doctrine of the Church, for it ignores the promise of Christ to be with his people in all its frailty. As with the sect view, this secular view assumes that the reality of the Church depends on our "good works." But the validity of the Church does not rise or fall with our good works. It exists by the promise and presence of Christ through Word and Sacrament. A fuller understanding of the relation of God, world, and Church looks more like this:

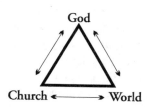

169

God's saving grace meets us through both the Church and the world. In the Christian community Christ opens our eyes to see who he is. In the world, Christ comes to us incognito wherever there are movements of freedom and peace (Matt. 25). We shall explore the Emmaus road passages subsequently for another view of this question. Here we note that the Church is *fully* the Church not only when it sees the Vision and hears the Word, but also when it goes into the world in pursuit of Shalom. On the other hand, the life with God in the world finds its fulfillment when it leads into the Christian community where the Purpose of God is revealed.

The Ministries of the Church

We are in the midst of a great debate in the Church today about the meaning of ministry. At one time, either in the dogmatic formulations of "high church" traditions or in the common practice of many avowedly "low church" ones, it was an unquestioned premise that ministry belongs to the ordained clergy. Whether this was defined in sacerdotal fashion as bestowal of the mark of priesthood by the laying on of apostolic hands, or functionally as the setting apart of some to the office of Word and Sacrament, or operationally as those who "run the church," the clergy were conceived as the Ministers, and the rest of the Christian community as Laity, a lesser breed.

In the past few decades this view of ministry has come under sharp attack in both theory and practice. Both the ascendency-submission pattern and the sharp distinctions of the earlier view have been challenged by a recovery of "the ministry of the laity."

Sometimes the ministry of the laity is interpreted to mean that there is no privileged caste, either ontologically or institutionally, and that all services by both clergy and nonclergy are of equal importance before God and in the life of the Church. At other times, the ministry of the laity is conceived as the complete mobility of functions within the Church, each person being empowered to perform any function. In other settings it is understood to mean that the real ministry of the Church is in the world, and thus the laity constitute the fundamental ministry of the Church, with the clergy serving as resources to, and enablers of, the laity in their secular mission. And at yet other times, the ministry of the laity is seen to be the only ministry, with baptism as the act of ordination, and the need for clergy in any sense of the word questioned.

A new vision of the ministry of the laity has had a salutary effect in many areas of the Church's life. But it has also contributed to the loss of a sense of identity among clergy. And the reaction against the oversimplifications of some of the more recent theories of the ministry of the laity has prompted a too quick return in some places to authoritarian clergy models. In the midst of these tendencies and countertendencies is a rising generation of women seeking ordination and equal participation in the Church as pastors. This crucial struggle carries with it the assumption that there is a unique and important meaning to the ministry of altar and pulpit.

The context for our discussion of the meaning of ministry is the nature and marks of the Church. As the ministry is viewed in the light of the Acts charter, both the wholeness and the particularities of ministry come into clearer view.

The General Ministry and Special Ministries

The Body of Christ lives by the breath of God, the Holy Spirit. The signs of its life are the gifts given to it by the Spirit: kerygma, diakonia, koinonia, leitourgia (see 156-59). Baptism, in one of its meanings, as entrance into the Church, is the seal of membership in this Body. Membership is to be understood in its most elemental sense as being one of the "members," one of the organs of this Body. Baptism, therefore, is ordination to the general ministry of the Church. It is a seal of a gift of the Spirit, the claim of God on a person to be a living member of the Body and thus to exercise some gift for the life and work of this Body. In baptism all are called to be living parts of the Body of Christ (1 Cor. 12:4-31; Eph. 4:7-16).

The growth of a member of the Body is the coming to consciousness of the gift that has been given and the faithful exercise of that gift. The gifts of the Spirit for the preservation and vigorous life of the Body are of two kinds. There are gifts that assure the *identity* of the Body, and there are those that guarantee its *vitality*. One kind of gift has to do with the *memories* and the other the *hopes* of the Church.

The gifts of kerygma and leitourgia, the telling and celebrating of

171

the Christian Story, are organs of the identity and memory of the Body of Christ. Without these gifts the Church falls into amnesia; it does not know who it is or where it has come from. Without them the Church cannot see its Vision or know its goal. Some within the Church are the custodians of the gifts of kerygma and leitourgia (1 Cor. 3:5; Acts 6:1-6; 2 Tim. 1:11). They do not monopolize them but they do guard and facilitate them. Preserving the memories of identity, they remind the Church of who it is . . . and whose it is. The Church requires stewards of the mysteries of God (1 Cor. 4:1). Stewardship is exercised by proclamation and celebration, by the custodianship of kerygmatic and liturgical gifts, by preaching the Word and administering the Sacraments. Stewards of identity exercise a special ministry within the general ministry of the whole people of God, "to stir into flame the gift of God" (2 Tim. 1:6). As a particular ministry signaled by the act of ordination, its gifts and functions are essential to the health and wholeness of the Church.

A body can see visions and speak a word and still be inert. A body is made to walk and work, run and dance, embrace and reach out. So, too, the Body of Christ. Its purpose is fulfilled not by its longest memory or its mellowest voice, but by its life and movement. The Spirit's gifts of this vitality are diakonia and koinonia. The beating heart, reaching hands, and moving feet of the Body are those signs of life. To ninety-nine percent of the membership of the Church are given these organs of vitality. The laity, those called to the upbuilding and outreaching in love of the Body of Christ, are the stewards of its vitality (Rom. 12:4-8; 1 Cor. 12:27-31; Eph. 4:11-12).

Because the Body of Christ exists to walk and work in the world, the ministry of the laity is in the foreground of the mission of the Church. The laity as the presence of the Church in the rhythms and structures of society, the places of work and leisure, governance, education, science, social change, marriage and the family, turn occupation into vocation as they live out their own priesthood. *How* this ministry is to be rightly exercised is still a moot point: as individuals in these systems and patterns? Or corporately in churchly or extra-churchly forms of Christian life and witness? *That* the laity are the leading edge of mission is not to be questioned. And *what* is to be done there is first and foremost the employment of the gift given by Christ, the serving ministries of rehumanizing love.

Baptism into general ministry claims and accredits the laity for mission in the world. If clergy, also baptized, are called by special ordination to their special ministry of kerygma and leitourgia, why are not the laity called and confirmed in a special way to the exercise of their particular gifts? Precedent exists for this kind of commissioning, and therefore some tacit recognition of the void in the consecration of laity to such churchly functions as church school teaching, choir participation, and other forms of intrachurch leadership. Some traditions ordain laity to the offices of deacon and elder, and commission them for mission in and through church agencies. Here and there, some laity are consecrated for ministry in their own secular work. We have a long way to go, however. The recognition of full membership in the Body entails setting apart, through special commissioning, its gift-ministries of diakonia and koinonia, as well as kerygma and leitourgia. The present practice of ordaining deacons is a timid step in this direction. But the ordination into the diaconate should be a consecration of called laity to servanthood both within and without the congregation, with special accent on missions without, the ministry to elemental human need, and therefore ministry with Christ in the world.

Our emphasis on different responsibilities for ministry should not be hardened into a rigid division of ministry. A living organism is an interrelated whole. Even more so is the Body of Christ, as is underscored by Paul's moving discourse on love in 1 Corinthians 12, directed to the different gift ministries mentioned in 1 Corinthians 12. No faithful stewardship of kerygma and leitourgia is possible that does not issue in diakonia and koinonia. Nor is there faithful stewardship of diakonia and koinonia that is not grounded in and illumined by kerygma and leitourgia. Further, an open Church is one in which each steward needs the other stewards and learns from them. And where there is weakness or lack of opportunity in one section of the Body, those with other gifts may feel the claim to move beyond their formal call to support and strengthen the Body at its point of need or opportunity. In recent decades of church history clergy have acknowledged the open-ended character of their own gift ministry by moving beyond kerygmatic and liturgical responsibilities to diaconal and koinonial ministry. From the 1960s on, a vigorous clergy involvement in the common life has taken place in diaconal movements of human rights, poverty, peace. In the same period ministrations of koinonia in counseling and small groups engaged many clergy. Correspondingly, many laity embarked on kerygmatic and liturgical ministries when clergy neglected those responsibilities, as in the leadership of laity in Bible study and theological inquiry, their growing interest in evangelism, and the search for a more meaningful spirituality.

Inasmuch as this movement beyond the particularity of gift does really achieve its purpose of interrelating gifts — the frontline involvement of clergy in justice and peace movements encouraging the laity to exercise their own ministry, and laity initiatives in biblical study and piety pressing the clergy for growth in their own stewardship of Word and Sacrament — this mobility of ministry is vital to the life of the Body. But when either clergy or laity usurp the other's role and thus neglect their own special call, such movement becomes a cancer growth that consumes the other Body parts and makes for death, not life.

To be *responsible* for the kerygmatic and liturgical gifts does not mean their monopoly. Clergy are charged with responsibility for these organs functioning within the Body, not their exclusive exercise. Stewardship of kerygma in mission and evangelism means that the minister of kerygma sees to it that the Good News goes forth from the Church. But it may be that the most effective sharing of the Christian Story is done by laity, either organized and trained by the Church or equipped to witness in a more individual way. In the same way, a diaconate of the laity is called to keep the human needs of the world and the congregation before the Church and facilitate its reach of neighbor love. In that ministry there will surely come a time when clergy can play a vital role. Ministry is stewardship, not overlordship, of a gift of the Spirit.

To set the foregoing exploration in the larger context of the continuing Work of Christ, we may summarize this understanding of the ministry in the following way.

The continuing Work of Jesus Christ in the Church is the same done in his ministry of life, death, and resurrection. The same Christ is present in the Body as Prophet, Priest, and King. Our ministry, therefore, as it shares in the continuing Work of his ministry, participates in that threefold office. The whole ministry of the people of God continues his ministry of Seer, Sufferer, and Liberator. It does so in the modalities fitting to the ministries of identity and vitality.

The ordained ministry of identity is an agent of the Work of Prophet as it proclaims the Word and clarifies the Vision in its custodianship of the kerygma. And it serves the Work of Priest in its stewardship of the sacramental mysteries and in liturgical leadership. It is an agent of the

Kingship of Christ in its role of enabler of the life of koinonia through both support and governance. And in each aspect of ministry is carried out the meaning of the word itself, diakonia, suffering servanthood.

The ministry of vitality given to the laity is the empowerment of the Body by the Spirit that enables it to walk and work in the world, embodies the office of Prophet (Seer) as it bears witness to Shalom by deed and word in the secular structures, and enriches the work of the stewards of kerygma by bringing a secular context to the biblical text. The Work of Priest (Sufferer) lives on in the laity's participation in the suffering servanthood of God in the world as they seek to live out the life of the Body in all the ambiguities and agonies of secular existence, and as they bring this experience to the liturgy, whose very center is the broken Body and shed Blood. In this understanding of the priesthood of all believers in the common ventures of life, Mary is the first to model such vocation, as Raymond Brown has pointed out (Luke 1:38; 11:28). The royal Work (the office of Liberator) is discharged when the laity are agents of liberation and reconciliation in the world and take responsibility for freedom and peace in the governance and life of the Church. Thus, the ministry of the whole people of God, shared according to their several gifts, is continuous with the threefold ministry of Christ in word and worship, Work, and redemptive suffering (Consultation on Church Union).

A final observation: all the gifts are given by the Spirit to the whole Body. It is the Body in its unity and totality, therefore, that tests and then sets apart the special ministries of kerygma, leitourgia, diakonia, and koinonia. While the personal call to be eye or mouth, hand or foot of the Body comes in the intimacy of one's communion with the Spirit, the public confirmation of that call and consecration in it come through the Christian community through its designated representatives in ministries of identity and vitality.

The dispersion of the power of the Spirit among all the people includes universality in the opportunity of the people of God to enter into any ministry for which personal call and publicly validated equipment have prepared them. The debate about the ordination of women to the ministry of kerygma and leitourgia has sharpened this question of universality of option. An unambiguous answer is given in the Petrine framework for ecclesiology. In the charter language of the Church he declares, "God says, 'This will happen in the last days: I will pour out on everyone a portion of my spirit; and your sons and daughters shall prophesy. . . . Yes,

I will endue even my slaves, both men and women, with a portion of my spirit, and they shall prophesy'" (Acts 2:17, 18). Because in Christ there is "neither male nor female," no ministry of the Church is denied to any part of the people of God.

Order and Orders

The form of government and the exercise of authority in the Church are long-disputed questions. Scripture does not give unambiguous direction in either matter, a fact that suggests the relative theological weight of church order and ministerial orders. While the Church is an article of faith and a chapter in the Story, its mechanisms are not. However, the intensity with which these issues have been discussed, the genuine contributions that various traditions have made, and the biblical clues on the question indicate that the well-being (*bene esse*) if not the being (*esse*) of the Christian community is at stake. We are helped along on the issue of orders by the 1983 World Council of Churches Faith and Order Commission document on this subject, and by the rich learnings from church unions and ecumenical ventures. We shall seek to integrate these learnings with our narrative framework.

As at Pentecost so also throughout Christian history, the local gathering of the people of God is where the kerygmatic, liturgical, koinonial, and diaconal gifts are given with constancy and predictability. For most people most of the time, here is where the Story is told and celebrated in life together and in mutual service. As the television medium is used more and more extensively in the propagation of faith, both its strengths and its limitations become more apparent. In this context the phrase "electronic church" can be seen to be a misnomer, for there is no pentecostal life together in worship and service. The congregation as the basic community expression of the Christian religion gives force to the argument for congregational polity or, at the very least, a place in church governance for the congregation.

As koinonia is a constitutive factor of the Church's life, and as the Christian community is far more than its first congregational expression at Pentecost, the life together of individual congregations must be joined in covenantal bonds, for these are already so joined before the eye of Christ. The Church is universal, extending far beyond the limited perspective of a local gathering. As the Body of Christ, the Church is composed of the single cells of congregations having their life from a larger organism. This supraparochial reality argues for the significance of presbyterial polity, in which the whole Church enjoys an existence in its own right with its commensurate institutions and agencies, and in which there is mutual accountability between the church local and the Church universal.

The third form of government, alongside congregational and presbyterial, is episcopal, and lies on the boundary between church order and ministerial orders. We shall deal with it, therefore, in the discussion of orders that follows.

As the congregation is the basic locale for the kerygmatic and liturgical graces, the ministry commensurate thereto does its work in that place. The ministry of identity befitting the congregation occupies the pastoral office or, in comparable language from Scripture and ecumenical formulation, is ordained to the order of presbyter. The Story is told and celebrated by this preaching and priestly elder in the midst of the worshiping and serving congregation. We have examined the characteristics of this office earlier in its general features. Here their focus is in the congregation.

The koinonial and diaconal gifts require their respective stewards. In ecumenical thinking the office of deacon is increasingly set apart for the execution of ministries of vitality. Ecumenical documents usually associate this office with the care of church efforts in service to the world, such as leadership in eleemosynary institutions and other social and educational ministries. This servanthood is usually expressed in extraparochial or supraparochial ways, as befits the issues and avenues of service. As such it represents a conception of the diaconate that is an advance on earlier views, which treat it essentially as a step toward clerical status. The next natural evolution of this concept is to relate it to the ministry of the laity. In this case the diaconate would be viewed as that corps of commissioned people of God who exercise their servanthood in their vocation, and not only those whose diakonia is carried out from an ecclesial base.

The direction in ecumenical conversation is toward a threefold order of ministry, including the office of bishop. Our exploration of ministerial orders connects with church order at this point, encountering the issue of episcopal polity. As the Church that tells and celebrates the Story is more than the local congregation, so too is the office responsible for the stewardship of those means of grace. The Church in its presbyterial expression is one way that leadership is carried out, as noted earlier. However, as representative bodies meeting on stated occasions — sometimes thought of as a kind of collegial episcopacy — they cannot carry out the day-to-day responsibilities of the church regional or provide the focus of personal leadership comparable at that level to the pastoral office at the congregational level. For the well-being of the Church at large, there developed a pastor to pastors and a pastor to congregations. This figure also came to be a symbol of the unity and continuity of the Body of Christ. The pressures of history and the needs of ecclesiastical existence have been such that this office appears in one way or another in most denominations, even when they avoid the word "bishop." To name it as such, to state clearly the function and status of the episcopal office, and to place the offices in a network of accountability to congregation and region are far better than to carry on the practice without theological warrant or critique.

The threefold order of ministry cannot be construed in a hierarchical fashion. How else could it be for those who take up Christ's ministry, the one who came "to serve and give up his life as a ransom for many" (Matt. 20:28)? The three are parallel ministries exercised in arenas commensurate with their respective calls. How the complexity of the interrelationships is worked out in practice and what its connection is with "apostolic succession" are issues that cannot be resolved here, but are very much on the agenda of ecumenical dialogue.

The Sacraments

The identity of the Church is sharpened by the central events of leitourgia cited in the second chapter of Acts, baptizing and breaking bread. They have been with us ever since as the rites of birth and nurture in the Christian community, baptism and the Lord's supper. These events of initiation and nourishment, the "mysteries" (1 Cor. 4:1), are the *sacraments* of the Church, "the outward and visible signs of an inward and spiritual grace." They are the sign language of faith, the visible Word that portrays and declares the Good News. They are the happenings that give visibility to the Vision of God. But they are gestures of the Church that *do* what they *say;* the sacraments are "effectual signs" that convey grace as well as display it. Sometimes this twofold quality is expressed in the idea that they are "signs and seals" of the Promise.

The ingredients of valid sacramental action are usually considered to be the matter or external element, the form or Word said in conjunction with it, the one who administers the sacrament, and the honest intention that this event be what it is biblically asserted to be. *Validity* of action becomes *efficacy*, the sacrament becomes salvific, when faith is present to receive the grace offered.

Through these signs the Holy Spirit seals God's people within the community of faith. Indeed, there are other visible acts through which the Spirit works to strengthen our ties to Christ and to one another: confirmation at coming of age in faith, marriage at conjugal union, ordination at vocation, confession and counsel — public and private — in the pilgrimage of faith, and burial at the end of our journey. These *ordinances* are radii from the sacramental hub. We focus here on the central acts, rising out of the ministry of Christ manifest in the originating events of the Church's birth, and integral to any participation in the Body of Christ. Here the Word becomes physical in the water, wine, and bread, creating and sustaining the Christian community.

Baptism

While there have been a few significant recent studies on baptism and some interest in its implications for ecumenism and mission, this rite still dwells in the shadows of contemporary Christianity. Moreover, its traditional importance and meaning have come under heavy attack, especially regarding the practice of baptizing the newborn. The demise in many places of a triumphalist mentality, the pluralist society in which the Church lives, the stress on the diaconal and koinonial credentials of the Christian community, a neo-universalist and eschatological framework for theology that is reluctant to make soteriological claims for the church, all work to put in question this entry point.

For all the modern uneasiness about baptism, any contemporary faith that takes the Scriptures seriously will have to come to terms with its many assertions about this rite. Baptism is described in the New Testament as the cleansing laver of regeneration (John 3:5; 1 Cor. 6:11; Eph. 5:26; Titus 3:5), the remission of sins (Acts 2:38; 22:16), being buried and rising again (Rom. 6:3-4; Col. 2:12), putting on or entry into Christ (Rom. 6:3; Gal. 3:27), engrafting into the Body of Christ (1 Cor. 12:13), the pouring out of the Holy Spirit (Acts 2:38; 19:1-6; 1 Cor. 12–13; Titus 3:5-6), and in general is associated with God's saving action (Mark 16:16; Eph. 4:5; 1 Pet. 3:21). When the Church's testimony is added to that of the Bible, similar high claims are found among classic interpreters: forgiveness of sin and divine illumination (Justin), "the seal of eternal life and our rebirth in God" (Irenaeus), the bestowing of the Spirit (Tertullian), freedom from the power of the devil (Origen), participation in the mystical Body (Augustine), unity with the Godhead (Athanasius), deification (Gregory of Nyssa), putting on Christ (Calvin), and bathing in Christ's blood (Luther). The collision between ancient wisdom and contemporary perception presses for a restatement. The vision motif provides us with a suggestive angle to view the meaning of baptism.

Baptism is the enactment of the Church's vision of parental embrace in the Prodigal Son story, "the open arms of the Father" (Aulén). Baptism declares that the eye of God rests on this child of God. It is itself a ray of the divine Light that reaches toward this "single one." But in this individuating reach there is a gathering as well as a calling. Baptism is the welcome of Christ into the community, the doorway into the household of faith.

Where the water is joined to the baptismal Word in the community of faith these things happen.

1. The baptized is taken from the shadows and brought into the pilgrim band moving toward the horizon Light. The direction in which this company moves is that in which the risen Christ can be seen by the eye of faith. In other metaphors, baptism is engrafting into the Body of Christ, the entrance into the new Covenant, translation into the Kingdom of grace, membership in the church.

2. The baptized is brought into a new *relationship*. The "I" of Christ makes a "Thou" of the baptized, signaled by the giving of a Christian name. The wide-open arms of God close in their reach toward this individual. Here is the self-presentation of covenanting Love. The offer of mercy effected on Calvary is particularized to this human being. The face of God is turned toward this person. Baptism is regeneration and new birth, unity with the Godhead. All these ancient terms point to a new bond forged between this self and the divine Self.

3. In baptism a personal *claim* is made and a *call* is issued. The baptizand now is invited to make response to the invitation of grace. Thus baptism is ordination to the general ministry, the call to servanthood.

180

It carries with it the impulse to special ministry as well, insofar as a unique gift is given by the Spirit to be exercised within and beyond the Body. Thus baptism is being buried and rising again with Christ, or putting on Christ. Baptism as call and claim is an indelible mark, the insignia that identifies the soldier and convicts the deserter (Augustine).

The environmental, relational, and imperative aspects of baptism are the work of the Holy Spirit. As membership in the mystical Body, and as individual relationship to its Head, the Spirit signifies and seals the action. Grace, not our works, makes baptism "illumination," the shedding of divine Light on one for whom Christ died and rose again.

Grace and Faith in Baptism

Grace in baptism is the self-offer of Christ and all his benefits. Faith is the reception of that Presence, the open arms of the daughters and sons responding to the divine reach. "Be it unto you according to your faith" is a sacramental word as real to baptism as to the supper. The presence or absence of personal faith does not materialize or destroy the reality of baptismal grace. Baptism is valid with or without our response. But it is not baptism "unto salvation" without personal faith. We are justified by grace appropriated in faith. The meaning of this great Reformation theme we shall explore in the subsequent chapter. Here we anticipate it by making a crucial distinction between the *offer* and its *acceptance*. The baptismal waters are the lens through which the divine Light is brought to focus on a single self, and on that called-out community. Whether that self or society opens its eyes to see the Light and walk in the Light depends on the act of faith, itself the fruit of grace.

"Faith comes from what is heard" (Rom. 10:17 RSV). This is why the proclamation of the Word is companion to the celebration of the sacraments. Faith is born in the conscious confrontation with the mighty acts of God in Jesus Christ. The believer comes to the baptismal event to accept the welcome of Christ there portrayed and enacted. Thus the Holy Spirit works faith in the preaching of the Word and seals it in this sacrament, binding the faithful to one another and to Christ. The grace of baptism, therefore, *saves* when it is received in *faith*. When the "Yes" of God in baptism is answered by the "Yes" of faith, it is "unto salvation."

As the love of God can turn to hot coals before its enemies (Rom. 12:20), so the divine Love that comes to us in baptism can be burning fire rather than healing Light, damnation and not salvation. And so the awesome reminder by Karl Barth that the casually taken ritual stands as a sign of judgment on the faithlessness of Western Christendom. But those who receive it in a faith busy in love receive it unto life and Light.

Household Baptism

If faith alone can receive the grace of baptism, then can the sacrament be administered to the newborn? While it is possible to speculate about the seed of faith in an infant, the high view of baptismal grace we have taken here demands serious attention to the preparation for this gift, and at the very least a profession of faith, one that is responsible only at the age of discretion. Is baptism then to be limited to the mature believer? Do the open arms of Christ reach out only to individuals who are "old enough to decide for themselves"?

"God setteth the solitary in families" (Ps. 68:6 KJV). Our individualistic culture finds this to be a hard saying. The ambiguous state of the family in contemporary society makes it further suspect. The corporate framework of biblical faith is not the conventional wisdom of modernity. But the theme that "no one is an island" is part and parcel of the Christian Story, expressing itself in a variety of ways, from the corporate personality of the people of Israel, through the koinonia of the Christian community, to the belief that the intercessory prayers of one can help another and that the faith of one can count for another (Matt. 17:14-21; Mark 2:3-12). The vicarious act on the cross itself attests to this truth. It comes to expression in the practice of infant baptism or, better, *household baptism,* the biblical word that puts the emphasis where it belongs, on the communal meaning. While a clear but not convincing case can be made for household baptism in five New Testament passages (Acts 2:38-39; 16:15; 16:31; 18:8, and 1 Cor. 1:16), and while there is no mention of the adult baptism of the children of believers (and such other arguments as parallels with Jewish proselyte baptism, the evidence for a fairly universal practice in the early centuries, etc.), the question must finally be resolved on theological grounds. If baptism is the sign and seal of the reach of God, and if the self is more than solitary, then a household reception of the divine Love is one way of responding to the beckoning of God.

The family that receives the divine invitation is an inclusive one. Those who represent the newborn child, making the act of faith for that child until he or she can make it personally at the age of discretion, and preparing the child for that option, are first and foremost the parents, to whose conjugal union the Spirit adds the child as a blessing. But the nuclear family does not exhaust the circle of support, extending as it does to "sponsors" or "godparents" and to the congregation itself, which takes the vows.

The corruptibility of the practice of household baptism is well known and much to the foreground of contemporary discussion, especially in lands where there is some form of state Church, but also anywhere that the Church has settled comfortably into its surroundings. The integrity of Church membership becomes a passionate concern where accommodation and mediocrity are the order of the day. To this end, the deepening of the meaning of a faith commitment within the congregation preparatory to the baptism of a child and the strengthening of the ordinance of *confirmation* deserve eminent attention. In the latter case, the confirmand is prepared to take on herself or himself the profession of faith, which receives the offers of baptism and through which the Spirit renders them "unto salvation."

To summarize the point of household baptism we return to the Acts charter: "Repent and be baptized, every one of you, in the name of Jesus the Messiah for the forgiveness of your sins: and you will receive the gift of the Holy Spirit. For the promise is to you, and to your children . . ." (Acts 2:38-39). The inclusion of the children of our household in this promise means that the pilgrim band moving toward the Horizon gathers to itself in baptism also its children. The sleeping child is carried in the arms of this company. But there comes a moment in that pilgrimage when the child must descend from the arms that have supported it, open its own eyes to the Light, and decide whether it will continue in that path. This is the journey of household baptism, begun vicariously in the bosom of the community and confirmed subsequently in the freedom of faith.

The apparent divergence of practice in the Church today is actually not as theologically polarized as it would appear to be, for the rite of "dedication" of children widely observed in adult-baptism denominations signifies the welcome into the arms of Christ represented by the baptismal waters. And the growing stress on the importance of subsequent training and decision where household baptism is practiced is recognition of the importance of the personal act of faith at the age of discretion.

Supper

The pentecostal flames burn again in "the altar fire" (Olive Wyon). As the Light of God invites us in baptism, it comes to strengthen us in the holy supper. Illumination happens because at the Lord's table we are guests proleptically at the heavenly banquet itself. Here is the presence of the Future. The eschatological hope is imparted in the eucharist, and we participate in things yet to come.

At the "last supper" Christ is Host, his disciples gather in communion with him and each other, and the wheat and wine of the earth are consecrated. In the upper room Christ gave his disciples a taste of the heavenly banquet, with its union with him and unity with humanity and the earth. And the price paid for that final victory, the sacrifice of Jesus and the suffering of God, is the modality in which the Future comes to us: through the medium of bread and wine, a broken body and shed blood.

Our reenactment of that meal in the sacrament gives like visibility to the divine purpose. In the Lord's supper we remember that event and the sacrifice to and through which it pointed toward Shalom. As such, it is a memorial of what has been and a whetted expectation for what is yet to come. Together with the first guests at the table who were present with the Host, who partook mystically of his sacrifice through the bread he broke and wine he poured, and who shared in the feast to come (Luke 22:14-19), it is for *us* also a *participation* in this Kingdom, as well as its recollection and anticipation (John 6:41, 48-51). In our celebration of the supper we keep company with the same Host and taste of the same feast of final liberation and reconciliation. We do it under the mode of a sobered hope by the same symbols of sacrifice. And the claim on the partakers and the praise that they offered for these gifts are ours as well. Let us examine these aspects of the holy meal.

Memory and Hope

The sacrament of a historical religion will be rooted in earthy happenings. Our supper points back through the upper room to the crucifixion. It is a "*memorial* of the blessed sacrifice of his Son." The participant remembers the formative event of the community's history and of personal pilgrimage. The meal fixes on the reality of suffering and death, its cost on Calvary and in Deity. But *this* historical religion by looking backward is thrust forward. The Lord's supper then and now is portent of the eschatological banquet with its celebration of the final coming together of all things. This is the sacrament of mourning and joy, memory and hope (1 Cor. 11:24-26).

Communion with Christ

This is the *Lord's* supper. He is the Host at this table. The Church that is his Body on earth takes its most decisive embodiment in this event of breaking bread and pouring wine. Here is not only memory and hope but also the real presence and thus *communion* with the risen and ascended Lord (1 Cor. 10:16). Here is where the Vision is seen with the eyes of faith. "He broke the bread and offered it to them. Then their eyes were opened, and they recognized him" (Luke 24:30-31). We come face to face at this table with the One who is to come, participating mystically in his glorified humanity. This is why the sacrament of the Lord's supper has always been considered by the Christian community "the innermost sanctuary of the whole Christian worship." The bond of the believer with the Lord is strengthened with greatest power, and the Vision is kept clearest by regular communion of guest with Host (1 Cor. 11:23-30).

Communion of Saints

The coming Kingdom is not an ethereal communion of "the alone with the Alone." It is a *life together* with the brothers and sisters in Christ (1 Cor. 10:17). As foretaste of that reconciliation among neighbors, the sacrament is communion now with all the visionary people, all those who see the Light and live in it. The children of Light are the saints of God, for saintliness is not spiritual virtuosity but living in relationship, turning to and walking in the Light that has shined toward us. The saints of God are the whole company of believers, present and distant, living and dead. At this table the communicant is joined to a worldwide fellowship and a time-long "cloud of witnesses" who have gone before us. Thus the communion of saints joins communion with Christ in a prolepsis of the eschatological life together. And as testimony to life together, the supper is claim as well as gift, calling us to challenge all the bondages and alienations inimical to the final vision of Shalom.

Unity with the Earth

The Vision includes the knitting together of all the ruptured relationships with nature as well as with self and society. Our neighbor the earth is represented in the sacrament by the wheat and the wine. The sanctification of the earth, the healing of the wounds it has sustained in this fallen world, is symbolized by the setting apart of these symbols in anticipation of that fulfillment. And our eating and drinking is an anticipatory union with that new heaven and new earth (Rev. 21:1-4).

Sacrifice

The New Jerusalem is yet to come, swords are yet to be beaten into plowshares, the new heaven and new earth are still to transfigure this groaning creation. Whatever sacramental participation we have Now in this Not Yet is in cruciform presence. Christ and all his benefits come to us through broken body and shed blood. It is as *sacrifice* that the future comes into our midst in the sacrament. The One who offers himself to us here is the crucified Lord. And all the healed relationships share in this ambiguity, a communion with brother and sister and union with the earth that is still under the sign of the cross, living toward the crown (Mark 14:24).

In this sacramental union we are joined to the One whose single perfect sacrifice is here re-presented to the eye of faith (Heb. 10:19-25). And we see the sacrifice for what it is, the bleeding body of Christ and the broken heart of God taking the consequences of our sin and communicating to us the forgiveness of sin in the bread and wine.

Thanksgiving

The sacrifice we make is of our praise and thanksgiving. We offer on the altar our gratitude for Christ and all his benefits, remembering the past deeds of God, anticipating those to come, and rejoicing in the Presence. This meal is the supper in which we join Christ in giving thanks (Luke 22:19). That the Vision given to us in this liturgy was, and is, and is to be makes this event, climactically, the *eucharist*.

186

Grace and Faith in the Supper

Grace in the sacramental meal is the self-offering of the Host and all his benefits. He is there by his promise, not our performance. That promise and presence is received by faith, and therein grace becomes "efficacious," and the promised renewing of relationship and refreshing of visions are fulfilled. As with baptism so with supper, this faith is itself a gift of grace. In prospect we act as if it were up to us; in retrospect we know it is of the Spirit. In this prospective context we speak of it as the fit preparation for the receiving of the sacrament. The gracious personal relationships of the supper require of the guests a readiness. Whether it is there or not will determine, not the Presence, but how that Presence will make itself felt, "unto salvation" or "unto damnation" (1 Cor. 11:29).

Preparation means penitence, the antechamber of faith. The cleansing of the heart is given form in the confession of sin before the rite. Preparation means belief in the promise of Presence and trust in the suffering Love there exposed, an inner act given outer expression in the confession of faith in the liturgy. Where there is authentic penitence and faith, the meal is one in which the Host's welcome is honored by the guest and the Host's blessing is on its partaker. A faithful response also is one that is claimed by the Shalom there shared; the authentic vision issues in mission. In the encounter with Christ comes a commission to serve in kind. A sign of the joining of grace to faith at the supper is the empowerment of the guest to keep company with the Christ of the table as he makes his way from room to road to be present there, incognito, as the crucified Lord in the sufferings of the world.

The six aspects of the eucharist noted here are variations on, and exposition of, the three refrains that appear in ecumenical conversation. As set forth in the landmark document of the Faith and Order Commission of the World Council of Churches, *Baptism, Eucharist and Ministry,* the holy supper is thanksgiving to the Father, communion with Christ, and empowerment by the Holy Spirit.

6. Salvation

The Spirit descends from the ascended Lord to form the Church and launch it on its mission. This continuing Work of Christ by the power of the Spirit brings *salvation*. "And I, when I am lifted up from the earth, will draw all people to myself" (John 12:32 NRSV). The word "save" is taken from a common usage that often means the accumulation or preservation of things, from money in the bank to time on a clock. In Scripture and the tradition of the Church something else is meant. There to be saved means to be rescued or delivered from a foe. It also signifies healing or making whole. Thus we are saved *from* something and saved *for* something. From what and for what?

In our discussion of the atonement, we have already met the enemies and the friends in this encounter. The Work of Christ is the beginning of the doctrine of salvation. Sometimes the atonement is treated as the *objective* aspect of "soteriology," which is complemented by the *subjective* side that deals with how salvation reaches us in grace and is personally appropriated by us in faith. Here we organize the chapters in the Christian narrative in a slightly different way in order to stress the unity of the Incarnation and the atonement in their own right and also to see those aspects of "Salvation Today" (the theme of a World Council of Churches inquiry) sometimes hidden from view in the notion of "subjective soteriology."

The distinction in salvation between God's action and its consequences is better expressed by the use of categories appropriate to the narrative character of Christian faith: the time segments of past, present, and future. As H. Richard Niebuhr is said to have replied to a zealous street evangelist who

188

asked him if he was saved: "I *was* saved by what Christ did; I *am being* saved right now; I *shall be* saved when the Kingdom comes." Salvation is a process launched in the saving events that take place in Jesus Christ. It continues into the present as the Spirit moves to deliver and make whole. It reaches a climax when the enemies of God ultimately surrender and the friends of God are finally brought together. We shall focus on the *present* dimension in this chapter. The historical roots of salvation have been examined in our discussion of the Work of Christ. And we reserve the exploration of the end point of the processes of salvation for the last chapter of the Christian saga, "Consummation." (It is possible also to interpret the chapters from Christ through Church and Salvation to Consummation as all parts of eschatology, the doctrine of the End, insofar as the future breaks into history in Christ and we live now in the tension between Already and Not Yet.) Here we address ourselves to the meaning of salvation in the "time between the Times."

The enemies of God are sin, evil, and death. The Work of Jesus Christ, the finished work accomplished once and for all in the life, teachings, death, and resurrection of Jesus Christ, is deliverance from these foes. Herein is the meaning of *salvation from*. They can no more imperil the Purposes of God; deliverance has *already* taken place. We are saved from their assaults — liberated!

The salvation accomplished for us in Jesus Christ is *reconciliation* as well as *liberation*. It brings together God, humanity, and nature. No more barriers exist to their friendship. Both God's favor and power have been turned toward us, and the breach has been healed. Herein is the meaning of *salvation for*. The Light of God has shined on the world, and that world shall be drawn into its intended unity.

Salvation Now

The tendency toward reductionism we have met in previous chapters appears here also. How passionate is the proselyting and how ready are the partisans to consign their opponents to damnation! Those who believe that the essence of salvation is deliverance from the judgment of God by the blood of Christ will hear of no other point of view. Those for whom salvation means liberation from political and economic oppression will call all else flight from reality and the opiate of the people. But the Story is more encompassing than either.

Salvation now, however conceived, comes to us by *grace* (Acts 20:24; Rom. 4:16; 1 Cor. 15:10). Grace is the ancient Christian term for the initiative taken by God, the going-before-us of Deity, the divine prevenience, priority. Grace is a gift of God, given not earned; we are *saved by grace* (Eph. 2:5). God reaches toward us first. Grace in the larger setting of salvation *already, now,* and *not yet,* is the flow of the healing waters from their source in the saving work of Christ toward the parched lands of the present and future. Grace extends to us through the deeds of God. Grace is the reach of Jesus Christ toward the present and future. And because this reach is to the present and the future, it is the work of the Holy Spirit. Grace is another word for the activity of the Spirit. Salvation now is the gracious work by the Holy Spirit of bringing Christ and all his benefits to us in this time and place.

Salvation from Sin

On Calvary God took the punishment for our sin. The divine Love absorbed the divine Wrath on the cross. Out of this suffering is born the mercy that covers our guilt. So Jesus Christ saved the world, liberating us from the bondage of sin.

But this freedom in Christ now available to us must be *received* by us. It is by God's personal grace that we are reached by the action that took place on Golgotha, the divine favor that accepts the unacceptable and loves the unlovely. The offer of forgiveness of *our* sin is communicated through the proclamation of the Good News. This Word of liberation from sin and reconciliation with God comes to us in the Bible and is set forth by the Church faithful to this Gospel. The image of speaking and hearing has been part and parcel of our understanding of this aspect of salvation, as grace is understood as a gracious personal Word.

Grace is also understandable in visual terms. Grace is the cross of the dying Savior, the open arms of suffering, Love receiving the sinner. Grace is the overflowing compassion of the parent welcoming the prodigal. Just as grace as Word is communicated to us in preaching, grace as Action is displayed to us in an "outward and visible sign," the sacrament of baptism. Envisioning takes form in visibilities, the open arms of the Church drawing us into life with God. The sacramental entry of the newborn into the Christian community is an expression of unconditional grace as a divine favor that is in no way contingent on our demonstrated

190

merits. So also the gifts of the Body of Christ, diakonia and koinonia as well as leitourgia, are gracious gestures of the beckoning God.

The open arms and the word of welcome invite response. Salvation now happens in our life when the embrace of God is received in trust. We enter those arms in the act of *faith*. Faith is our response to God's initiative. It is made possible by the same grace that reaches toward us, now empowering us in turn to reach out to God. *We are saved by grace through faith* (Eph. 2:8).

To be saved from sin, right now, is to receive in faith, by the power of the Holy Spirit, the offer made by God on Calvary. It is to be made "right with God" after having been "in the wrong." Another way of speaking about this new relationship to God is *justification*. To be justified is to receive the pardon offered by God on Golgotha. The declaration of pardon to humanity now becomes the declaration of pardon to this believer, justification by grace through faith.

While our language forces us to speak about faith as a *response* to grace, and our practice suggests that we appeal for a human decision of faith, Christian piety grasps the grace-faith equation in other terms. "In my labors I have outdone them all — not I, indeed, but the grace of God working with me" (1 Cor. 15:10). This "I . . . not I" paradox (Donald Baillie) expresses the sense that faith (and its issue, labors of love) is a choice to which we are called, one that is ours to make. Yet, we make it not on our own power, but only by grace. Put another way, in *prospect* we feel it is all up to us, but in *retrospect* we know that it was all of God. It is not "partly us, and partly God," not even "some us and mostly God" as the variety of synergisms and semi-Pelagianism in Christian history have suggested. Jonathan Edwards said it this way: "In efficacious grace we are not merely passive, nor yet does God do some and we do the rest. But God does all, and we do all. God produces all, and we act all. For that is what he produces, *viz.* our own acts. God is the only proper author and founder; we are the proper actors." Psychologically, prospectively, linguistically, we enter the faith movement as the actor in this drama; theologically, retrospectively, and spiritually, we know who its Author is. We are, therefore, justified by *grace,* which expresses itself in us as *faith.*

The Pilgrimage of Grace and Faith

A great gift that Martin Luther brings to the Christian community is his exploration of the depths of the soul's struggle with the meaning of justification. We are indebted as well to that tradition of piety which testifies to the experience of personal salvation by grace through faith for mapping this terrain of Christian spirituality. The perennial encounter with the Christ of faith may come to us in our way and time through the wrestle with social visions as well as individual commandments, but the issues of sin and grace remain the same.

Luther felt the claims of the Law and sought to pursue its perfections, a quest that led him into the rigorous self-abnegations of monasticism. The Christ who beckoned from on high seemed to be reachable only by the ascent of the ladder of moral and spiritual achievement. Yet the grasp of each rung brought with it the self-congratulatory whisper, "Good work, Brother Martin!" The act of righteousness became the occasion for self-righteousness. Sin in its ugliest form, spiritual pride, kept company with the climb toward virtue. The harder he tried, the more intense the temptation, and the more despairing the pilgrim. Luther's sensitive conscience saw the face of Christ astride the rainbow above as full of wrath and prepared for punishment. In this impossible struggle to attain the righteousness demanded of us, how can we find a gracious God?

In the search of the Scriptures carried on in the midst of this pilgrimage he found his answer. Righteouness — being right with God — is not a prize won by the moral and spiritual athlete. He learned from Paul: "I am not ashamed of the gospel . . . because here is revealed God's way of righting wrong, a way that starts from faith and ends in faith; as Scripture says, 'he shall gain life who is justified through faith'" (Rom .1:16-17). Righteousness cannot be earned by good works since it is freely granted by God in Christ, and receivable by us in trust. We are "justified by Christ's sacrificial death" (Rom. 5:9), and we appropriate this gracious act through faith. Hence, the fighting words of the Reformation, *justification by faith*.

In this pilgrimage, the Law plays an ambiguous role. On the one hand, it is "in itself holy, the commandment is holy and just and good" (Rom. 7:12), a statement of the divine intention for the race, of love to God and neighbor. And Luther read the decalogue in the light of Christ's counsels of perfection with monastic rigor. But the Law becomes something more than a sharp and clear imperative when it strikes home to us as fallen creatures: "When the commandment came, sin sprang to life . . . sin found an opportunity in the commandment, seduced me, and through the commandment killed me" (Rom. 7:9-11). The perversity in the human heart uses the mandates of good for its own ends. Not only does it prompt us to want to do what we are told not to do, but our obedience to it stirs up the vainglorious pretension that exudes "Thank God I am not as others!" (Luke 18:11). Yet, in this struggle, the Spirit turns our abuse of the Law into a sound "schoolteacher" use, the apprehension of our plight, the realization of our lethal inclinations: "What I do is not what I want to do, but what I detest. . . . For I know that nothing good lodges in me — in my unspiritual nature I mean — for though the will to do good is there, the deed is not. The good which I want to do, I fail to do; but what I do is the wrong which is against my will. . . . Miserable creature that I am, who is there to rescue me?" (Rom. 7:16, 17-19, 24). Our sojourn with the Law brings us to despair about ourselves. But by grace this despair grows into repentance, a wrenching loose by the power of the Spirit from the bondage to the self, and finding a new freedom in faith. Repentance is turning *(metanoia)* from the powers of night and toward the Light.

The response of faith to God's gracious pardon is both *assensus* and *fiducia*, both *assent* and *trust*. It is assent, an affirmation, a belief, a Yes! to the telling of the Christian Story about the suffering Love on Calvary that takes away the sins of the world. It is a commitment of the mind to the Tale that is told about the journey of God into the world to obliterate our guilt by an act of holy Love.

But this belief is not only intellectual. It is a profound inner event, an act of "soul," in which the self hurls itself on the mercy of God. Thus faith is *trust* as well as belief, one that engages the deepest level of emotion and the total being of the believer. Trust does not exclude the mind's assent. The love of God that is the act of faith is one of the whole self done with "all your heart, with all your soul, with all your mind" (Matt. 22:37).

Grace and Faith in Present Contexts

The pilgrimage of faith continues. The struggle with the Law, the reach of grace, and the truth of justification are enacted on ever-changing terrain. The dreams of perfection that drew Luther into the monastery may be found also in our time as visions of liberation and reconciliation, personal, social, and cosmic. An era of hope believes it can bring the Kingdom of God into its history, and its visionaries pursue this righteousness in a variety of ways. By political, social, and economic transformation or personal self-renewal and New Age pieties, freedom and peace can be won. The quest for righteousness continues in these efforts in secular and spiritual salvation. By whatever route, salvation is sought by goodwill and good works.

For the serious pilgrim who heeds these imperatives, there comes a moment of truth, Luther-like. Our best efforts collide with a recalcitrant world — both without and within. Honest self-examination alerts us not only to the shortfall, but also to the pretension and self-righteous fury that cloak our own self-serving interests. This moment of perception of the ambiguities of self and society can lead to despair and retreat, the occupational hazard of visionaries whether they pursue their dreams in a monastery or in a movement. This torpor that counsels retreat from the vision, or the vanity that hides its own vulnerability is on a continuum with the sins of concupiscence and pride spoken of in the classic tradition. But the slide into lethargy or the imperial claims of self-sufficiency are themselves rooted in the deeper fact of our fallen nature, the idolatry of the self, the substitution of one's own visions for the divine Vision.

Freedom from our apathies and arrogance comes when the pilgrim learns of the broken heart of God that takes the other side of the cross, the accepting Love that lies behind the demanding Law. The dreamer can face the realities of sin and evil. In this encounter the imperiled visions are themselves renewed, regrounded in both a realism about self and society and a hope in the God who empowers Shalom. The Word of pardon and peace belongs as much to those in quest today as to Luther and to Paul.

Pardon and Power

Personal salvation is *power over* as well as *pardon of* sin, *Christus in nobis* as well as *Christus pro nobis*. The Reformation's emphasis on the depth and stubbornness of our sin makes it rightly suspicious of any claims of virtue, leading as they do to self-congratulation and "works-righteousness." This sobriety in its extreme form, however, may fall prey to an abstract and excessively juridical understanding of grace. Grace is *sanctification* as well as *justification,* the making of persons whole (holy) as well as declaring them forgiven. Grace is power as well as pardon. Salvation is liberation from the act of sinning as well as from the guilt of the sinner. Where the Spirit has brought the believer into a new relationship with God, the same Spirit confirms this bond with grace on grace. "The harvest of the Spirit is love, joy, peace, patience, kindness, goodness, fidelity, gentleness, and self-control" (Gal. 5:22). The greatest fruit of the Spirit is love. The sanctification intertwined with justification is growth in the life of love and its issue, good works.

Faith is a seed planted and nourished by the Spirit that springs up in the fruit of love. By these fruits the reality of faith is demonstrated. Or in our visual language, salvation is not only seeing the Light but seeing *by* the Light. It is seeing in that Light the wretched of the earth. It is the vision of the neighbor in need as well as the vision of God. The works of love are directed toward our wounded neighbor who cries out for help and also our neighbor the earth, scarred and ravaged. And the works of love that flow from faith have at their core the love of God as well as the love of neighbor. This is the life of piety directed toward Deity, in and through the life of service toward the neighbor in need.

We would have learned poorly from the great insight of the Reformation if we did not add to this hope for progress in good works the realism that sin always clings to the healthiest of spiritual and moral growth, stunting it and pulling it back on itself. Indeed, advances in sanctification are themselves occasions of temptation, as "the saints" regularly testify and the self-satisfied "righteous" regularly demonstrate. The grace that must finally save us is the mercy that reaches from the other side of a gap left unbridged by the longest stretch of our good works.

By *faith* we receive the saving grace of God that delivers us from guilt and sin. In *love* we participate in the victorious struggle of God against the principalities and powers of evil. To this aspect of the saving work of Christ we next turn.

Salvation from Evil

Christ prays, "Deliver us from evil." That prayer is answered. Through him God has delivered us: as sin meets its match in Christ, so do the demonic principalities and powers. The suffering Love that covered guilt also cowered the armies of darkness. Wielding the sword of the cross, Christ invaded the realm of the rebel authorities and angels. These powers, which we have characterized en masse as Evil, range from the intimate enemies that afflict body, mind, and spirit, through the historical forces of political, economic, and social tyranny and vast natural perils of disease, pollution, earthquake, fire, and flood to the more mysterious minions of a fallen supernature. The liberation won in the life, death, and resurrection of Christ ended our bondage to these powers. But liberation is a process begun then, continuing now, and completed only in God's final Future.

Wherever the world is freed from foes that separate humans from humans, nature from itself, humanity from nature, and all or any from God, there our Deliverer is present and active. Wherever the barriers of evil are removed and the life together of Shalom breaks through, there the hidden Christ present by the power of the Holy Spirit brings the mighty from their seats and defeats the demonic. The Son of God, exalted to the right hand of the Father, rules over all powers that seek to challenge the divine regency.

Where Christ is liberating now is where Christ was liberating in the days of his flesh. And his work is done with the same weapon of suffering Love with which he vanquished the enemies that beset his world.

In his Galilean ministry Christ exorcised the demonic powers that enslaved persons, and healed the sick. Wherever and however bodies and minds are mended today, by the methodical sciences or imaginative arts of healing, often by the best of modern medicine but also mysteriously, there is the same Christ touching the infirm. Here is the light of Shalom penetrating the darkness, burning away by the hot fires of its love the enemy powers.

As liberation is freedom from the ills of the flesh, it is also freedom from the cares and oppressions of the world. The New Testament word to us is that Christ our contemporary is to be found, incognito, wherever the hungry are being fed, the prisoner attended, and the naked clothed (Matt. 25:34-46). This ministry is no genteel benevolence but is fraught with the same kind of conflict and struggle that Christ faced. This is made clear in Christ's declaration of war against the powers and principalities at the inception of his ministry. "The spirit of the Lord is on me because he has anointed me; he has sent me to announce good news to the poor, to proclaim release for prisoners and recovery of sight for the blind; to let the broken victims go free, to proclaim the year of the Lord's favour" (Luke 4:18-19). In this battle he engaged structures of power, a political-economic-military-ecclesiastical complex that saw his claims of lordship as a threat to its own tyrannies and that finally brought him to court and to death. Yet not without important skirmishes that give us a clue to his present work: the driving of the money changers out of the temple, forewarning us of the corruptions of economic power, and, through the confrontation with Caesar, putting us on notice to the onslaught of political power. Salvation now is the presence of Christ the Liberator, wherever the shackles of human bondage are being torn off and the oppressed set free. In our time we discern his footprint in the struggles of the developing nation to be liberated from colonial domination, the ravages of hunger, and its own internal political tyrannies. And we see it wherever there is the struggle of the ethnic, racial, and religious minority, the unfree majority, the unrepresented young, the ignored elders, exploited women, the trampled class and caste. Christ is alive and at work wherever "the least of these" raises a cry of anguish and hope.

"Where the Spirit of the Lord is, there is liberty!" (2 Cor. 3:17). Liberation in the Christian vision is all-encompassing. It can settle for no partial perceptions of the disenfranchised, enlarging our horizon to see the present work of Christ in the empowerment of the old as well as the young, the oppressed sex and race as well as class, the middling citizen as well as the minority group, the disabled as well as the dispossessed.

Christ is present not only in victories but also defeats, in times of agony as well as hope. He is Sufferer as well as Liberator, victim as well as victor, experiencing the anguish of the oppressed, the cold, the hungry, and the homeless. He is the God-Man of sorrows acquainted with our grief (Isa. 53:3). And as one who knew the abandonment of the Father on the cross, the Son participates in the sense of God-forsakenness that attends so much human misery. The cost of liberation is the pain of co-suffering with those in chains.

Our consciousness of the range of evil has been raised in this time of ecological sensibility. Liberation is freedom from the poisons and imbalances of earth, air, and water caused by the arrogance and shortsightedness of humanity, and also the hostilities to Shalom that are endemic to a nature red as it is in tooth and claw, sundered as it is by earthquake, fire, disease, and decay. The eyes of faith also see in this realm of nature evidence of a cosmic Lord. The New Testament bears witness to One who stills the storm and marks the sparrow's fall. The story of Christ walking on water is the testimony of a faith that nature, too, comes under the lordship of Jesus Christ.

As grace brings mercy to the sinner now, so the same grace of God delivers from evil now. We are saved by grace from sin and saved by grace from evil. And as we are called to participate now in the salvation from sin offered to us, so we are also beckoned to enter into these healing streams. The entrance to one is by faith, to the other by love.

The Saving Presence of Christ

As in the tale (Matt. 25) of the sheep and the goats, keeping company with Christ in the world means participating in the sufferings of and struggles for the hungry and the hurt. We are companions of the hidden Christ as we keep step with him in his ministry to the tribulations of this world. The Samaritan who reaches to bind up wounds is in fellowship with Jesus Christ.

The relation of faith to love and thus to the revealed and hidden Christ is suggested by the Emmaus Road story (Luke 24:13-35). In that episode the disciples experience two different relationships with the risen Christ. On the road they travel with a stranger who "caused their hearts to feel on fire" (Luke 24:32). In the upper room at the end of the journey, the stranger identifies himself at the table: "He broke the bread and offered it to them. Then their eyes were opened and they recognized him" (Luke 24:30-31). Christ is present with us "on the road" and "in the room." We keep company with him in profile, as our comrade in acts of mercy and struggles against the powers of evil. Neighbor love puts us on the road alongside the incognito Christ who is present wherever the hungry are fed, justice is done, and peace is made. But we also meet him face to face in the intimate encounters, the disclosures of identity, personal piety, and Christian life together. At the holy table in sacrament, word, worship, and prayer, faith opens our eyes to recognize him and opens our ears to hear the Word in which he says who he is. In the life of the Church, Christ encounters us by grace through faith as an I meets a Thou. In the life of the world, Christ meets us by grace through love as an I travels with the He.

Those who serve the broken, the hungry, and the oppressed but who do not know him or confess his name nevertheless do keep company with Christ. They participate in *that aspect* of Christ's saving work, deliverance from the powers of bondage and estrangement. Those who do know him and confess his name yet fail to follow him from the room to the road in ministry to and with Christ among the neighbors in need are judged with the eschatological rigor of the Matthew passage. By the same token, those who do not personally know Christ as the Liberator from sin and guilt, the One who discloses himself in Word and Sacrament, have yet to participate in the fullness of his atoning Work. Herein lies the Church's evangelism mandate.

Authentic *faith* will know the Christ of the road as well as the Christ of the room; true faith is busy in neighbor love. A fulfilled *love* will learn to know and love God as well as neighbor; it will travel with Christ to the upper room.

As faith is impossible except by the gracious initiative of God, so love cannot be manufactured by human effort. A love that participates in the suffering and liberating activity of the worldly Christ is a gift of grace. Wherever salvation happens, it is not earned but granted. We are saved by grace.

The Works of Love

The graced love that puts us in touch with the hidden Christ expresses itself in different ways. It manifests itself in the works of *heaven, earth, and hell.*

Heaven

The works of heaven are echoes of the self-abnegation of Christ. They take the form of cheek-turning, coat-sharing, second-mile love that *will be* in heaven, that *was* in Christ, and that *is* in the heart of God. Here is eschatological love, the perfection for which we are ultimately intended, an agape of selfless behavior that matches Christ's own Agape.

In the perfection of the Realm in which God is all in all and there is no sin or evil, the reach of this love is reciprocated in kind: Love evokes love. But on earth in this time before the Kingdom's coming, sin and evil take their toll. In such an unfulfilled world the powers of darkness trample selfless behavior; perfect love ends on a cross. Samaritan cheek-turning to the bandits on the Jericho road during an assault will result in two victims instead of one. The failure to recognize this, rooted as it is in a too sanguine view of human nature and history, results in an ethical *perfectionism* unable to set bounds to the rampages of sin and evil. The perfect ethics of heaven cannot be exported in packaged fashion to earth.

But radical selflessness in behavior does have relevance to day-to-day decision making. The perfect Law of love embodied in Jesus Christ is the lure and judge of all lesser conduct. It is a Vision that attracts us toward the conformation of our life to the divine Agape. It keeps us off balance, goading us to higher approximations of selfless conduct in both personal and social relationships. And it judges us for our shortcomings. Thus the Law of love exposes us as the sinners we are.

The evidences on earth of selfless conduct serve to sharpen our perception of the heavenly goal. Those who pursue the perfection of the Sermon on the Mount are witnesses to the final Vision and a conscience to the larger society. And in special historical moments, cheek-turning purity translated into nonviolent strategies for social change, as in the movements of Gandhi and King, may have intense historical significance. But these times pass, and even their moment of ripeness is not unfree of practice that sits uneasily with the theory (as when one marches in non-violent protest protected by the guns of the National Guard). In the matter of day-to-day decision making in which all available choices lead to some harm to someone, we take Heaven as our reference point, as guide and judge, but must make our way along the rutted and poorly marked trails of the earth.

Earth

The work of love on earth is to translate moral vision into the realities of conflicting claim and counterclaim, of the world's intractable self-regarding tendencies. Love in this land means setting bounds to the destructive possibilities and expansionist inclinations of human nature. It means pro-tecting the weak from assaults of the strong. And it means aspiring toward whatever measure of mutuality can be achieved in this world of competing claims. These forms have shaped earthly love: moral law, code, and covenant. *Moral law:* Human societies, for all their differences, share common perceptions of fundamental right and wrong given in the covenant with Noah; their survival depends on the pursuit of values that set limits to the lethal tendencies of the race. Among these universal imperatives are justice, freedom, order, and mutuality. Moral law in the hands of Christian love reads justice as equality of option to fill every need, freedom as liberation from all tyranny, order as the civilizing boundaries that make social existence tolerable, and mutuality as the community necessary for a human life together. *Code:* The more general moral laws are particularized in the Exodus code of the biblical communities, the decalogue. Like moral law, these imperatives are mandates of the earth that presuppose the fractious material of which we are made. Hence their construction as "Thou shalt nots." In its three-thousand-year laboratory the people of two covenants have learned that such acts as murder, stealing, adultery, and lying rend the fabric of human life. *Covenant:* The human community and the biblical communities have also learned that there are social structures integral to survival and humanization, as, for example, the state and the family. Commitment to the state by Christian love is an acknowledgment of the need, on the one hand, to set limits to the self-interest of humans living together, and on the other, to make possible human growth. Its vision of Shalom will predispose it to the kind of state in which freedom and justice for all, and a community supportive of the needs of each, is the rule. Commitment to the family by Christian love will mean a conjugal union with children as the way sexuality finds expression and the next generation is born and nurtured.

Out of the general laws, codes, and covenants of earthly love come a wealth of derivative guidelines with greater specificity. Thus from the universal axioms of moral law grow "middle axioms" that take on special relevance in a particular time or place. "Justice" becomes justice for black citizens in housing, education, and voting; "freedom" becomes freedom for the undeveloped country under colonial domination; "order" becomes order for an urban community paralyzed by crime. And beyond these is the hammering out of perspectives on new moral issues prompted by technological innovation or other developments for which there is no obvious lore either in the human community or in the biblical communities: medical issues such as abortion and euthanasia and biomedical issues such as the creation, control, and extension of human life.

What is common to all the wisdom that grows out of the experience of earthly love is its communal matrix. Whether it is learning from the experience of the human race as in universal moral law, or fresh formulations within the biblical peoples past and present, "the community" is at work in honing the guidelines for conduct on the earth. As such this life together reflects both the communal vision of Shalom and the realism that knows that in a fallen world the sin in the self has to be subjected to public tests and corporate scrutiny.

Reductionism rears its head on earth as well as in Heaven. In earthly love the temptation is *legalism*. The legalists give unthinking loyalty to the laws of earth. As absolutists they remain unchallenged by the higher possibilities of heavenly love, on the one hand, and on the other, they do not allow for the "exception to the rule" made necessary by the life of love in hell. To this latter perilous terrain we now turn.

Hell

Hell is that circumstance in which both the horns and all the cloven feet of the devil appear (Reinhold Niebuhr). Hell is confrontation with the full malignancy of the powers of sin, evil, and death. Satan and his hordes do not play by the rules of the game. Therefore, in hell one cannot look up in a book of the codes, laws, and covenants what must be done. Here we face the exception to the rule.

Yet the Light penetrates even the shadows of hell. The stars of Agape and Shalom shine in this night. Our attitude and behavior take their bearings from these orientation points. Decision making in hell is the union of faith with lethal fact, love with ambiguous circumstance. Agape-Shalom, therefore, lives contextually in the land of the demons. It makes judgments case by case as it is given Light by the Spirit of love. Let us examine some cases.

In heaven selflessness evokes selflessness and its fruit is mutuality. In hell selflessness is exploited as weakness and the innocent are slaughtered. In this attack on the Vision of freedom and peace, and the violation of the earth's laws of humanity and justice — let us say, in a case of political tyranny — Agape must be translated into behavior that "resists the powers of evil." The right of revolution, in 1776 in the American colonies or in 1976 in African colonies, becomes an option in Christian ethics. Just revolution has its counterpart in macrocosm in "just war" and in microcosm in "just abortion," however severely restricted the former in our awesome nuclear context, or carefully interpreted the latter amid the rampant oversimplifications. In other no less oppressive circumstances, when the political covenant of law and order (Rom. 13) descends to hell (Rev. 13), the ethical imperative may be the nonviolent civil disobedience of the first-century martyr or the twentieth-century resister. And in yet another example of the limits of earthly covenants, when the powers of evil have so destroyed partners and offspring in the bonds of marriage and family, it is a work of love to sever the ties.

"Situation ethics" thrives on the ambiguities of context and the limitations of codes, reminding us of the hell in which Love is our only Light. Yet as with each insight in ethics, the temptation to absoluteness is overpowering, ironically even in a perspective that disavows it. Christian ethics cannot be reduced to *situationism* any more than it can be to legalism or perfectionism. Contextual ethics must itself be taken contextually, and that context is hell. It is not a norm for day-to-day decision making, for in the continuities of earth the corporate lore of the biblical peoples and the human community serves as a critical resource.

One other gift of Heaven, in addition to the dispositional Light of Agape, that makes its presence felt in hell is the communal theme of Shalom. The self-serving agendas that are always operating, and especially so when we bracket the codes and covenants of earth and choose to live by Love alone, come under public scrutiny when the brothers and sisters are partners in painful exceptional choices. Thus the choices of violence or nonviolence in challenging the oppression of the state should be done in mutual conversation and consolation with the brothers and sisters in faith. That presence of "the other" is, of course, at work as well in the counselor or pastor at hand as third party in the hell of marital breach. Decision making in extremity calls in the community.

The three motifs in Christian ethics we have discussed can be visualized in this way.

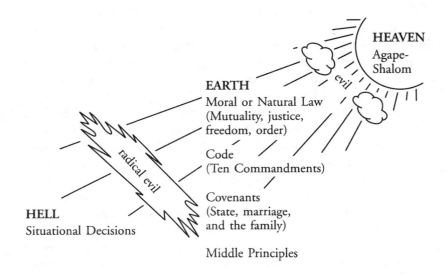

HEAVEN
Agape-
Shalom

EARTH
Moral or Natural Law
(Mutuality, justice,
freedom, order)

Code
(Ten Commandments)

Covenants
(State, marriage,
and the family)

Middle Principles

HELL
Situational Decisions

radical evil

evil

Salvation from Death

And what of the "last enemy," death, and salvation *now* from death? On the face of it, our enemy death is mortality. The present preoccupation with death and dying surely understands it that way.

In the broad Christian tradition death is mortality, the fact that our days come to an end as a tale that is told. But it is also more than that. The death that is the "wages of sin" is, in its deepest sense, *separation from God.* And in its broadest purview it is estrangement of all the intended partners to Shalom: God, humanity, and nature. Death is alienation. It is the enmity of the world toward God and itself. And, in turn, it is God's sorrowful judgment on this rebel creation.

As the fracturing of all our intended relationships, death is the destruction of the divine Dream. When sin and evil swagger, and especially when they make their all-out attack on the Light that comes into the world, the shadows of death lurk about us. At the point in human history when the Light of God was extinguished on Golgotha, there was a death *in* God. The fading of the Vision of God portends the demise of the world, the abandoning of the Great Experiment in Shalom. The wages of sin and evil are death and damnation.

The flickering inner light, the image of God in us, sustained by Noah's covenant, is not so dim that it cannot at least disclose something of the shadows to be seen. Hence the fear of mortality. Indeed, mortality is a sign of the peril to the Purpose of God. Now in an era of lengthened time perception, the anxiety about the finitude of persons is extended to the finitude of history and ultimately the cosmos. Thus the futurist warns of ecological disaster or nuclear holocaust, and the scientist speculates about the heat death of the universe. Fear of death, and times preoccupied with mortality in any of its expressions, is loss of confidence in the future of God, expectation of the slaughter of Hope.

In the Christian Story the Good News of salvation from death is bodied forth in the resurrection of Jesus Christ. God *has* triumphed over the power of death! The Dream did not die on Calvary.

The resurrection of Christ is more than an announcement. It is an event of triumph itself. If sin and evil were whipped on Calvary, then the "last enemy, death" met its match on Easter morning. As death is nothing less than mortality, so the empty tomb declares that finitude is not the last word. The death of this body, and also of this history and this cosmos, is not the end toward which the world moves. Our history in time, as self or society or universe, does not conclude as a tale futilely told. The finish is not the finale.

As our earlier discussion indicated, the freedom conferred on us at Easter is far more than breaking the shackles of mortality. In its profoundest meaning it is liberation from the *consequences* of sin and evil: the alienation from God and the partners of God. Liberation from death *is* reconciliation. In the resurrection, the world is granted in an anticipatory way the unity with God, humanity, and nature that will be its final destiny. The risen Christ is the down payment on that time of ingathering, a preview of the "coming attraction." The Future of God is assured. And the way to that future is the suffering Love that triumphed over sin and evil, and now the last enemy, death.

What then of the process of liberation as it reaches us now, salvation *now* from death? What is achieved for us in the resurrection of Christ is communicated to us by grace, by the Holy Spirit that empowers the risen Christ to beat down death in our own time and place. The risen Christ is the enabler of new life in the world. He brings God, humanity, and nature together. Wherever the power of death and darkness is in retreat, there is life and Light, the risen Christ. Wherever reconciliation happens, there death is in flight. After resurrection all the manifestations of unity in the world are the work of a triumphant Providence. The reconciling action of the risen Christ means that death does not control the future of persons, history, or nature. Here in this phase of its pilgrimage toward fulfillment, time is open to fresh possibilities. As God's Dream has been reborn, so it is right that we, too, should dream. The empowered vision of God is given a new lease on Life by the resurrection; our hopes for this world have a foundation in the renewed nature of things.

Christian *hope* is legitimated by the resurrection then, and the life and work of the risen Christ now. As we are saved from sin by grace through faith and participate in the salvation from evil through love, so we share in the liberation from death by hope. Hope reports an open historical future, and eschatological hope an open final Future. Hope knows that mortality is not the last fact. But more, hope is our perception that alienation is not our destiny. Hope is seeing the coming together of all things. To hope is to catch sight of the fulfilled Vision and to track the rays of its Light from the future back into the present. By hope we participate not only in the suffering but also in the victories of God in the world.

While the eyes of hope perceive the Light to be, that same Vision sees what human sight also knows: the persistence of sin and evil, and the stubborn fact of physical death. Arrogance and apathy still work their ways in the self; history and nature are under constant attack from the demonic powers; mortality still is our portion, and estrangement is everywhere to be seen. The pall of death, in every sense, hangs over this fallen world. Hope is no illusion of instant sweetness and light. Hope is not utopian; we do not live at the Noontide when all the shadows pass, but in the half-light of the Already–Not Yet. Hope's symbol is a Dawnburst, not Sunburst, for dark shadows are still on the land. Hope is *sober* hope, not giddy fantasy. And it knows that its rising sun metaphor is at best ambiguous, for there is no gradual dispersal of the clouds as Sol rises to meridian. Each historical advance is harassed by the continuing gloom, the resistance of the powers of night that continue to the End of time. "If it is for this life only that Christ has given us hope, we of all men are most to be pitied" (1 Cor. 15:19). Hopes for *this time* between the Times are modest, the expectation of rays that pierce the darkness, signs and portents of that which is yet to come. The final conquest of death awaits the full Day.

But the "sting of death" is taken away by hope. We know that mortality can do us no final harm. The estrangements of this world cannot erase the Unity that awaits us. And the removal of the sting of death also means the freedom to quest for anticipatory victories that an open future promises in *this world*. To face our own approaching death and the world's demise without the anxiety of defeat is already in a profound sense to conquer death. And to be able to look for and rejoice in the victories of Shalom in our history is a like triumph.

Hope has a way, itself, of making a contribution to these victories. While despair *paralyzes,* hope *mobilizes.* Because the future is open the hoper strides toward it. Because the risen Christ is Lord, those forces that appear to the eye of ordinary sight to be impenetrable are "dust and ashes" to the eye of faith.

The end point of liberation from death and therefore the reconciliation of all things is the final chapter toward which the Christian Story moves, "Consummation," the everlasting Life in which the shadows of death finally disappear. The fulfillment of the promises of God mean nothing less than that all the enemies are brought under the feet of Christ.

The Good News of salvation Now is a *word of faith* about the mercy offered to us on Calvary that covers our sin and guilt, a *work of love* that keeps company with the Presence in the world, and a *vision of hope* of a future opened by the risen Christ.

Salvation by Christ Alone?

Some awesome claims have been made in the last three chapters of *The Christian Story.* They center on the unique Person and Work of Christ, their consequences and implications. The very structure of the narrative, as well as explicit doctrines rising from it, makes three assertions of particularity. In Jesus Christ a *deed* is done that reverses the direction of the history of God with the world: sin, evil, and death have been overcome in the being and doing of Jesus Christ, and the reconciliation of God, humanity, and nature has thus been effected. In this same series of saving events a *disclosure* has been made of the One who does this deed, and the meaning of the deed in relation to the trajectory of the biblical narrative has been given. Thus a singular revelation is made. Those who respond to the deed and disclosure as it comes to them in the stream of proclamation, celebration, fellowship, and service that flows from the coming of Jesus Christ are offered *deliverance* from the bondage of sin and guilt. Here is redemption by grace through faith. In the teaching, liturgies, prayers, hymns, and confessions of classical Christian faith, these three unquestioned assumptions constitute the "scandal of particularity." The definitive claims about *reconciliation, revelation,* and *redemption* are simply and memorably expressed by the Johannine Christ: "I am the way, the truth, and the life; no one comes to the Father except by me" (John 14:6).

The omnipresent experience of religious pluralism in a world knit together by modern technology has raised serious questions about these historic declarations of Christian particularity. When the window opened onto the world by television and the increasing contact among once isolated cultures show us "the long search" of the world's religions for salvation, the impressive spiritualities and moral insight of other religions come into view. How can we any longer maintain that Christianity is unique and salvation is to be found only in a Galilean carpenter? The contemporary experience of religious pluralism, "plural shock" (kin to the other children of modernity, culture shock and future shock), has resulted for many in christological heart failure. It shows up in a variety of re-formulations of Christ's role in the burgeoning literature on the relation of Christianity to other religions. One such reconceptualization of the meaning of Jesus Christ holds that there is a common core of truth below the level of our particular religious histories and heroes, a universal en-counter with the holy, "unthematized" in its essence, and given diverse intellectual expression in the various religious traditions. Jesus Christ be-comes, in this view, one among many equally legitimate cultural mani-festations of a common depth dimension. Another view questions this commonality of religion, insisting instead on a diversity of experience and perception, yet urges that the best in each tradition be discovered and joined together in a global faith. Christianity makes a contribution to this synthesis, but requires the correction and completion that must come from other religions. Yet another view attempts to maintain a loyalty to the Christian religion, but acknowledges that salvation is to be found in all high religions and people of goodwill, except that Jesus represents the highest expression of the universal grace, a Mt. Everest in a chain of lower peaks of truth, different in degree but not different in kind. In all of these perspectives, the three claims to particularity integral to the Christian narrative disappear, and the Gospel erodes at its very center.

Others determined to maintain the nonnegotiables of unique recon-ciliation, revelation, and redemption have only disdain for the questions raised by modern pluralism. Thus an imperial view holds fast to the singular deed, disclosure, and deliverance in Jesus Christ, and is prepared to consign to eternal damnation all those who either do not hear the Word and make their decision for Christ or are foreordained to eternal damna-tion. To do otherwise in this view is to deny the Word of God. While rightfully defending the uniqueness of Christ, however, an imperial sin-gularity denies the universal dimension of the Gospel.

Unsatisfied with both those who compromise Christian claims to particularity and those who deny the new questions of universality raised by religious pluralism (really not so new, since the early Christians faced the same issues in a spiritually hungry Mediterranean world and in relation to a parent religion), others seek a way to affirm both particularity and universality. Influenced by Karl Rahner in the Roman Catholic tradition and Karl Barth in the Protestant tradition, those who hold these views have sought to maintain the singular claims of reconciliation and revela-tion, indeed in very different ways, given Barth's denial of revelation

208

beyond Jesus Christ and Rahner's acknowledgment of it in anticipatory ways. Through these perspectives they attempt to show how the unique reconciliation wrought and revelation given by God in Jesus Christ have universal consequences. For Rahner and those who follow him that means an "anonymous Christianity" in which a universal grace related to the Absolute Savior works salvation in all people of goodwill. For Barth there is a decisive saving work of God in Christ but one that has universal consequences, rendering all humans "virtual" brothers and sisters in Christ, although only those given the biblical revelation know of this work and are called ("vocation") to share the news. (Barth, finally, rejects "universalism" — universal selection — for only God can decide whether the "virtual" becomes the final.) Both of these conceptions and their many current variations represent a serious attempt to respond to the issues raised by modern pluralism, contrary to the rigidities of an imperialist Christianity, acknowledging either explicitly (Rahner) or implicitly (Barth) that a new historical perspective requires response to these critical questions and possibly the development of Christian doctrine. Further, we have spoken here of a universal grace of the incognito Christ that saves from evil those who respond to him in love, a refrain that is similar at one point to Rahner's discussion of universal grace. While these views are worthwhile attempts to struggle with these momentous issues, we find them finally unsatisfactory, however, for they qualify or eliminate the third nonnegotiable of particularity — personal redemption, life, salvation by grace through confession of faith in Jesus Christ. There is another way to maintain the classical scandal of particularity and at the same time be open to the "scandal of universality" implicit in the biblical testimony. Since it draws heavily on eschatological themes, we shall deal with this perspective in the following chapter.

7. Consummation

The Christian narrative moves to its climax, the account of the "last things." Eschatology, the doctrine of the consummation, deals with Christian teaching about the culminating chapter of the Story. For many people the turning of the final page of life has to do with our own personal end. What is the meaning of death? What happens to me when I die? Where now is that deceased loved one who was so much part of my life? Can we communicate with the dead? The issues of "death and dying" have come dramatically to public consciousness in recent years. This preoccupation with mortality has been further accented by the medical and biomedical issues surrounding our personal end, questions running from organ replacement and the establishment of the moment of expiration to the humane treatment of the terminally ill and comatose.

Often the subject of eschatology is treated in the foregoing context and therefore understood to mean the belief in "life after death." And the Easter Sunday sermon will confirm it with intimations of immortality. Eschatology becomes here, or in the funeral homily, the declaration of postmortem existence. In the wider religious and cultural discussion, belief in the future life may range from theories about the immortality of the soul to New Age assertions about reincarnation.

In contemporary theology some more attuned to the claims and burdens of history seek to relate eschatology to the present world — the time before, not after, death. New eschatologies stress the this-worldly aspects of the future. Theologies of liberation and political theologies interpret eschatology to mean the hopes we can have for a just and peaceful tomorrow.

210

Still another point of view of eschatology can be found in which the notes of finality and decision are considered to be stark confrontation with Christ in the present moment. Right now, as one is encountered by an ultimate choice, the end is present with us, one before which we stand accused and called to decision. Under the influence of the existentialist thought of Rudolf Bultmann and others seeking to demythologize the cosmologies and chronologies of the biblical eschaton, the presentizing of eschatology is declared to be compatible with the modern mind.

There are things to be learned from all of these reinterpretations of New Testament eschatology that have to do with personal death, historical hope, existential choice. Yet they all fall short of the main point of this final chapter of the Story. This End is characterized by both meanings of the word *end — telos* and *finis*. The narrative has a *purpose* and it has a *conclusion*. And there is a point of convergence of these two: a Finale toward which history moves and at which its purposes will be fulfilled. The Story moves from invitation through alienation and connection to intersection and convergence. There is no responsible reading of it without the "last things" beyond the *finis* of our personal existence and the *telos* within history or existential choice. The penultimate matters of our personal death, the futures within human history, and the choices we are called to make point beyond themselves to the final End, and are in turn illumined by this fulfillment of the Purpose of God. Last things thus merge into the "next-to-last things," the absolute future into our personal, historical, and cosmic futures.

Mystery and Modesty

What does the Christian message have to say about the End? First, we must be clear about what it does *not* say. In periods of uncertainty and peril, there is a strong temptation to claim to know far more about the times and seasons than befits the modesty of classical Christian Faith (2 Thess. 5:1-2). The history of the Church is replete with movements that responded to crisis times or circumstances with detailed forecasts of the how, when, where, and who of the end. Thus eschatology becomes *apocalypticism* with its blueprint, timetable, map, and cast of characters, all in a soon-arriving cataclysmic conclusion. Most often, the lush imagery of contemporary apocalyptic takes the form of a *premillennialist* scenario, especially in its "pretribulationist" version, in which events in the present move toward the "rapture" of believers, a tribulation of holocaust proportions, the return of Christ to establish a thousand-year Kingdom in this world, succeeded by a final revolt of the powers of evil, their overthrow, the coming of a new heaven and a new earth, and the going of the damned to the everlasting fires. *Postmillennialist* views read the same texts differently, forecasting the Kingdom within history before Christ's final return. And *amillennialist* conceptions, less sanguine about both the postmillennialist possibilities of history and the premillennialist claims to a God's-eye view of the consummation, construe the apocalyptic imagery symbolically and see sin and evil persisting to the End. Here we follow in the tradition of the latter while respecting the insights of the other views. "Travelogue eschatologies" (Hans Schwarz) do not represent the mainstream of Christian teaching about the future, for Jesus' own counsel has been decisive: "About that day and hour no one knows" (Mark 13:32). Responsible tellers of the Story observe this counsel and acknowledge that "We see through a glass darkly" (1 Cor. 13:12 KJV). The glass is not transparent, giving us a full and clear view, but translucent. We have enough light by which to see and to discern some of the shape of things to come.

While the Christian epic does not yield up encyclopedic knowledge about the *how, when, where,* and *who* of the consummation, it does give us bold affirmations about the *that* and *what* of the matter. In this respect the doctrine of the End is much like the doctrine of the Beginning. The factuality and form of creation and consummation are the things of interest to the Storyteller. *That* God shall fulfill the divine Intention, *that* history moves toward its Omega, is fundamental to the meaning of the Christian saga. *What* the dimensions of that fulfillment are is equally important. The latter is summarized in the classic creeds of the Church. The Christian community has focused on the central biblical refrains: *the resurrection of the dead, the return of Christ, the last judgment, everlasting life.* These compose the kernel of Christian teaching about the End. They are the "last things."

The kernel is surrounded by a husk. The color and sheen of this covering have a way of attracting the seeker, sometimes causing him or her to settle too quickly for the surface instead of probing to the center. Here we find a range of rich metaphors and images — the Anti-Christ, a thousand-year reign of peace, golden streets and pearly gates, numerology, and apocalyptic cosmology — in which the great affirmations are housed. Three things should be noted about them:

212

1. They are not dominant or ubiquitous New Testament motifs, but random assertions.
2. They rise out of particular historical circumstances (Nero, Rome, etc.), helping to shore up the faith of the early Christians faced with oppression and martyrdom.
3. Most of them fall short of being eschatological affirmations since they do not deal with the transfiguration *of* the world, but with events *in* the world. Christian eschatology is not secular forecasting but the futurology of the World to Come. While these exuberant scenarios provide material for the armchair speculations and sometimes frenzied imaginations so popular in periods of travail in human history, Christian thought about the End has in the main chosen to be reserved about the details, focusing rather on the centralities of resurrection, return, judgment, and eternal life.

Science and Faith

What is the relation of Christian eschatology to the projections of the scientific community? Does the former not intrude on the terrain of the latter by making statements about this time-space continuum? Should not the faith community confine itself to inner space or transtemporal realms so that faith and reason do not collide with one another? This policy of accommodation has been a favorite one since Immanuel Kant laid the groundwork for the distinction between fact and value, with reason taking responsibility for one and our spiritual and moral intuitions for the other.

Science and faith do have different foci and fields of inquiry. Yet theories emerging out of both the science community and the faith community may come into conflict. A case in point is the debate about creation. There is a legitimate division of labor here between science, which deals with the particulars of the origin of the world, and faith, which is concerned with its meanings. Yet what cannot be given up in this debate is the *source* of this creation and also the *fact* of its beginning, as noted in the first chapter. If it is a real saga with which we have to do, then the latter is as important as the former, something not always recognized in Christian apologetics. The reason it was not given its due is that the regnant theories of the origin and growth of the universe have posited a beginning.

213

Evolution is out of a point in time, so both evolutionary theory and the Christian Story point toward an inception.

The bearing of this nineteenth-century debate on eschatology comes in the affirmation of an end point as well as a beginning point. This is a necessary faith statement. What is not of the essence of faith is how the world reaches its termination. Indeed, if the scientific accounts and those of the Story do not agree, we must choose the best light we can get from scientific sources, as we have done with the question of the origins of the world. And that can include projections of a thermonuclear holocaust or environmental exhaustion as it pertains to this planet, or a theory of entropy about the running down of the universe itself. Eschatological faith speaks fundamentally about the nature and meaning of the end and is not tied to one or another scenario of natural or historical evolution or devolution. And it can live with the prognostications of the human community about the how and when of the end as well as of the beginning.

Themes Bashful and Bold

In the primitive Christian community the last things tended to arrange themselves in a certain sequence with an obvious logic: first the resurrection of the dead, then the return of Christ, then the combination of the two — a judgment by Christ of the resurrected dead — then everlasting life. Several things have happened to this early scheme as each subsequent generation sought to use it to shed light on its own future. A tendency developed to accent one or another of these motifs: *judgment* of evil by Christ in times when oppressive forces loom large; *resurrection* of the body in times of heady spiritualization of the faith that ignored things material and fleshly; *everlasting life* in times that call for words of hope. Also different aspects of one or another of these motifs were brought to the fore according to the needs of the hour or the inclinations of the interpreter. Thus everlasting life came to be interpreted as a vision of God granted to the redeemed, an image powerful where the quest for truth or mystical experience was to the foreground; again, a full-blooded restoration of the poor to their rights in times of social struggle and in the throes of the oppression; plentiful crops, singing mountains, a joyful creation replaced a world of disease and drought and a groaning creation; eternal rest in times of weariness of body and spirit.

214

While each of these exercised a certain power with those to whom it was addressed or among those for whom these metaphors had special meaning, the same images for other folk and other times proved to be meaningless, or even stumbling blocks to faith. Thus an affluent and activist culture finds it impossible to believe that the goal of history is "eternal rest," an image that becomes a favorite target for skeptics, who take pleasure in pointing out how boring such a heaven is. To realize that the appeal of this imagery is to oppressed people who are not so fortunate as to have middle-class creature comforts, nor the attendant energy or leisure, is to be less disdainful of these hopes of the hopeless. It is also true that other biblical images of the End suggest anything but bovine serenity. Last things include a lively city, a festive banquet, the growth of seeds and kingdoms. We need to honor all the motifs, without reducing eschatological faith to just those that reflect our limited experience.

The Resurrection of the Dead

The Christian Story cannot be what it is unless all that ever has been participates in the culmination. Every thread of history is gathered up and woven into the final tapestry. When the time of fulfillment comes, consummation reaches into every nook and cranny of the past. An awesome thought!

The *resurrection of the dead* means that God brings into existence again the least and the last. The dead are not lost but recovered and placed as actors in the final scene. All things are in the last things (1 Cor. 15; Acts 24:15; John 5:28-29).

Resurrection includes our bodies. This assertion needs to be underscored in those times and places in which more elusive spiritualized versions of the faith or popular religion have tended to denigrate the body both here and hereafter. The phrase *resurrection of the body* in the Apostles' Creed was connected with the repudiation of a world-denying and body-rejecting Gnosticism and Docetism. It recurs in periods that ignore the issues of justice for trampled victims whose bodies are racked by hunger and pain. The resurrection of the body "comforts the afflicted" as well as "afflicts the comfortable." Glittering generalities about the final state, or elusive talk about "the immortality of the soul" devoid of biblical earthliness, are no part of the realistic hope of the New Testament.

215

The resurrection of the dead has *already* begun. Jesus Christ is the first of this new race. What he was at Easter we, too, shall be. The resurrection appearances of Jesus are in both continuity and discontinuity with his pre-Easter being. While the New Testament accounts portray a Jesus visually the same as his Galilean self, the flesh so perceived is not of equivalent temporality and mortality. Hence Paul's paradoxical description of our own resurrection bodies: "What is sown in the earth as a perishable thing is raised imperishable. Sown in humiliation, it is raised in glory; sown in weakness, it is raised in power; sown as an animal body, it is raised as a spiritual body . . . flesh and blood can never possess the kingdom of God . . ." (1 Cor. 15:42-44, 50). The prolepsis of the universal resurrection in Jesus Christ points toward the imperishable but embodied selfhood that shall be ours as well.

The resurrection of the dead in this tale refers to unbeliever as well as believer, the damned as well as the saved (Rom. 14:10). Nothing and no one escapes the last things. The resurrection of the dead is both final resolution and final reckoning, good news and bad news. It not only consoles but also warns that there is no place to hide in either the convenient theories of disappearance into nonexistence ("annihilationism") or the pleasant illusions that twittering birds and laughing nymphs are all that await us as we go to an eternal Forest Lawn.

The Return of Christ and the Final Judgment

The Apostles' Creed asserts, "He will come again to judge the quick and the dead." Christ lived in a fallen realm as a suffering and crucified figure. As the world reemerges now in a new frame of reference, it must deal with the one who has preceded it to a new plane of history (1 Thess. 4:16). Now Christ at this culmination point is not victim but victor! The King who indeed reigns in heaven in the time between the Times now comes at the end of this age into a transfigured history and into his complete glory. The great Day ends the night. The shadows disappear, and even the dawn passes away as the Sun ascends to its place at the meridian.

When the Son of God shines in the new world, everything comes to light. All that ever was is exposed for what it is in the radiance of Shalom. Dark alleys are no longer hiding places. The world shall know who its friends have been all along — God, neighbor, and nature. We shall see them in the

Light. On the other hand, we shall see ourselves for what we really have been: "He will bring to light what darkness hides" (1 Cor. 4:5).

The coming of Christ is linked with judgment, for the flight of the world from its true goal must be reckoned with. Judgment is exposure to a searching Light. Such radiance burns as well as shines. Predictably, therefore, images of fire recur within the history of eschatological preaching and teaching.

As Jesus Christ is our Judge, we enter fully into the light of Shalom. All of us must stand that scrutiny, both believer and unbeliever. "For we must all have our lives laid open before the tribunal of Christ, where each must receive what is due to him for his conduct in the body, good or bad" (2 Cor. 5:10). What can this stern declaration mean, one that is a refrain in the New Testament? The biblical imagery gives us a clue. To be judged "in the light" is to see with total clarity what we have been. The first fact apparent is our slavery to the powers of sin, evil, and death and our alienation from neighbor, nature, and God. To see the ugly fact of our self-centeredness and its effects with blinding clarity is an excruciating pain. More so, indeed, for those who have made professions of loyalty to Shalom and have given lip service to liberation and reconciliation. What deepens the agony of this self-disclosure is the other fact that comes clear in this moment of judgment — that the light of judgment is the light of Love. The harshest judge of a conscience that knows what it must do or what it should have done is to know the hurt it has caused. To know that we have broken faith with the One who has brought us to be, and to know the suffering we have caused God, is horror indeed. The hot fires of last judgment are the "burning coals" of the divine Love (Rom. 12:20). The divine Light lets us see the injury we have done to God. On the other hand, the New Testament tells us that there will be joy in heaven for the deeds of Shalom that are disclosed by this same luminescence (Rev. 20:12). In those acts of "life" Christ will be receiving back the fruits of his own grace.

The wrath of God on judgment day falls on the agents of bondage and alienation. In the parable of the sheep and the goats Jesus reserves for them his direst warnings. Those who have not fed the hungry, clothed the naked, cared for the sick, the prisoner, the stranger, will have to answer to the Christ they spurned in the least of these brothers and sisters (Matt. 25:41-46). Thus the vindication of justice, the final accountability of the people and powers that trod on the poor, despoiled the needy, and dehumanized all those of low degree is an eschatological promise.

Good works are honored in the Eschaton, but final judgment will not be made in terms of the deeds done (John 3:16). Only by faith are we "saved from the wrath that is to come" (1 Thess. 1:10). That faith is trust in Jesus Christ. He is our Savior as well as our Judge. The Christ who comes to judge the quick and the dead is the Shalom that suffers for our sake, taking away the sins of the world. The divine Love is more ultimate than the divine Wrath. That is the ground for his unceasing quest for us and finally taking on himself the judgment that is ours on Calvary. Jesus Christ is by that reach of suffering Love the one who stands between us and the Wrath we so genuinely deserve.

How then do we stand before the judgment seat of Christ our advocate? We stand only as we are behind him, yes, *in* him. He is the advocate of the Father's Love before the Father's Wrath. We are saved from the wrath by that participation. The act of this affiliation is faith. Only as we have him as our shield can we stand in the latter day.

Faith, of course, is no faith unless it expresses itself in works. Faith is not just belief — even "the devils have faith like that" (James 2:19) — but belief busy in love. Without the love that expresses itself in works there is no faith. That is why in Matthew 25:31ff. the tests of authentic faith are the works of love. What counts on the last day is a faith demonstrating its reality in love — feeding the hungry, visiting the prisoner, seeking justice, making peace (1 John 3:15-18).

Judgment and the Knowledge of Christ

What of those who have not heard this Good News and therefore have not had the opportunity for Christian faith? The Gospel of John declares: "God so loved the world that he gave his only begotten Son so that whoever believes in him shall not perish but have everlasting life" (3:16). Are the nonknowers of Jesus Christ denied "life" and destined for everlasting death?

In our earlier soteriological inquiry we examined the two meanings of salvation in Scripture: salvation from sin and its consequences of judgment before God, and salvation from evil and its ravages within and without. The universal grace of God makes and keeps life in this world livable by bringing forth in responsive selves the fruit of love. Thus salvation by grace from the powers of evil and death is a gift given wherever there are signs of historical Shalom. But our responses to this omnipresent grace even when positive are so tainted by self-serving impulses that, before the purity of divine Love, we stand exposed for what we are. "No one is righteous, no, not one" (Rom. 3:10). No human love is so free from the bondage of the will that it can claim sinlessness before the One who is of purer eyes than to behold iniquity (Hab. 1:13 KJV). There is only one cure for this sickness unto death, "the medicine of immortality," the gift of *fullness* of life pointed to in the Johannine text. This is eternal life with the eternal God — salvation by grace through faith that comes from hearing and believing the proclaimed Good News.

Imperial views of soteriology and eschatology close the matter here with their logical conclusion: those who have not been reached by the Gospel in this world — or who have not been predestined to salvation — are presumed to receive eternal damnation. We shall return to a consideration of these perspectives later, questioning their premises.

Another point of view holds that those who have not heard the Gospel are judged by their response to the light of conscience. However, this idea is difficult to reconcile with the universality of the fall and the rejection of salvation by works. An heir of this latter view, the "anonymous Christianity" discussed earlier, holds to a stream of universal grace flowing from the Absolute Savior Jesus Christ, empowering persons of conscience in an act of love that is itself implicit faith, thus conforming to the biblical affirmation of salvation by grace through faith. But the texts of the New Testament on this subject overwhelmingly assert faith to be an explicit confession and not a covert one: Matthew 8:10-13; 9:1-8, 19-22, 28-38; 10:32-33, 37-40; 11:27-30; 12:36-37; 17:19-20; Mark 2:5-12, 34; 8:34-38; 9:23-25; 10:52; 11:22-26; Luke 5:20-25; 7:9-10, 50; 8:48-50; 10:25-28; 15:7; 18:29-30; John 1:12-13, 16-18; 3:3-8, 16-18, 28, 36; 4:10-14, 22, 42; 5:24; 6:29, 33-40, 47-51, 53-58, 68-69; 10:10; 11:25-26; 12:25-26, 50; 14:1-7, 23-24; 15:1-11; 17:1-5, 25-26; 20:30-31; Acts 2:36-39, 47; 3:17-19; 4:11-12; 8:21-22; 10:43; 11:13-18; 13:38-39, 48; 15:6-11; 16:30-34; 20:21, 32; 26:16-18; Romans 1:16-17; 3:21-22, 25-31; 4:3-17; 5:1-2, 8-11; 6:23; 8:28-30; 10:9-13; 11:1-6, 11, 13-14, 21-22; 1 Corinthians 1:9, 18-19, 21-24; 3:15; 5:5; 6:9-11; 15:1; 2 Corinthians 2:14-16; 4:4, 14; 5:18-21; 6:2; 7:9-10; 8:7-9; 10:7; 13:4-5; Galatians 1:4; 2:15-16, 19-21; 3:6-14, 22-29; 4:4-7; 5:4-6; 6:8-9, 15; Ephesians 1:4-7; 2:3-5, 8-9, 13, 16, 18-19; 3:10-12, 17-19; 4:30-32; 5:8; Philippians 2:12-13, 15-16; 3:8-11; Colossians 1:12-14, 20-23, 26-28; 2:2, 6, 12-13; 3:1-4, 12-13;

1 Thessalonians 1:9-10; 2:11-12, 16; 4:12, 14, 16; 5:5, 23-24; 2 Thessalonians 1:3-10; 2:10, 12; 3:1-2; 1 Timothy 1:16, 19; 2:3-6; 4:1, 16; 5:8; 6:12; 2 Timothy 1:5-10, 18; 2:11-13, 15; Titus 1:1-3; 3:5-8; Hebrews 4:2-3; 5:9-10, 12; 6:5-6; 7:24-25; 9:14-15; 10:32-36, 39; 13:20-21; James 1:17-18, 21; 2:5, 20-26; 5:20; 1 Peter 1:5-9, 19-23; 2:23; 4:17-19; 5:10; 2 Peter 1:3-4, 10-11; 1 John 1:1-7; 2:1-3; 3:1-4, 23-24; 4:9-10, 13-15; 5:4-5, 11-33; 2 John 1:9; Jude 1:20-23; Revelation 14:12. Further, the very structure of the Christian narrative, while acknowledging a grace that makes and keeps life human (thus rendering possible the very conditions for continuing the Story), treats the fall in such a radical and universal way that our human love cannot win salvation before God or constitute the equivalent of faith.

"Universalisms" and "neo-universalisms" have their own kind of answer to this question at hand, one we shall presently address. Yet others, discussed earlier, so qualify the claims of Christian particularity that the issue we are here examining does not appear.

We have postponed some of the discussion of this soteriological question to our chapter on consummation because eschatology plays an important part in the struggle with this question. Early in the history of Christian thought, attention was given to the saving work of Christ that continues beyond the doors of death. We find this theme in the Apostles' Creed in the phrase "He descended into Hades," the place of the dead. This view is based on 1 Peter 3:19-20, 1 Peter 4:6, and a cluster of related passages (Eph. 4:8-9; John 5:25-29; Matt. 8:11; 12:40; Luke 13:28-30; Heb. 9:15; Rom. 10:7; Rev. 21:25). Some early church fathers, as well as some nineteenth- and twentieth-century theologians working out of a missionary tradition sensitive to other cultures and religions (for example, the "Andover theory"), laid the groundwork for an eschatological perspective on the destiny of those who have not heard the Good News. "For this is why the gospel was preached even to the dead, that . . . they might live in the spirit like God" (1 Pet. 4:6 RSV). They believed that the wideness and length of God's mercy would deny no one the hearing of the Gospel, a word of invitation extended by the glorified Christ to those who have not been reached by the earthly Body of Christ. That offer is made by the same vulnerable Love that does not force its will and way on anyone, and thus in the eschatological encounter grants the right to respond with a No as well as a Yes.

If the soteriological issue posed with increasing insistence by modern religious pluralism is viewed in this eschatological perspective, the particularity of classical claims to salvation by Christ alone and faith alone can be maintained, together with the universal aspects of Christ's saving work. Particularity is grounded in historical event and choice, but universality is not circumscribed by our earthly institutions and timetables. Those who respond in faith to Christ's eschatological word may indeed be the "other sheep of mine, not belonging to this fold" (John 10:16).

"And so all Israel will be saved" (Rom. 11:26). Paul's struggle with the relation of Christian claims to salvation to other worldviews made a special place for the role of Israel (Rom. 9–11), and so must we. The connection between Christ and Israel is different in kind from that between Christ and other world religions or people of goodwill, for Christian faith comes itself from "the root of Jesse" (Isa. 11:1). Theologians have puzzled over Paul's suggestion that all Israel, in fact, will be saved, proposing that in the time between Good Friday and Easter Christ descended into the place of the dead to preach to the elect patriarchs and matriarchs. Another view held that a proleptic form of faith saved believers in Israel since Abraham is identified as the very "father of faith" (Rom. 4:11). Can it be that Israel then and the faithful Jew now as heirs of Abraham have an implicit faith in Christ insofar as they respond to the saving deeds of God in the midst of this people? Is this a faith whose source in Christ is disclosed eschatologically, so that what was hidden may be revealed? Our speculations finally join those of Job and Paul in their counsel of modesty before this ultimate mystery, "Who has known the mind of the Lord?" (Rom. 11:34 RSV).

Hell and Damnation

What is the fate of the faithless? What is the destiny of those who have turned a deaf ear to the Word, a shut eye to the Vision? As in other Christian teachings, so here, too, theology has been drawn in two directions, each with its biblical warrants and simple and clear-cut scenario of the End.

221

Scenario 1: Light and Darkness

Clearly a majority opinion in traditional Christianity, this view of the End forecasts a double destination for the human race: the faithful go to Heaven and everlasting bliss, the faithless go to hell and everlasting damnation. The saved receive their reward in the Kingdom and the sinners receive their due, the fires of eternal judgment. By a strict reading of the arithmetic of both the New Testament ("Straight is the gate, and narrow the way, and few there be that find it") and the empirical calculation that only a small portion of world's population have even the opportunity for the choice of explicit faith, this option (one that has not, to date, acknowledged the proclamation of the Good News by the glorified Christ discussed earlier) must be prepared to consign the better part of the human race to the curse of everlasting punishment.

Scenario 1 has been expressed in a variety of ways, from hard- to soft-line interpretations. In a harsher form double destination can mean a double *predestination,* in which God foreordains some to eternal life and others to eternal death. In a milder form the distinction is made between the eternal salvation of the faithful and the cessation of existence, the nothingness of death, for the unworthy — "annihilationism."

Scenario 1 is able to assemble a set of New Testament texts that speak of hell and damnation for the sinner and Heaven for the saved, the future division of the sheep and the goats, the fires of eternal hell for those who in this life have gone astray (Matt. 25:31-46; 10:28; Luke 16:19-31; John 3:36; 5:25-29; 2 Thess. 1:9; Heb. 6:8; 9:27; Rev. 14:10-11). Built on these texts, and shaped by a theory of punishment and reward, quid pro quo, this view assigns to some a destiny of Light and casts others into the outer darkness.

Scenario 2: Light and No Darkness

Clearly a minority opinion in historic Christianity but a popular option on the margins of the Church, Scenario 2 is rooted less in biblical texts and more in an appeal to the logic of the divine love and also in a more sanguine assessment of human nature. It holds that there is no hell and damnation but only a future of love and light. There are no damned, for all shall be saved.

The belief in universal salvation and no damnation — "universalism" — is usually associated with a confidence in the essential virtue of human beings. If human nature is basically good, there is no reason for dire forecasts of hell and damnation. We deserve a better fate. Another version of universalism is based more on the goodness of God than the trustworthiness of human nature. A God of love, it is asserted, would not punish humans in such a fashion. "God forgives. That's his business." The goodness of human nature and the goodness of God, one that precludes eschatological judgment, are joined as presuppositions in much modern universalism.

The timetable and conditions vary in the different expressions of universalist belief. For some, a simple deism links immortality with God and virtue as the three convictions at the core of all religion, and assumes that joyful afterlife is our immediate and common destination. For others seeking to honor the biblical passages on judgment, a temporary punishment after death gives way to universal redemption. And for others, of "neo-universalist" persuasion, God's judgment on sin is affirmed but all die in Christ on Calvary and are raised with him unto universal salvation.

Scenario 3: Light Overcoming Darkness

At many points along the way in our narration of the Christian Story we have found a polarization between reductionist views and the search for an excluded middle that holds in creative tension themes that would prefer to be autonomous and finally imperialistic. We meet this duality again on the present question and seek the elusive unity.

As often is the case, the excluded alternative is more difficult to state than the trim and simple, and therefore oversimple, polarities. This is especially so with regard to the third eschatological option. Because it has to do with what is yet to be, talk about it must carry the same modesty and mystery appropriate to the subject of eschatology as a whole. The modesty is increased and the mystery deepened in this aspect of eschatology by two additional considerations:

1. The biblical material to which we go for final perspective moves in two different directions. Depending on the texts, a case can be made for certain themes in both scenarios.

2. In dealing with the future, and eminently so with the ultimate Future, the sovereign freedom of God is fundamental. God will be who God will be. We cannot tell God how to exercise that freedom. All our projections here, as they are built from the New Testament and from the trajectory of the Christian narrative itself, stand under this "eschatological proviso." Scenario 3 is an "article of hope," not a clear doctrinal "article of faith."

Scenario 1 is right in its serious assessment of the reality of sin and its demand for accountability. The righteousness of God is not a divine indulgence that overlooks the horror of human sin. We are responsible for our turning away from the Light and our own plunge into the night. Judgment falls on our pride, punishment for our faithlessness and idolatry.

Scenario 1 fails to relate this necessary emphasis on judgment to the forward momentum of the saga toward the fulfillment of the divine purpose. To believe in that end when "God is all in all" is to affirm that there is no last resisting rampart, no unconquered territory. In the biblical End all enemies are put under Christ's feet (1 Cor. 15:26) and "all," in the words of the hymn, is the "death of death and hell's destruction." How is it possible to declare this kind of final victory of the Lord of Lords and King of Kings and still maintain the fact of accountability and punishment? We shall presently explore this difficult but crucial excluded middle. (See also Matt. 19:28; John 12:32; Acts 3:21; 1 Cor. 3:13-15; 15:22-28; Eph. 1:9-10; Phil. 2:10-11; 1 Tim. 2:4; 2 Pet. 3:9, 13.)

Scenario 2 is right in its instinctive resistance to the assumption of Scenario 1 that God creates a human race only to consign it in large measure to everlasting perdition. But this loving scenario contesting a loveless one is finally too naive about both the virtue of humanity and the indulgence of its Maker. It does not measure the depths of sin in the human heart or the accountability to God for this lethal resistance. It does not know how profoundly the heart of God has been broken by this breach of faith. The righteousness of God holds humanity responsible for its abuse of freedom, and that means the coming of the night of punishment for those who have turned aside. Yet how can the love of God be reconciled with the biblical assertion that sin will not go unpunished by the righteousness of God?

In answering this question we must remember how the *setting* of the Church's thinking has influenced the way the Story is told. Enlightenment views of a noble human nature and a nonjudgmental deity have contributed to the universalism of Scenario 2. Cultural assumptions have also had their effect on the understanding of punishment to be found in Scenario 1. The milieu of traditional theories of hell and damnation has been a punitive and retributive judicial theory and penal practice. Punishment was "pay back" for the criminal. Punishment as rehabilitation of the offender for return to responsible participation in society was unthinkable. New Testament teachings on divine punishment were read in the light of the culture's practice of retributive justice.

That there are other ways of accountability and other methods of executing punishment than the punitive practices of another day is a common assumption in contemporary penology. Indeed, current ideas of rehabilitation and restoration may well have had their rise out of fermenting work of the Christian vision of redemption challenging secular notions of retribution. Be that as it may, the eschatological affirmation of the Christian faith cannot be controlled by cultural categories, past or present. But the change in these categories serves to make us more critical of the too easy assumptions that the Last Judgment must look just like the judgment rendered in a sixteenth-century British court and meted out in the cruelties of prison and scaffold.

Another clue to avoiding the oversimplification of Scenarios 1 and 2 is found in the time line of the biblical narrative. As in the parallel question of theodicy discussed earlier, so, too, here we have to do with a vulnerable Love that leaves the human partner the maneuvering room of freedom, but a stubborn Love that persists in unswerving pursuit and an empowered Love that will not relent until the "Hound of Heaven" has ended the chase. Thus evolves a Story of the moves and countermoves of God in pursuit of the divine purpose. Death itself is no barrier to a resolute Love, as we have seen in the postmortem Petrine texts and the descent of Christ into the place of the dead.

The disengagement of punishment from its retributive context and the affirmation of the Christian faith as a tension-filled narrative that takes time seriously and moves to the real fulfillment of the promise of redemption are elements in our third scenario. In this view judgment is utterly real and punishment of sin on the day of judgment ineluctable. Indeed, the light of that day brings with it the fire of the divine Love, as in the visual and verbal art forms of the Christian tradition. But fire can temper and cleanse. The flames of divine Love can purge and refashion, and the winds of the Spirit can winnow that chaff. While there are no biblical warrants for the teaching of purgatory as it is held in traditional Roman Catholicism, the passage to which it points (1 Cor. 3:13-15 NRSV) does speak of the last Day's fire that "will test what sort of work each has done." In the midst of his long discourse on eschatological hope in the fifteenth chapter of 1 Corinthians, Paul speaks of the acts in the final drama of redemption as eschatological struggle and cleansing: "For as all die in Adam, so all will be made alive in Christ. But each in his own order: Christ the first fruits, then at his coming those who belong to Christ. Then comes the end, when he hands over the kingdom to God the Father, after he has destroyed every ruler and every authority and power. For he must reign until he has put all his enemies under his feet. The last enemy to be destroyed is death . . . so that God may be all in all" (1 Cor. 15:22-27, 28 NRSV).

The New Testament passages that portray in vivid colors the judgment on sin make unmistakably clear our accountability to the righteous will of God. Written in the midst of persecution from without and the risk of defections from within, they serve as warning and prophylactics, heightened in rhetoric by the life-and-death circumstances and the perils to the survival of the faith community itself. The stridency of these admonitions, which not infrequently call to decision with the promise of everlasting curse and everlasting blessing, should not prevent us from searching for the truth within the hyperbole. And to see that truth as the *possibility* of the lasting but *not* everlasting fires of divine Love does not take away from the same evangelical Word that is part of the Church's mission today. On its positive side, the offer of salvation by grace through faith is the invitation to participate *now* in the eternal life that shall be then. And its refusal is a reckoning *now* with the judgment that is and shall be until all things are put under the feet of Jesus Christ.

The judgment on that Day in which the sun of Shalom rises over all is one in which the fires of liberation and reconciliation refine and its light so burns away the shadows that the last darkness is overcome. The God whose "will it is that all men should find salvation and come to know the truth" (1 Tim. 2:4) has the power of the Holy Spirit to keep that promise and accomplish that Dream. The agony of this final contest of light and darkness cannot be understated, as the proponents of Scenario 1 have been at pains to point out. There *is* hell and judgment. But the last word in the Christian Story is not that of a half-accomplished purpose, but of a promise kept and a Vision that becomes Reality.

Does the assured fulfillment of that divine purpose include *apokatastasis,* the certainty that what 1 Timothy 2:4 declares to be God's desire — universal salvation — will also be God's deed? Two things prevent us from carrying the themes of postmortem redemptive punishment into the doctrine of universalism. One is the freedom of a majestic and mysterious God to make that final decision, a choice that cannot be determined by our theological blueprints. The other is the divine self-restraint with its awesome power to forego the coercion of human beings granted the freedom to resist the divine purposes. Yet the same conviction that has refused to give us a universalist dogma, an "article of faith," does give us an "article of hope." Christians have a right to *hope* that eternal death means the burning love of an eternal God cleansing the dross as only eternity can do, a lasting but not everlasting death. Here is a modest Christian hope, with its eschatological proviso, leaving all to God's final, mysterious Purpose.

Everlasting Life

As we began the biblical epic with the Vision of God, so we conclude there. In the end, the Vision becomes Reality. The promise of Shalom is kept. The world that God brought to be out of the divine Hope reaches its fulfillment, the Kingdom comes, and God's will *is* done on earth as it is in Heaven.

If the wages of sin and evil are death, then liberation from these foes is life. And their destruction is *everlasting life.* How can humanity still trapped in the valley of the shadow of sin, evil, and death understand what this Light and Life mean? For our dimmed vision there are the translucent metaphors of the book of Revelation. Here in the final accounting of the final event we receive some illumination, albeit in the stained-glass colors and shapes of this terrain. The rich imagery of the Apocalypse, to be taken for what it is, symbols from this world that let in the light of the world to come (not seeing "face to face"), gives us our clues. They express the reconciliation of all things that issues from the liberation of all things.

1. *Reconciliation of Humanity with God.* "How blest are those whose hearts are pure; they shall see God" (Matt. 5:8). When the purifying work

of liberation is completed, its gift to us is the *vision of God*. John portrays this beatific vision in the richest images at hand: "There in heaven stood a throne, and on the throne sat one whose appearance was like the gleam of jasper and carnelian; and round the throne was a rainbow, bright as an emerald" (Rev. 4:3). Now the long-blind eyes are opened and we behold this ineffable Light. We face the One from whom we had turned, so that we may live and love in communion with God.

To see the Envisioner is to see the Vision: "I saw standing in the very middle of the throne . . . a Lamb with the marks of slaughter on him" (Rev. 5:6). And to see by the Spirit the Father of the Son is to exult "Thou art worthy, O Lord our God, to receive glory and honor and power. . . . Worthy is the Lamb, the Lamb that was slain, to receive all power and wealth, wisdom and might, honor and glory and praise!" (Rev. 4:11; 5:12). To see the Light is to celebrate. The joy of thanksgiving, portended in our eucharistic worship, is the service of worship and praise that issues from seeing.

2. *Reconciliation of Humanity*. Seeing the Light is seeing *by* the Light as well; the biblical portraiture of fulfillment has a horizontal as well as a vertical dimension. We see in the Light of the glory of God the brothers and sisters in Christ. The estranged shall dwell in unity: "By its light shall the nations walk, and the kings of earth shall bring into it all their splendor" (Rev. 21:24). The Vision given to us is described in Revelation not only in interpersonal metaphors of life together in joy and love but in social and political images. The powers as well as persons of this world will come together and give obedience and praise to their Maker and Redeemer. "He showed me the holy city of Jerusalem coming down out of heaven from God. It shone with the glory of God; it had the radiance of some priceless jewel, like a jasper, clear as crystal" (Rev. 21:10-11). The pearly gates and golden streets, disdained by both the spiritual and secular, are in fact important symbols of the earthy and corporate hopes of the Christian faith. Nothing is too worldly, for ultimate redemption includes the bringing of all things under the feet of Christ, including the principalities of this world, which have used their power and glory for their own ends. Now the kingdoms of this world shall give way to the Kingdom of God, and the new city will displace the tyranny and injustice of the old metropolis. We have noted earlier the ethical imperatives that this vision of a new city generates as we are called to set up signs in this world to the just and peaceable Kingdom to come. Thus the book of Revelation main-

tains the communal, corporate, and structural hopes of the prophetic tradition of the Old Testament. The new city and Kingdom to come are the world of Shalom, in which swords are beaten into plowshares and spears into pruning hooks and there shall no more be the trampling of the poor or the waging of war.

The portrayal of everlasting life juxtaposes the wrongs and hates of the world to the justice and love to come. But there are continuities as well as discontinuities in Christian hope. Signs of life as well as the pallor death are to be found *in* this world, earnests of the Realm that are not destroyed but ennobled and fulfilled at the consummation. One such firstfruit of the Kingdom is the conjugal union spoken of eschatologically in the marriage service: "So live together in this world that in the world to come you may have life everlasting." While on the one hand we know that "at the resurrection men and women do not marry" (Matt. 22:30), on the other the use of conjugal and familial metaphors to express the ultimate Rule suggests that the richest unities in this life will participate in the final reconciliation. Such union is a candle lit in a dark world. When the Day comes it will not be extinguished but drawn into a larger radiance. "Love never ends."

3. *The Reconciliation of Nature.* The Apocalypse places "living creatures" around the throne of God in its vision of things to come. And John declares, "I saw a new heaven and a new earth" (Rev. 21:1), a revivified nature that includes crystal waters, abundant crops, and flourishing forests whose "leaves . . . serve for the healing of the nations" (Rev. 22:2). Thus the New Testament continues and completes the prophetic vision of Shalom in nature, in which the wolf and the lamb lie down together, the child is a friend of the snake, and the desert blooms. The creation no longer groans but rejoices, for "I heard every created thing in heaven and on earth and under the earth and in the sea, all that is in them, crying, 'Praise and honor, glory and might, to him who sits on the throne and the Lamb for ever and ever!' " (Rev. 5:13).

God's is a cosmic Vision. Its fulfillment is the restoration of all things. The ecological imperative of the Christian faith is grounded in this hope of God for the created order. As with the healing of the nations, so with the ministry of compassion to a wounded earth, we are beckoned to set up Franciscan signs here and now to the new creation.

We have a synoptic vision of the everlasting life that brings an end to the death we see about us in that panorama of liberation and reconcil-

229

iation lifted before the eyes of faith at Christian burial: "I saw a new heaven and a new earth, for the first heaven and the first earth had vanished, and there was no longer any sea. I saw the holy city, new Jerusalem, coming down out of heaven from God, made ready like a bride adorned for her husband. I heard a loud voice proclaiming from the throne: 'Now at last God has his dwelling among men! He will dwell among them, and they shall be his people, and God himself will be with them. He will wipe every tear from their eyes; there shall be an end to death, and to mourning and crying and pain; for the old order has passed away!" (Rev. 21:1-4).

After Death — Interim Eschatology

What happens to us immediately after death? As confident chronologies and cosmologies about the end of time proliferate in an era uncertain about its future, so, too, do self-assured descriptions of our destiny after the last heartbeat. Postmortem existence is a favorite topic of the cult and the occult. Its territory is carefully mapped by mystical cognoscenti, many of whom claim to have precognition or periodic reports from those who have arrived before us. Compared to the charts and graphs of these seers, the small candle lit by the Christian faith seems unimpressive indeed. But as with the last things, so also here with the next-to-last things, we do see through a glass darkly, and the counsel of mystery and modesty is our best guide.

The pattern we have discerned in other Christian teachings, being pulled from two sides — spiritual and physical — is also manifest here in the penultimate arena of eschatology. Two very different views have emerged around these poles, ones that have claimed Christian credentials as vigorously as have their christological counterparts, Docetism and Ebionitism. View 1: The first and more dominant point of view declares that on death an indestructible part of the self, the soul, detaches itself from the body and returns to God: the "immortality of the soul." The merging of the soul with Deity can be conceived in more impersonal terms on the analogy of the drop of water being absorbed into the ocean of Spirit. Or it can be interpreted in more personal terms as the communion of the soul with God. Sometimes this destiny of the self is considered the final one, with little or no connection to the eschatological themes of resurrection, return, and judgment, as is pointed out in Oscar Cullmann's famous study of the question "The resurrection of the body or the immortality of the soul?" Teaching about the immortality of the soul is traceable to Greek philosophical assumptions negative about the world of time and space, matter and the body, and therefore hopeful of the release of the soul from this "prison house."

Though the attempts are constant to force this teaching of the immortality of the soul into the Christian system, so much so that many pulpits in an acculturated Christianity offer it as the yearly Easter diet, it must finally be declared indigestible. Christian faith has too profound and critical an understanding of human spirit to consider it the "divine" segment of the self worthy of immortality, and too high a view of the body to disdain and separate it from our final destiny. Both something less and something more must be said about our penultimate and ultimate futures.

View 2: A forceful "neoorthodox" criticism of the immortality of the soul has been made and a clear alternative offered by the bold assertion of the psychosomatic unity of body and soul in Hebrew thought. Associated with it is the belief in the resurrection of the body at the end of history; thus, "when you're dead, you're dead." On death our body and soul, being inseparable, disintegrate and die to wait on the end, when we shall be reconstituted and resurrected in the flesh.

Sundry interpretations of "secular Christianity" are glad to have some traditional allies at this point, for they, too, affirm that death is the end. The difference from the neoorthodox eschatology is that there is no belief in a final resurrection.

Other variations of this view include the belief that the time between death and the end is as a "twinkling of the eye," on the analogy of sleep, as in several New Testament texts (Luke 8:52; 1 Cor. 15:20; 2 Pet. 3:4). Some have spoken of the continuance of the dead "in the mind of God," or more recently, in the language of computer technology, in the "memory bank" of God, available for "printout" on the last day.

The criticisms by View 2 of View 1 are to the point. The affirmation of the resurrection of the dead as the end is surely a faithful reading of the Story. But a theme in the first view echoes some notes in that saga that are missing in the second. It has to do with the bond forged by grace through faith with the believer. By faith we live and see the Light. Such a union with God is described in the Gospel of John as "eternal life" (John 3:36; 5:24; 6:40). What is eternal is indestructible. This union cannot be broken. Death does not sever the tie that binds us to eternity. There is a "putting on of immortality" (1 Cor. 15:53) by faith active in love more powerful than our mortality. Death cannot separate us from the life and love of God (Rom. 8:38-39).

What is the state of life in this postmortem union with God, the "interim" between death and the final resurrection? Some say this is an illogical question since there is no "time" in eternity; dying into the presence of the eternal God is the arrival of the End itself. Others declare that we return to the dust at death only to be raised on the last day. Yet others believe that this is a period in which the soul lives without a body, waiting to be clothed fully at the resurrection of the dead.

Two sets of passages inform the doctrine of the future on this point, the "asleep" texts mentioned earlier and the "awake" texts (Luke 16:19-31; 23:43; Rev. 6:9). Both strands, paradoxically, assume the passage of time in eternity. While Greek modes of thought find that association unthinkable, the time-drenched and Incarnation-grounded biblical faith does not. The love of a vulnerable God is such that the condition of our temporality can be taken into the divine being itself in order to achieve the divine purpose. The narrative of faith continues into eternity.

The asleep references in the New Testament seem to suggest the absence of self-awareness in the interim state and thus corroborate the view of "soul sleep," or existence only in the divine mind until the resurrection of the dead. Some argue, however, that "asleep" is a metaphor for death, expressing its visible manifestation and not making a theological judgment about the condition of the self after death. Further, the awake passages appear to express in a richer way the continuance of eternal life established and experienced in faith. And our earlier discussion of the Petrine text on the proclamation of the Gospel to the dead, and the Pauline suggestion of the winnowing fires of divine love in the world to come, presupposes some kind of conscious existence. Again, as John Mbiti and other Third World theologians remind us, the classical Christian teaching about "the communion of saints" is too easily forgotten by a secular Western theology and must be recovered in our dialogue with cultures that have a sense of relationship to the dead. The "cloud of witnesses" who have gone before us in some mysterious sense still surround us as they make their own pilgrimage toward Shalom. On balance, therefore, and assisted by our narrative framework, we view the journey of the postmortem self as in both discontinuity and continuity with its earthly pilgrimage and its ultimate destiny. While awaiting the fullness of resurrection portended in the Easter Christ, death marks a stage on the way to that end, one in which the self is in some way alive and responsible in a fashion we cannot comprehend, "having and not having" who and what we shall be.

Our metaphor of light is a clue to how we might perceive the Already–Not Yet paradox of the interim state. The light of the divine Vision shines from the end of history toward us. But this is no cold and distant radiance. Its rays penetrate our terrain. It comes as revivifying warmth. Light shining *on us* is also power working *in us*. Just as personal salvation is not only pardon but also power, justification productive of sanctification, so the eschatological favor of the ultimate future pours into our penultimate future as power *now* over death — eternal life on earth and after death. Those empowered to see the Light and walk in the Light traverse the shadowy valley in hope. As a summary that both honors the mystery yet affirms the majesty of the eternal life that death cannot destroy, it is impossible to improve on Paul's own ecstatic utterance. For this reason it is the climax of the service of Christian burial: "Who shall separate us from the love of Christ? Shall tribulation, or distress, or persecution, or famine, or nakedness, or peril, or sword? . . . No, in all these things we are more than conquerors through him who loved us. For I am sure that neither death, nor life, nor angels, nor principalities, nor things present, nor things to come, nor powers, nor height, nor depth, nor anything else in all creation, will be able to separate us from the love of God in Christ Jesus our Lord" (Rom. 8:35, 37-39 RSV).

Historical Hope

If Light streams from the future toward us *after* death, so it does *before* death. Jesus insistently struck this note in his own teaching about the Kingdom of God. Here in *this world* there are signs of the coming of Shalom, as the sick are healed, the blind see, the captives are released. Easter confirms and transfigures these intimations of the coming Reign of God. The resurrection is the foundation of Christian hope for portents and earnests of the Not Yet.

When speaking of historical hope, the doctrines of salvation and consummation merge. Eschatology at this point lies on the boundary of soteriology. The chapter of the Story on salvation speaks of the thermal current of grace flowing in the lives of persons and in the structures of history and rhythms of nature. The eschatological chapter points forward to the possibilities of that grace in all the little tomorrows that stretch toward the final Tomorrow. Christian hope seizes this prospective work of the Holy Spirit, its charter for dreaming dreams and seeing visions.

That hope includes the possibilities of personal growth in grace, the pilgrimage of Christian turning to and walking in the Light that we have earlier explored. But it reaches far beyond to look for and hope for what the Spirit can and will do in the environment of nature and the theater of history. Thus both the givens and the perils of nature do not confine or define the future. That future is open to possibilities of historical Shalom in which the blind do see, the deaf hear, and the lame walk, as dreamed and envisioned in the still blue-sky forecasts of medical and biomedical futurism. And that same tomorrow is not closed to the social and political hoper who is able to say with Martin Luther King, Jr., "I have a dream!" Visions of liberation and reconciliation in the world are part of what penultimate hope is all about. It has taken the "theology of hope" to remind us of this kind of Light and Power that penetrated our human future.

Eschatological dreaming for our personal, social, and natural futures is lured by the Great Vision, but it is also grounded in reality. We live in the half-light of the Already–Not Yet, at Dawn, not High Noon. The last chapter does not tell of the building of the Kingdom of God by us in this world. The Commonwealth awaits the coming of and culminating Work of its Lord. As the Spirit gives us strength to erect signposts to the New Jerusalem, we struggle with the powers of sin, evil, and death that continue their harassments. Christian hope, therefore, is *sober* hope aware of the impossibilities as well as the possibilities of the historical future. Its visionary realism knows that the best and brightest of human advancements are plagued with ambiguity, afflicted by the temptations to arrogant power, corruptible and mortal. It tempers the giddy expectations of both the technological futurist and the political visionary with sobriety about sin, evil, and death. And it warns the moral and spiritual perfectionist about self-righteous fury and fanaticism. But visionary realism is not cynicism. While perceiving the shadows ahead in the corridor of the future, it knows that Jesus Christ has torn down the "No Exit" sign at its end and shouldered open its dark door. While it is not thrust wide open to instant sunshine everywhere, there is a crack of light in the historical future. The powers of darkness do not control tomorrow or Tomorrow. Despair about the future paralyzes. Hope mobilizes.

Epilogue: God

"Immortal, invisible, God only wise,
In light inaccessible hid from our eyes."

"I am the Alpha and the Omega, says the Lord God, who is and who was and who is to come" (Rev. 1:8). Our telling of the Christian Tale began with the Prologue's portrayal of the eternal origins of the drama of salvation in the Godhead. As the Story has unfolded, what was implicit in its beginning has become explicit. The character of the God who envisions and empowers takes form in the deeds that fulfill the Vision. Now we go beyond the sketch of the nature of God given in the Prologue and paint a portrait of the chief Actor who emerges from the drama. While traditional theology positions the doctrine of God early in its development, anticipating themes from subsequently expounded beliefs (for example, the Person and Work of Christ), here in conformity with our narrative structure we have chosen to use Prologue and Epilogue as the appropriate places to introduce and conclude reflection about the nature of Deity. In the Prologue the sparse trinitarian framework gives us resources to launch the epic. The Epilogue draws on the rich material of the history of God so recounted to fill out that picture.

The inner-trinitarian Life in which the Christian drama originates — Purposer, Purpose, Power, Father, Son, and Holy Spirit — expresses itself in missions commensurate with the Modes and Persons of God's being. Purposing begins in the Purposer's/Father's mission of creating and preserving, as we have seen in the chapters "Creation," "Fall," and

235

"Covenant." The Purpose and Word become flesh in the liberating and reconciling mission of the Son at Bethlehem, in Galilee, on Calvary, and on Easter morning. And the redeeming work of the Holy Spirit, the Power of God, is to be seen in the birth of the Church, in the rush of the winds of salvation, and in the consummation of the divine intention.

The first mission of the Trinity includes both the bringing to be of the divine partner, the world, and its preservation. Its grace is revelatory as well as formative, for the Light of God shines on nature and in humanity. God also keeps company with the world in its rebellion against the divine intention. Providence supports the Purpose in the maelstrom of history and nature and sets limits to the destruction that the powers of sin, evil, and death would wreak on the world.

The mission of the Son, the eternal Light, comes to a turning point in the Incarnation and atonement. The Vision becomes flesh and discloses the intention of God in the life and ministry of Jesus, is assailed by the full hatred of the world on Golgotha, makes the wrath of humanity serve the intentions of God by a cross of suffering Love that defeats sin and evil, and finally brings life to the death of Hope on resurrection morning. Liberation from the enemies and reconciliation of the friends take place in the Person and Work of the Son of God.

The Holy Spirit brings the liberation and reconciliation accomplished for the world in Jesus Christ *to* the world and works them *in* the world from Pentecost to consummation. The doctrine of the Spirit, pneumatology, has been implicit in our charting of the work of the Power of God in the sending of the beams of Light and Life from the Easter horizon across the world. The Spirit makes the Word known and experienced in the birth, life, and witness of the Church, the flow of its saving grace in persons, history, and nature, and in the final coming of Shalom. The Spirit's work is the effective redemption from sin, evil, and death in the time between the Times and at the End of time.

While the operations of the triune God manifest themselves in these three great divisions of the Christian Story by the foreground activity of one or another Person, the mission of each interpenetrates the others. ("The works of the Trinity are one." — Anselm.) The Logos of God is partner to creation and companion to Providence, and is active in redemption. The Spirit is the Power that brings newness to be at the beginning as well as at the end, and conceives the Son at the center of the Story. And in all the actions of Purpose and Power is to be found the presence of the Purposer.

As the Tale unfolds, certain attributes of God emerge that character-ize all the Persons. We shall identify them as the formal and material qualities, sometimes referred to as the metaphysical and moral attributes. The academic nature of this kind of cataloguing grates on the proper sense of mystery that should attend our talk about God. Let all these descriptions be understood, therefore, as modest glances toward a Light whose inner reaches are finally "hid from our eyes."

Formal Qualities

Subjectivity

The God of the Christian Story is a Subject. The events we have traced rise out of a self that purposes and chooses. The ground of these happenings and of all being is the inner spontaneity of the divine Subject. The forevision of God and the deeds done to consummate that intention bespeak freedom, awareness, self-direction. Here is the living, willing Spirit, and therefore the *personal* God (Exod. 3:14; Eph. 1:9, 11).

A cloud of ambiguity envelops many discussions about the divine subjectivity. A strong and important mystical tradition, in alliance with Hebraic and Reformed concern to protect the sovereignty of God, declares that all anthropomorphisms, including that of human selfhood, are not finally worthy of the God who is above all our formulas. Yes, both mystery and majesty require us to describe subjectivity, and all the other qualities we attribute to God, as analogies that faith employs to describe the inde-scribable. However, either a certain kind of secularization or an extrabiblical mysticism disguised in these proper modesties also disavows anthropomor-phism and counsels us to translate personal metaphors ("necessary for piety") into more literal philosophical descriptions of the divine, such as the abso-lute, all, depth, process, and ground. There is both methodological and theological error here. Methodologically, it assumes that faith supplies only the emotive symbols, and philosophy the cognitive meanings. But faith is, as we have noted, both *assensus* and *fiducia,* both an *assent* of the mind and a *trust* of the heart; it uses *meaningful* metaphors that carry within them crucial, albeit not exhaustive, cognitive implications. Moreover, what are declared to be literal philosophical terms are themselves also metaphors, drawn from areas of experience that are consistently subpersonal.

Theologically, the right reserve about personal metaphors does not mean the denial of the real subjectivity of God. God is *at least* personal, but inexhaustibly *more so*. God is not less than our own self-directing, purposive, free, choosing selves. The God of the Christian saga is an envisioning, acting self, the abysmal depths and plenitude of whose subjectivity can only be hinted at by our frail figures.

Transcendence

All that we have said abut God the Subject could be interpreted to mean a macrocosmic person complete with body parts, as indeed Deity has been portrayed in three-level cosmologies and in Mormon and Swedenborgian traditions. While the word *transcendence* is employed to mean a variety of things, we use it here to describe Deity as incorporeal. The God who acts in our history is not one being among other beings, but Another who transcends space and time. God is a Spirit. The divine Other stands over against the world even while being a full participant in its history (John 4:24; Col. 1:15; 1 Tim. 1:17).

Transcendence includes two classical attributes: *infinity* and *eternity*. The Infinite is not exhausted by finitude. God is not in space, but space is in God. As Eternal, God is not in time, but time is in God. While it is common to express this transcendence of space-time by speaking of God as "outside of space" and/or God as "before and after" time, both statements assert what they are seeking to deny, for they use spatial and temporal metaphors (outside, before, after) to express the nonspatiality and nontemporality of God. "Apophatic theology" may be the best way to deal with this enigma, using a negative statement to point toward our meaning: God is not spatialized or time-bound (Deut. 32:40; Job 11:7-9; Ps. 90:2; Matt. 6:13).

Immanence

While God does not have a body, the psychosomatic unity of human selfhood does provide an analogy that points to the immanence of God in the world. As human subjectivity expresses itself in, with, and throughout our bodies, so the transcendent subjectivity of God is immanent in the patterns, processes, and events of this world. The Christian narrative is unintelligible apart from the assumption of the busy presence of the purposing God in nature, selves, historical happenings and structures, and in a singular fashion in the Person and Work of Jesus Christ. Immanence is an abstract label for the sum of these involvements: the warm currents of grace that flow in the cosmos, holding it together, bringing it to new levels of creativity and wholeness, resisting the powers inimical to it, calling and claiming each individual through the traces of the divine Purpose that we have not been able to expel from our consciousness, setting boundaries to the destructive powers of evil in history and nature, acting in the events and illuminations of Israel, taking flesh, liberating, and reconciling in Jesus Christ, empowering the Church to see the Light and bear witness to it, and coursing through the world with signs and portents that point toward the final coming together of all things. Immanence is our description of these happenings that were, and are, and are to be in our time and space. In this history God has not willed to be God without this relationship with us and participation in our world.

Immutability

The unchangeableness of God has been vigorously called into question in recent theological discussion. "Immutability" suggests the marks of the Greek philosophical climate — dispassionate and ahistorical. As we have noted, this *apatheia* does not cohere with affirmations about the passion of Christ or the vulnerable responsive love of God intrinsic to the Story.

For all that, the quality of *steadfastness* at the heart of this ancient insistence on the unchanging nature of God is part and parcel of the Gospel. Philosophical categories and aristocratic cultural models of passionlessness do not adequately convey this important conviction that "immutability" intends. Ancient gods were volatile and idiosyncratic (reflecting cultural dispositions and temperament). Ancient theologians were concerned to distinguish their understanding of God from these tendencies, and did so in words that sought to portray the undeviating commitments of God. These cultural borrowings, while preserving the note of constancy, added to it the idea of "impassibility" and prevented the biblical understanding of divine vulnerability and relatedness from reaching theological consciousness. About this we shall say more presently. For now it

239

is important to underscore the divine perseverance. God will not be deflected from the course. While the ways of pursuing the purpose may vary according to the resistance mounted by the world, the divine mind does not change, and the intention to pursue this course to its end point remains unswerving. This Story is about a stubborn God, steadfast in purpose, "immutable" (Ps. 102:27; Mal. 3:6; James 1:17).

All-Sufficiency

The Power of God is able to accomplish the Purpose of God. Herein is the belief in the divine *all-sufficiency*, expressed in three classical "omnis" — omnipresence, omniscience, and omnipotence.

Traditional theology has sometimes expressed the all-sufficiency of God in terms of a speculatively established idea of what a supreme Being ought to be like. Thus notions of power drawn from human experience become the touchstone for defining divine Power. All language in theology bears the marks of its experiential habitat. But the Christian understanding of God is not derived from general human experience, but from the deeds of God done in the midst of that experience. Therefore, our language about God undergoes a transformation in the light of that special history of God with us. We do not extrapolate the meaning of divine all-sufficiency from our experience of human sufficiency. All-sufficiency, then, does not mean a human quality to the nth power, but all-sufficiency as God defines it by the deeds done to accomplish the divine end. We shall interpret the omnis from within the framework of the Story.

Omnipresence: "Where can I flee from thy presence . . ." (Ps. 139:7). God is everywhere we choose to go in flight and in need. God tracks us to the ends of the earth. We are never out of reach. God moves in all things to achieve the divine ends. Nature as well as history, the cosmos in its extent and depth, are penetrated by the Presence. Our discussion of the immanence of God has touched on the range of God through the vastness of outer and inner space. God is there actively bringing Shalom to be. God has all-sufficient presence to assure the divine Purpose (Jer. 23:23-24; Acts 17:27-28).

Omniscience: God has all-sufficient knowledge to assure the divine Purpose. The figure of the all-seeing Eye has been a favorite one in Christian art and interpretation. All that ever has been, touching the divine intention, is within the divine purview (Matt. 10:29-30; Acts 2:23; Rom. 11:33).

Divine knowledge in its all-sufficiency includes not only the awareness of things that have been, and the things that are, but also the things that will be. Divine wisdom includes foreknowledge, forevision. Does the foreknowledge of God mean that all we do is charted and known beforehand? In its strictest construction the omniscience of God includes an omnipotence of God that has foreordained a yet-to-be-executed pattern known by the divine omniscience. In a more modest form, the freedom to choose is really ours, but the all-seeing Eye knows what that choice is to be. If what is to be is to be, the distinction between these two scenarios seems to be little more than verbal.

Genuine human freedom in a narrative response to the divine beckoning requires that those choices must have their own integrity. How so, given the divine omnis? Our choices are hidden, *by God's choice*, even from the divine Eye. Does the belief in the omniscience of God and the all-sufficiency of the divine knowledge require the kind of total exposure assumed by what is usually meant by foreknowledge? That would be so if foreknowledge were our human kind of knowing speculatively extended to its limits. But we have said this rational projection will not control our understanding of the attributes of God. Rather, the frame of reference will be the Story as it unfolds. By this biblical criterion, foreknowledge means the grasp by God of the Future that will be. God both foreknows and foreordains that Shalom shall be — divine election in that encompassing sense. The foreknowledge of God is grounded in the confidence God has in the Power of God, the Holy Spirit, to fulfill the eternal Purpose of God. Further, that foreknowledge must include the range of options the world has to respond to the divine invitation, and therefore the resources God has to deal with those responses. The omniscience of God in this context is the foreknowledge of the possibilities of choice, the scenarios of divine response and the ultimate outcome of the struggle between the human No and the divine Yes. What further is stipulated has more to do with speculation about the Deity than close attention to the Storyline. What has been added over and above these affirmations grows out of a wedding of Christian faith with cultural assumptions about what "omni-ness" ought to mean and is therefore regularly influenced by imperial models of power. This is eminently true of notions of omnipotence, with which we shall presently deal, but its effects are also to be seen here in the understanding of omniscience. Yet any notion of omniscience that takes the Story as its frame of reference must allow for the genuine freedom of the world to maneuver out of the range of the divine reach and for that lively set of moves and countermoves made by God to deal with this flight. All the "omnis" must be understood so as not to constrict the genuine overagainst-ness of the world as that is described in the divine drama. It is a real drama, and not a marionette show.

Omnipotence: "Almighty God . . ." Intrinsic to Christian piety and inseparable from the Christian Story is the belief in the divine om-nipotence. As with the other "omnis" we live with the tension between the world's conceptions of all-ness and the understanding of it from the perspective of the Christian faith, or more exactly, how the metaphors of absoluteness drawn from human experience are transmuted by the revela-tion in Jesus Christ. The significance of this transmutation comes forcefully home in our conception of the divine omnipotence. And around the issue of theodicy the Christian meaning of the power of God takes its clearest form.

By extrapolating from a fragmentary human experience of power — the capacity to influence things — we interpret divine omnipotence to mean the power to effect and control all things. But this abstract notion of total power, if pressed to the limit, contradicts certain fundamental assumptions about God: Omnipotence cannot mean the power of God to sin, lie, or die, to draw a straighter line than that between two points, to make two and two equal five, and to make wrong right. Definitions of divine power must be commensurate with who God is.

Other givens than those mentioned also must be taken into account in understanding omnipotence in Christian context. One of these is the narrative framework for understanding power. A genuine drama, a real struggle, entails the world's defiance of God's intention. Omnipotence cannot be conceived as an instant control everywhere. "Allness" of power has to do instead with a time line pointed toward a goal and climax. The almightiness of Deity is that God *shall* be all in all. And more, that on this time line God is even now proceeding toward this consummation of the divine purpose.

In conventional ideas about omnipotence, human notions are regu-larly projected into the Story. In the ancient world the Oriental potentate furnished the model of omnipotence, and so God becomes the one who by fiat and force exercises immediate and universal sway. At work here as well are machismo assumptions from a patriarchal society. But God is neither an autocratic regent nor a take-charge Western sheriff. The Creator does not act by force or fiat but by a vulnerable Love. Indeed, this Redeemer and Consummator shall be "all in all," but only so along a journey of stubborn Love that stretches into eternity itself.

When omnipotence is understood in this framework, and therefore eschatologically, the agonizing question of theodicy is put in perspective. Implicit in the traditional formulation of the "problem of evil" by Epicurus in the third century B.C. was the assumption of divine omnipotence according to the model of imperial (and masculine) sovereignty. This assumption has been unquestioned in much of the subsequent discussion of how the three themes in theodicy — the power of God, the goodness of God, and the reality of evil — can be reconciled. No wonder the insistent question: What kind of God tolerates or ordains such horrendous historical, natural, and personal evil? This quandary assumes a god made in our image of power. The God of this Story, not our own tale, is One who gives freedom to the creature to respond to the Creator. The power of God expressed in the act of creation was not only the power of creativity, but also of self-limitation. God willed the world to have a fiatless freedom. Life together is real only if freely chosen. Divine love does not program its responses. The self-limitation of God is the risk that the world will say No. The history of God and the world is the biblical account of what God does about the abuse of that freedom. Its center point is the act of ultimate vulnerability when God plunges into the world at Incarnation and receives the ultimate rebuke on the cross. Yet in so receiving it, God displays the sovereign power of this vulnerable love by overcoming on the cross and in the resurrection the resistance of sin, evil, and death, and beginning the process of winning the world in fact as well as in principle. "God's weakness is stronger than human strength" (1 Cor. 1:25 NRSV). The recalcitrance of the world shall be met and God shall overcome. This eschatological conquest includes the transformation of time and space and thus the final redemption of the world from sin and evil and their issue, death. Almighty God has all the power necessary to fulfill this divine purpose. What kind of power that is — vulnerable Love — and how that power is exercised — on a time line and in a drama — are determined by those data of Christian faith and not our images of potency. The word in the Christian vocabulary for this power is the *Holy Spirit*. God as the Power to fulfill the Purpose is the ultimate meaning of omnipotence in the Christian Story, the Spirit of the Son and the Father, and therefore the Spirit of suffering Love.

The narrative treatment of Christian doctrine, as well as the view of omnipotence developed here, has its implication for understanding the concept of election. In our discussion of the Trinity we viewed foreordination in the broad sense as the divine determination and promise to fulfill the primal vision — through tension to resolution. But narrative as such, and the specific epic we have seen developing from creation to consummation, and especially touching the meaning of divine power, points us in a special direction for the understanding of personal election. No conception of foreordination that empties Christian teaching of movement, tension, or purpose fits the saga we have watched unfold. The divine vulnerability that makes possible the real action and actors engaged in real drama cannot be reconciled with overbearing views of Deity shaped by cultural assumptions of either political or sexual hegemony. Thus a supralapsarian conception of election, in which before creation some are marked out for salvation and others for damnation, is ruled out, for the dynamic interplay of narrative character and events is rendered a charade. The infralapsarian view has a place for some of the moves and countermoves of narrative by placing election after creation and a self-determining fall. But it also closets drama to the time and place of an ancient decision settling all accounts, evacuating thereby the historic dynamism of the rest of the biblical narrative from creation to consummation. The same denarrativizing is to be found in modern neo-universalisms, which hold that all humanity is elected in Jesus Christ, both in fact and in principle. An alternative to the gridlock of these double- and single-destination views treats election confessionally as "truth for me," the poetry of the experience of grace. As such it speaks the language of drama and its openness, but at the same time it reduces Christian claims to "symbolic truth," neglecting the assertional content of "the truth of the symbol."

Does narrative drive us finally to stress openness and the role of personal choice so much that election itself is rendered either inoperative or innocuous in meaning? No, for *biblical* narrative requires us to hold together the Power of the Purpose of God, the Spirit of the Son that bears the story along and assures its consummation, with the genuine elements of openness and resistance that constitute narrative action. We therefore confront the same paradox we have met already in our analyses of Incarnation and grace. Here it expresses itself as an election of persons as well as purpose, which brings together the divine and human decisions in an inextricable and mysterious unity. We can explore but we cannot finally explain this double affirmation. The history of the controversy about election is strewn with the abortive explanations that stress foreordination to the exclusion of freedom, and vice versa. Biblical narrative on the one hand insists on the openness of the future, and on the other on the God who guides it to its proper end according to divine power and purpose, and not our will and ways.

Material Qualities

Shalom

The purpose that emerges from the events of the Story, the content that fills the formal attributes of God, is the Vision of peace and freedom. Running like a red thread through the narrative is the beckoning of God. This invitation presupposes the freedom of the world to respond, a gift of answerability granted in creation. The gift is given with the goal of communion in view. The freely chosen life together of God and the world is the end of this vast adventure.

The clarity of the purpose and promise of Shalom comes to us in the prophetic tradition (Ezek. 34:25-29; Isa. 32:16-17). In the prophet's imagery, the Vision is portrayed against the background of the world's resistance to the divine intent: swords beaten into plowshares, wolf and lamb together, the child with its hand over the viper's nest. Similarly the patriarch's Law is couched in "thou shalt nots," which also assume the resistance of the world. The Vision comes to us in our ambiguous history in struggle with the enemies that have arisen to contest the divine purpose, and as overcoming the alienation that has set in between the world and God. The primal Vision of freedom and peace becomes, after the fall, the hope of liberation and reconciliation. God's Yes related to the world's No becomes liberation from the bondage of sin, evil, and death and the reconciliation of humanity, nature, and God.

Implicit in the Vision of God as it expresses itself in the history of God and as interpreted by the biblical seers are certain fundamental originating attributes. The purpose of Shalom is rooted in qualities in the abysmal selfhood of God. If Shalom is the goal of the history of God, what is this ground of the history of God?

Love

The will-to-Shalom is the divine Love. Love is the caring intention from which the creation and redemption of the world arise. The Love of God brings the world to be, preserves it, enters into enemy territory, suffers its worst assaults, and never lets it go.

The depths of this Love are revealed in the face of the heights of our resistance to it. The divine Love is not only the quest for community with the world, but the faithful pursuit that is undeterred by the lovelessness of its object. God loves the enemies that break the divine heart. God loves the sinner. Here is in-spite-of, unconditional, unmerited Agape. The history of God is carried by this undeviating Agape. The history of God is carried by this undeviating Agape, receiving into itself the world's hates and hurts. This is the Love that "bears all things . . ." but "never ends" (1 Cor. 13). As such it is gracious Love, going before the world, and not turned aside by whatever No may be said.

The care spilled out unreservedly on the world in each chapter of the Christian Story is a Love constitutive of the divine Life itself. This Love expressed in the missions of God from creation to consummation is a Love finally grounded in the inner-trinitarian Life itself. God is the Life Together of Father, Son, and Holy Spirit. The Persons are in such loving interrelationship that the Three *are* One. God is sociality, community, coinherence, coequality — perfect Love. The "immanent Trinity" is the basis for the "economic Trinity." What we encounter in the deeds of God comes ultimately from the relationships within the Godhead. Within and without, "God is love" (John 3:16; 1 John 4:8-12).

Holiness

Divine love is not divine indulgence. The God who invites response is the God who holds the world responsible. God holds accountable those who choose to turn aside. We have to do with a *righteous* God, a *holy* Love.

The accountability intrinsic to invitation is manifest in the judgment

246

of God that attends rebellious response. The wages of sin and evil are death. Our resistance earns the rebuke of God in the darkening of the image of God in us and our loss of perception of the grace of God around us. Human sin in alliance with the fallen powers and principalities brings in its wake historical movements of a Providence that casts the mighty from their seats and calls to account those who grind the faces of the poor. The Providence that watches over our history brings judgment on recalcitrant selves and societies. Such is the "wrath of God." The boundary set to the limits of rebellion is at work in both self and society as the "law of love" that takes its toll on the imperial ego or nation; "love or perish." The wrath of God in the central chapter of the Christian Story is the bar of judgment on Calvary. Here the world is called to account for its assault on the Hope of God. It appears again at the Last Judgment. The divine righteousness brooks no challenge to its claims. No understanding of the love of God does justice to the deeds of God that does not also include the holiness of God (Deut. 32:4; 1 Pet. 1:16; Rev. 4:8).

Suffering

How can the just and judging God persist in love in the face of the world's rejection of the gracious invitation? This enigma has produced the predictable alternatives that sacrifice either love or holiness: either God is finally holy and therefore an unloving consigner of the adjudged to the everlasting fires, or God is loving and withdraws the judgment that rebellion merits. At the center of the Christian saga there is a more profound wrestling with this mystery. On the cross judgment does fall on the world. Yet we do not receive it, for it falls instead on the One who comes among us. God suffers our punishment in the Person of Jesus Christ. The Vision of Shalom dies. Yet as a seed falls into the ground and is transformed (1 Cor. 15:36), so the death in God of the divine Dream is transmuted into one reborn in suffering Love. The broken heart of God carries the world to its reunion with its purpose. Suffering Love is triumphant Love. The divine grace is not a cheap overlooking of our recalcitrance, but a costly love whose passion takes into itself the pain of our punishment. In the language of Luther, on the cross the blessing of God overcomes the curse, the love of God receives into itself the wrath of God. A suffering and triumphant Love bears the world toward its promised End. Suffering

Agape is the ground and Shalom is the goal of the history of God (Rom. 8:32; 2 Cor. 5:19; 1 Pet. 1:19-20; Rev. 13:8).

Mystery and Meaning

Our understanding of the divine attributes comes to us as God acts in our history, as those deeds are perceived and interpreted for us by the biblical prophet and apostle, and as they are illuminated in the Church's experience and our own encounter with reality. The words and images we use to convey these understandings are taken from our language and experience of presence, knowledge, power, love, justice, suffering. As such they carry with them all the limitations of the human matrix. Faith distinguishes them by an increase of magnitude — thus our impotence compared to God's omnipotence — and more important by reverse of their common valuations — our calculating love compared to God's unconditional Agape. Thus our words capture something of the meaning of the deeds of God, enough to allow us to see through the glass of vision what God has done, is doing, and will do, enough to bring us to our knees in repentance, faith, and adoration. The discipline of theology serves as a resource to the preaching and teaching Church, the believer, and the inquirer, so that by the power of the Spirit that glass may be diaphanous to the divine Glory.

Yet when the whole Story is told and all efforts at theological clarification are made, we confess to seeing through a glass darkly. This epic adventure is not over: only at the consummation do we see "face to face." What we say about the being and doing of God for now is in terms of the figures of time, not eternity. The biblical idiom is always normative for Christian theology, but the prophetic-apostolic testimony even in its privileged role is "the language of Canaan," rooted in its historical setting. And the retellings of the old, old Story in the translations of contemporaneity have their manifest fragility and transiency. Thus whatever recounting is done will never exhaust the heights and depths of the divine Truth. We are given enough Light to make our way, but we can make no claim to have penetrated the full reaches of that Glory. Living in this Pauline penumbra, we must finally echo the Apostle's words: "O depths of wealth, wisdom, and knowledge in God! How unsearchable his judgments, how untraceable his ways! Who knows the mind of the Lord? . . . Source, Guide, and Goal of all that is — to him be glory forever! Amen" (Rom. 11:33-34, 36).

Appendix 1

How the Dawn Came: *A Short Story*

In the beginning, God had a dream. The world is bathed in the divine Light. Creation and Creator are at one. There is joy and peace in Eden.

Some have pictured it as a campfire scene. God is the roaring blaze. Humanity is a circle of dancers, arms linked, eyes watching each other, at home in the silent woods, celebrating the fire-Light.

But reality shatters the dream. The people love Night more than Light. So all in the circle spin around on their heels, drawn by the Powers of Darkness. The about-face breaks the bonds. Facing outward, the people can't find each other anymore. Nor can they see the Light. Nature takes on a fearsome look as the distorted shadows of the lonely dancers play on the forest round about. This is not what God wanted! The "wages of sin" are the death of the dream.

The dream, though, will not die. A spark from the blaze finds its way to each dancer. An inner light keeps alive God's Hope. In each there is a flickering "image of God." Will that glow turn the world around?

God's long-suffering Love will not let us go. More light comes — a rainbow sign! A promise that God will not give up on us. And more — a path shown to a promised land . . . and a people called! The breath of God blows on a spark and brings into being a "pillar of fire" to lead Israel away from Night toward the true Light. To this people comes the law of a new land, commandments of turning to God and neighbor. In the people's midst rises a company of visionaries — prophets, seers of Light.

They point to freedom and peace — Shalom — a world where the circle is reknit, where swords are beaten into plowshares, where wolf and lamb lie down together!

But the people wander and go astray. Their prophets declare that the Day of the Lord will be Darkness, not Light.

Yet God keeps promises. Shalom *will* come to pass!

What will turn our willful world around? Sparks and pillars do not do it. We must be found *firsthand.*

The people who walk in darkness see a great Light. The dream becomes *flesh* and dwells among us, "full of grace and truth." Light shines in the face of Jesus Christ! We behold its glory. Shalom is born in Bethlehem . . . and lives in Galilee. The sick are healed. Justice is done. Sin is forgiven. Good News is preached. Hope is rekindled. The Realm of God is *here* as well as near. Christ our Liberator has come! Christ is our peace — the Light of the *world.*

When Light comes close to those in the grip of gloom, it sears the flesh. Shalom in our midst shames our shut-up ways. Love's coals burn the enemies of Light. The disarrayed dancers recoil. The powers of evil brace for battle. On a lonely hill, Night again descends; Christ is crucified; the Dream dies.

"On the first day of the week, at early dawn, they came to the tomb. . . ." Empty! Death can*not* bury the Dream! On the cross, the powers of death meet their match! Sin is forgiven! Easter heralds the defeat of Night. Christ is risen . . . a new *Day* breaks.

The Dawnburst makes its mark. Its rays warm the backs of the wandering dancers. Some slowly turn . . . and sight the Sun. They see the Light!

With Light comes Life. They live by its power, in faith — trusting in the mercy of God, hoping for the Not Yet, pilgrims on a new path.

An about-face to the Horizon brings new vision. Dawn People discern the neighbor in need. They see *by the Light* as well as *see the Light.* And they cannot pass by the wretched of the earth.

Dawnlight brings pilgrims together. They see the brother and sister in Christ as well as the forgotten and forlorn. No solo travelers; they form a family. And to others they call, "Come join us to see this Light and follow this Way!"

Dawn is not Noonday. There are still shadows on the land. Sin persists and death is our common lot. The promise fills the sky, but the meridian when all the clouds are gone awaits a Yet to Be.

As we live in the half-light of an already–not yet, God's Story merges with our stories. We now become characters in the unfolding plot — seeing the Light, seeing our companions in it, seeing the victims on the Jericho road *by* it, and pointing others *to* it.

And so unfolds the marvelous Story we have to tell, the song we have to sing:

> The darkness shall turn to the dawning,
> And the dawning to noonday bright.
> And Christ's great kingdom shall come to earth,
> The kingdom of love and light!

Appendix 2

The Revival of Systematics

Since the publication of the 1984 edition of *The Christian Story*, over fifty full-scale systematic theologies have appeared in English, variously identified as "systematics," "dogmatics," "introductions," or "constructive theology." Each work, like this one, attempts to cover all the basic topics of Christian belief.[1] Given the diversity today in both church and society, they do it from a variety of perspectives. In this Appendix to the third edition, a survey and interpretation of the systematics revival in English-language works replaces the bibliography that appeared in earlier editions.

Why the widespread interest in the comprehensive study of Christian teaching? Why so, when in the recent heyday of "secular theology," and in our more current "postmodern" period, systematic theology is said to be either unnecessary, wrong, or impossible?

One reason has already been given in the Introduction: the need for pastors and teachers to help parishioners in understanding the church's

1. For a survey of this phenomenon, see the author's essays "The Surge in Systematics: A Commentary on Current Works," *Journal of Religion* 73, no. 2 (April 1993): 223-37 and "In Quest of the Comprehensive: The Systematics Revival," *Religious Studies Review* 2, no. 1 (January 1994): 7-12.

---

*The substance of this survey appeared in *Interpretation* 69, no. 2 (April, 1995).

faith in a time of the vigorous advocacy of *other* worldviews. So the cry from the heart in many congregations: speak about our own basics![2] The growth of congregations' seasonal and long-term study groups on the essentials of Christian faith is a sign of the times. The surge of new volumes in the field of systematics is an important resource for pastors and teachers in their work on the theological ABCs.

A second reason for the revival of systematic theology is implicit in the first. The quest for Christian self-understanding is inseparable from knowledge of the theological heritage. Loss of identity in the church is like amnesia in persons. Finding out who one is, in either case, means recovering one's memory. Our identity as Christian believers is bound up with the retrieval of historic faith. While systematic theology is more than that — having to do with present interpretation as well as the recovery of past identity — it gives attention to all the standard topics, the *loci communes* — the "common places" of historic teaching. In this work, the "loci" are described as *chapters* in the Christian Story. As such, they follow the course of Scripture, the flow in the historic creeds and confessions of the church, the beliefs that are part and parcel of our worship and hymnody. These are the topics covered in the writing of systematics/dogmatics over the centuries. Even with our present theological diversity, they turn out to be the same subjects dealt with in all the new books in systematic theology.

A third reason for the current interest in basic theology is a natural companion to the first two. Identity is not only who we were, but who we *are*. We live in the *now*, not the *then*. Christian convictions have to be communicated in the setting of our own time and place. As circumstances change, what has been said about church basics earlier and elsewhere has to be interpreted anew.

The towering figures who did that interpreting in the earlier decades of the twentieth century — Barth, Brunner, and Tillich, for example — are gone, and no new giants have appeared. What we do have in the new momentum in systematics is a generation of teachers, many of them senior or mid-career, most of whom are responsible for introductory courses in theology in their schools, who believe the time has come to restate the ancient

2. Dorothy and Gabriel Fackre, *Christian Basics* (Grand Rapids: Eerdmans, 1991, 1992, 1993) with a video course based on the book produced by Andover Newton Theological School.

faith in terms of the challenges of this day and age. And the very character of our time as pluralistic — many traditions and points of view jostling one another — accounts for the outpouring of *different* approaches to theology.

The updating and "contextualizing" of the essentials has prompted the relabeling of systematics as "constructive theology" in some quarters. This description suggests a point of view that gives pride of place to the contemporary context. As such, it is a signal of a *type* of systematics among the variety to be discussed. In any case, all the projects in this field have taken rise from the desire to have the faith *understandable* as well as *recoverable*.[3]

Types of Systematic Theology

The Christian Story takes its place as a conversation partner around the new, lively and ever-enlarging table of current systematic theologies. To locate its seat, we examine some of the other place cards. The participants and points of view fall into three categories. Using self-designations found in many of the current works, they sort out into *evangelical, ecumenical,* and *experiential* types. We do not deal directly in this introductory book with either the theologians or their works, but they will appear in the succeeding volumes on specific doctrines.

Evangelical Systematics

In the sixteenth century, the word "evangelical" described the mainstream Reformation churches, and it still does in the names of some national churches. Evangelical faith was marked by its formal and material principles: the authority of Scripture and justification by grace through faith. "Evangelical" today refers to a subsequent movement shaped by pietism, the Great Awakenings, and revivalism that intensified and interiorized

---

3. Two of the four features of the teaching of systematics in seminaries and university divinity schools discovered in the writer's research are "retrieval" and "contemporaneity." The other two are commitment to the church as the context of systematic theology and the fact of diversity. See the writer's "Reorientation and Retrieval in Seminary Theology," *The Christian Century* 108, no. 20 (June 26–July 3, 1991): 653-56.

these two Reformation principles. Contemporary evangelicalism is characterized by (1) strict allegiances to and interpretations of Scripture and (2) intense personal appropriation of justifying faith in a "born again" experience.[4] For all the variety — from evangelistically oriented to "justice and peace" emphases in matters of mission; from "inerrantists" to "infallibilists" in biblical interpretation; from premillennial to postmillennial and amillennial views (and their variations) in eschatology — the *commonalities* of rigorous biblical authority and personally intense soteriological piety continue to be defining characteristics of modern evangelicalism.[5]

Self-identified evangelical systematicians were among the pioneers of the current systematics recovery. (G. C. Berkouwer's volumes on individual Christian doctrines preceded the current outpouring, but he is, arguably, ranked among the earlier "giants.")[6] While evangelicalism's premier theologian, Carl Henry, did not begin his *God, Revelation and Authority* as a systematics, it turned out to look very much like one by volumes five and six, covering as it did almost all the standard topics.[7] In 1978, Donald Bloesch's two-volume *Essentials of Evangelical Theology* appeared and was widely used by evangelical pastors.[8] Currently, Bloesch is at work on a new seven-volume systematic series, *Christian Foundations,* with the first two volumes now in print: *A Theology of Word and Spirit: Authority and Method* and *Holy Scripture: Revelation, Inspiration and Interpretation.*[9] About the same time as the works of Henry and Bloesch, Dale Moody wrote *The Word of Truth* with a breadth of scholarship that gave it entree

---

4. See the writer's "Evangelical, Evangelicalism," *The Westminster Dictionary of Christian Theology,* ed. Alan Richardson and John Bowden, rev. ed. (Philadelphia: Westminster Press, 1983), 191-92.

5. For an examination of a range of views in the interpretation of Scripture, see *The Christian Story,* vol. 2, *Authority: Scripture in the Church for the World* (Grand Rapids: Eerdmans, 1987), 60-156.

6. G. C. Berkouwer, *Studies in Dogmatics* (Grand Rapids: Eerdmans, 1962–1976).

7. Carl Henry, *God, Revelation and Authority,* vols. 1-6 (Waco: Word Publishing Co., 1976–1983).

8. Donald Bloesch, *Essentials of Evangelical Theology,* vols. 1-2 (San Francisco: Harper & Row, 1978, 1979).

9. Donald Bloesch, *A Theology of Word and Spirit: Authority and Method* (Downers Grove, IL: InterVarsity, 1992) and *Holy Scripture: Revelation, Inspiration and Interpretation* (Downers Grove, IL: InterVarsity, 1994).

well beyond the Baptist seminaries for which it was intended.[10] Shortly after these earlier ventures, Millard Erickson wrote *Christian Theology*, a learned, three-volume work, currently more widely used as a required text in systematics in evangelical seminaries than any other.[11]

These initial ventures were succeeded in the late 1980s and early 1990s by a number of substantial evangelical works, some of them multi-volume, and each with a special angle or audience. Paul Jewett wrote the substantial first volume, *God, Creation and Revelation,* of a projected series cut short by his untimely death, including sermons by a pastor, Marguerite Shuster, to illustrate doctrinal themes.[12] The first volume of James Leo Garrett Jr.'s carefully developed two-volume *Systematic Theology* came out about the same time, directed to both a Southern Baptist audience and a broader constituency; and the second followed five years later.[13] Gordon R. Lewis and Bruce A. Demarest coauthored the three-volume *Integrative Theology,* representing an attempt to bring systematic interests together with biblical, historical, apologetic, and cultural concerns.[14] Biblical scholar Wayne Grudem, with a stress on the accessibility of doctrine in hymns, worship, and general application, wrote *Systematic Theology: An Introduction to Biblical Doctrine.*[15] Coauthors Alan F. Johnson and Robert E. Webber in *What Christians Believe* also sought to blend historical, biblical, and systematic areas of inquiry.[16] Robert Lightner took up premillennial interests in *Evangelical Theology: A Survey and Review.*[17]

---

10. Dale Moody, *The Word of Truth: A Summary of Christian Doctrine Based on Biblical Revelation* (Grand Rapids: Eerdmans, 1981).

11. Millard Erickson, *Christian Theology,* vols. 1-3 (Grand Rapids: Baker Book House, 1983–1985). The wide use of these volumes was discovered in the writer's earlier cited research.

12. Paul K. Jewett, *God, Creation & Revelation: A Neo-Evangelical Theology.* With sermons by Marguerite Shuster (Grand Rapids: Eerdmans, 1991).

13. James Leo Garrett, Jr., *Systematic Theology: Biblical, Historical and Systematic,* vols. 1, 2 (Grand Rapids: Eerdmans, 1990, 1995).

14. Gordon R. Lewis and Bruce A. Demarest, *Integrative Theology,* vols. 1-3 (Grand Rapids: Zondervan, 1987, 1990, 1994).

15. Wayne A. Grudem, *Systematic Theology: An Introduction to Biblical Doctrine* (Grand Rapids: HarperZondervan, 1994).

16. Alan F. Johnson and Robert E. Webber, *What Christians Believe: A Biblical and Historical Summary* (Grand Rapids: Zondervan, 1989).

17. Robert Lightner, *Evangelical Theology: A Survey and Review* (Grand Rapids: Baker, 1990).

James Montgomery Boice's earlier *Foundations of Christian Faith* came out in a revised edition in 1986.[18]

Some evangelical works have very explicit ecclesial frameworks. William W. Menzies and Stanley M. Horton's *Bible Doctrines* was written from "A Pentecostal Perspective."[19] Richard Rice's mid-1980s volume, *The Reign of God*, stressed its "Seventh-Day Adventist Perspective."[20] William J. Rodman's ambitious three-volume systematics, *Renewal Theology*, was written "From a Charismatic Perspective."[21] The earlier-mentioned works by Moody and Garrett were in the Southern Baptist tradition. Stanley Grenz's *Theology for the Community of God*, while introducing an evangelical audience to Pannenbergian themes, is a self-consciously Baptist work.[22] A. J. Conyers's *A Basic Christian Theology* stands in the same Southern Baptist tradition.[23] R. J. Rushdoony defends a "reconstructionist" reading of the Calvinist tradition in his two-volume *Systematic Theology*.[24]

The quality of current evangelical scholarship is getting increasing recognition in the academy. In the field of systematics, for example, British theologian Alister McGrath was commissioned by Blackwell to write *Christian Theology: An Introduction,* now serving as a historical theology/systematics text in commonwealth universities.[25] He is also currently writing a multi-volume work in systematics.

18. James Montgomery Boice, *Foundations of Christian Faith,* rev. ed. (Downers Grove, IL: InterVarsity Press, 1986).

19. William W. Menzies with Stanley M. Horton, gen. ed., *Bible Doctrines: A Pentecostal Perspective* (Springfield, MO: Logion Press, 1993).

20. Richard Rice, *The Reign of God : An Introduction to Christian Theology from a Seventh-Day Adventist Perspective* (Berrien Springs, MI: Andrews University Press, 1985).

21. William J. Rodman, *Renewal Theology: God, the World, and Redemption; Systematic Theology from a Charismatic Perspective,* vol. 1; *Salvation, the Holy Spirit and Christian Living,* vol. 2; *The Church, the Kingdom, and Last Things,* vol. 3 (Grand Rapids: Zondervan, 1988, 1990, 1992).

22. Stanley Grenz, *Theology for the Community of God* (Nashville: Broadman and Holman, 1994).

23. A. J. Conyers, *A Basic Christian Theology* (Nashville: Broadman & Holman, 1995).

24. Rousas John Rushdoony, *Systematic Theology,* 2 vols. (Vallecito, CA: Ross House Books, 1994).

25. Alister E. McGrath, *Christian Theology: An Introduction* (Oxford: Blackwell, 1993).

Ecumenical Systematics

About the same time that evangelicals returned to this genre, "ecumenicals" also showed new interest in theology-in-the-round. An ecumenical systematics strives to honor the historic faith and its biblical grounding, but gives extended attention as well to the contemporary context and enters actively the current ecumenical exchange.[26]

As Berkouwer anticipated the ecumenical revival, two other continental authors ventured on the systematics task in major multi-volume works, Helmut Thielicke's *The Evangelical Faith* and Otto Weber's *Foundations of Dogmatics.*[27] Hendrikus Berkhof, long active in the ecumenical movement, sought to restate Reformed theology in contemporary idiom in his 1978 *Christian Faith,* a durable work now in a revised edition.[28] Later, Jan Milic Lochman wrote a self-designated "ecumenical dogmatics," *The Faith We Confess.* [29] In this country, Owen Thomas wrote *Introduction to Theology* from an Anglican point of view, with a subsequent companion piece, *Theological Questions.*[30] Geoffrey Wainwright, a key drafter of ecumenical documents (among them sections of *Baptism, Eucharist and Ministry*), wrote the one-volume *Doxology* as a systematics in a worship framework.[31] The first edition of *The Christian Story* in 1978 was part of this initial foray in the field.[32]

The ecumenical momentum went forward throughout the 1980s and continues to the present time. Systematic works in specific ecclesial traditions have become a feature of ecumenical as well as evangelical

---

26. Ironically, in spite of professions of ecumenicity, the theological reach of much ecumenical systematic theology does not engage the work of evangelical theologians.

27. Helmut Thielicke, *The Evangelical Faith,* vols. 1-3, trans. and ed. Geoffrey W. Bromiley (Grand Rapids: Eerdmans, 1974–1982): Otto Weber, *Foundations of Dogmatics,* vols. 1-2, trans. Darrell L. Gruder (Grand Rapids: Eerdmans, 1981, 1983).

28. Hendrikus Berkhof, *Christian Faith: An Introduction to the Study of the Faith,* trans. Sierd Woudstra (Grand Rapids: Eerdmans, 1979, 1986).

29. Jan Milic Lochman, *The Faith We Confess: An Ecumenical Dogmatics,* trans. David Lewis (Philadelphia: Fortress Press, 1984).

30. Owen C. Thomas, *Introduction to Theology* (Cambridge: Green, Hadden & Co., 1973; Wilton, CT: Morehouse-Barlow Co., 1983) and *Theological Questions: Analysis and Argument* (Wilton, CT: Morehouse-Barlow Co., 1983).

31. Geoffrey Wainwright, *Doxology* (Oxford: Oxford University Press, 1980).

32. Gabriel Fackre, *The Christian Story: A Narrative Interpretation of Basic Christian Doctrine* (Grand Rapids: Eerdmans, 1978, 1984).

systematics. One of the first of these was the two-volume *Christian Dogmatics,* edited by Carl Braaten and Robert Jenson and written with eight other Lutheran authors.[33] *Responsible Faith,* a one-volume systematics by Hans Schwarz, was another Lutheran contribution.[34] The 1993 *God–The World's Future* by Ted Peters, a self-declared "postmodern" effort, reflects its Lutheran matrix.[35] Daniel Migliore, in dialogue with liberation theologies, writes as a Reformed theologian in *Faith Seeking Understanding.*[36] John Leith's *Basic Christian Doctrine* is also a systematics in Reformed perspective, grounded in the author's long-time work in the history of doctrine.[37] Gordon Spykman's *Reformational Theology* stands in the Calvinist stream, appropriating the Dutch Christian philosophical and cultural traditions of Abraham Kuyper and Herman Dooyeweerd.[38] Anglican bishop Hugh Montefiore writes out of his tradition in *Credible Christianity,* but with the concerns of the "Gospel and Culture" movement associated with Lesslie Newbigin.[39]

Roman Catholic systematics had its fresh start also in the late 1970s. Karl Rahner, while numbered among the great figures of the century for his many publications and great influence, never wrote a Roman Catholic *summa* comparable to Barth's *Dogmatics.* But his 1978 *Foundations of Christian Faith,* with its philosophical prolegomenon, helped to launch a parallel systematics recovery and reinterpretation in Roman Catholic circles.[40] Richard McBrien's *Catholicism,* just re-published in a revised edition, has had a large academic and church readership, with its effort to bring the *aggiornamento* program of Vatican II into the teaching of doc-

33. Carl E. Braaten and Robert W. Jenson, eds., *Christian Dogmatics,* vols. 1, 2 (Philadelphia: Fortress Press, 1984).

34. Hans Schwarz, *Responsible Faith: Christian Theology in the Light of Twentieth Century Questions* (Minneapolis: Augsburg, 1986).

35. Ted Peters, *God — The World's Future: Systematic Theology for a Postmodern Era* (Minneapolis: Fortress, 1992).

36. Daniel L. Migliore, *Faith Seeking Understanding: An Introduction to Systematic Theology* (Grand Rapids: Eerdmans, 1991).

37. John Leith, *Basic Christian Doctrine* (Louisville: Westminster/John Knox, 1993).

38. Gordon Spykman, *Reformational Theology: A New Paradigm for Doing Theology* (Grand Rapids: Eerdmans, 1992).

39. Hugh Montefiore, *Credible Christianity: The Gospel in Contemporary Society* (Grand Rapids: Eerdmans, 1994).

40. Karl Rahner, *Foundations of Christian Faith: An Introduction to the Idea of Christianity,* trans. William B. Dych (New York: Seabury Press, 1978).

trine.[41] More recently, Frans Jozef van Beeck has begun a multi-volume work in Roman Catholic systematics linking "creed, code and cult."[42] Francis Schüssler Fiorenza and John Galvin assembled a group of leading Roman Catholic theologians (Avery Dulles, Catherine Mowry LaCugna, David Tracy, and others) to write on the major doctrines in the two-volume *Systematic Theology: Roman Catholic Perspectives.*[43] More recently, Avery Dulles engages a range of Christian thinkers from the fathers to the twentieth-century giants and then offers his own "systematics synthesis" in *The Assurance of Things Hoped For.* [44]

Other ecumenical works alongside Roman Catholic and magisterial Reformation traditions have appeared. Thomas Finger's two-volume *Christian Theology: An Eschatological Approach* stands in the left-wing Reformation stream.[45] James McClendon, Jr.'s two-volumes, *Systematic Theology: Ethics* and *Doctrine,* draw on a Baptist heritage.[46] Michael Pomazansky writes out of the Eastern Orthodox tradition in *Orthodox Dogmatic Theology.*[47]

"Ecumenical systematics" is obviously a capacious rubric. Some who place themselves within it stretch the boundaries toward either the evangelical or the experiential type on either side. One self-defined ecumenical, Thomas Oden, gives a "paleo-orthodox" turn to most Christian doctrines in his three-volume *Systematic Theology,* drawing primarily on patristic, medieval, and Reformation writers and questioning much contemporary effort in reinterpretation.[48] On the other hand, a wing of ecumenical theology that

41. Richard McBrien, *Catholicism* (Oak Grove, MN: Winston Press, 1981); rev. ed. (San Francisco: HarperCollins, 1994).

42. Frans Jozef van Beeck, *God Encountered: A Contemporary Catholic Systematic Theology: Understanding the Christian Faith,* vol. 1 (New York: Harper and Row, 1988); *God Encountered: The Revelation of the Glory,* vol. 2, part 1: *Fundamental Theology* (Collegeville, MN: Liturgical Press, 1993).

43. Francis Schüssler Fiorenza and John P. Galvin, eds., *Systematic Theology: Roman Catholic Perspectives,* 2 vols. (Minneapolis: Fortress Press, 1991).

44. Avery Dulles, *The Assurance of Things Hoped For: A Theology of Christian Faith* (New York: Oxford University Press, 1994).

45. Thomas Finger, *Christian Theology: An Eschatological Approach,* 2 vols. (Scottdale, PA: Herald Press, 1985, 1987).

46. James Wm. McClendon, Jr., *Ethics: A Systematic Theology* and *Doctrine: Systematic Theology* (Nashville: Abingdon Press, 1986, 1994).

47. Michael Pomazansky, *Orthodox Dogmatic Theology,* trans. Seraphim Rose (Wichita, KS: Eight Day Books, 1994).

48. Thomas Oden, *The Living God: Systematic Theology,* vol. 1; *The Word of Life:*

finds a significant place for Scripture and tradition also gives major attention to one or another aspect of contemporary experience. Gustavo Gutiérrez both pioneered in the systematics recovery and sought to reconstruct Roman Catholic theology in the context of Latin-American struggles for justice in his groundbreaking *Liberation Theology.*[49] With like concern for contextuality, but in North American Hispanic purview, is Justo Gonzalez's systematics cum history, *Manana: Christian Theology from a Hispanic Persepctive.*[50] Fred Herzog in *God-Walk*[51] and Douglas John Hall in his projected trilogy, *Thinking the Faith, Professing the Faith,* and *Confessing the Faith*[52] are striving to situate classical faith in the North American context in dialogue with liberation concerns. Christopher Morse's *Not Every Spirit* underscores the "disbeliefs" required by Christian faithfulness, with special attention to issues of gender and sexuality.[53] Currents in philosophy play a large role in some ecumenical works, as in the influence of process thought in Kenneth Cauthen's *Systematic Theology: A Modern Protestant Approach*[54] and Langdon Gilkey's *Message and Existence.*[55] The widely used seminary textbook edited by Peter C. Hodgson and Robert H. King, *Christian Theology: An Introduction to its Traditions and Tasks,* includes writers who fall in both the ecumenical and experiential categories, depending on the extent to which today's experience requires a "new paradigm" for systematics.[56]

Notable among ecumenical theologians writing now in this genre

Systematic Theology, vol. 2; *Life in the Spirit: Systematic Theology,* vol. 3 (San Francisco: Harper & Row, 1987, 1989, 1992).

49. Gustavo Gutiérrez, *A Theology of Liberation: History, Politics and Salvation,* trans. and ed. Sister Caridad Inda and John Eagleson (Maryknoll, NY: Orbis, 1973, 1988).

50. Justo L. Gonzalez, *Manana: Christian Theology from a Hispanic Perspective.* Foreword by Virgilio P. Elizondo (Nashville: Abingdon Press, 1990).

51. Fred Herzog, *God-Walk: Liberation Shaping Dogmatics* (Maryknoll, NY: Orbis, 1988).

52. So far, Douglas John Hall, *Thinking the Faith: Christian Theology in North American Context,* vol. 1; *Professing the Faith: Christian Theology in a North American Context,* vol. 2 (Minneapolis: Augsburg and AugsburgFortress, 1989, 1994).

53. Christopher Morse, *Not Every Spirit: A Dogmatics of Christian Disbelief* (Valley Forge: Trinity Press International, 1994).

54. Kenneth Cauthen, *Systematic Theology: A Modern Protestant Approach* (Lewistown, NY: E. Mellen Press, 1986).

55. Langdon Gilkey, *Message and Existence* (New York: Seabury Press, 1979).

56. Peter C. Hodgson and Robert H. King, eds., *Christian Theology: An Introduction to its Traditions and Tasks,* new updated ed. (Philadelphia: Fortress, 1994).

are Jürgen Moltmann and Wolfhart Pannenberg. Of worldwide influence, both have joined in the recovery of systematics, although Moltmann refers to his five-volume project as "systematic fragments." Each has taken eschatology as an organizing theme, although in different ways. Moltmann's *Messianic Theology* project (*The Trinity and the Kingdom, God in Creation, The Way of Jesus Christ,* and *The Spirit of Life,* so far in translation)[57] draws out the sociopolitical import of the coming Reign of God at every doctrinal juncture. Pannenberg's *Systematic Theology,* two volumes now in translation, is distinguished by its stress on the coherence of Christian claims with a universal rationality and, finally, their eschatological verification.[58] When speaking of the premier theologians, do we add here the reappearance of Karl Barth himself in the first volume of his never-before-translated *The Göttingen Dogmatics?*[59]

Experiential Systematics

The word and concept "experience" are notorious for the variety of interpretations current and possible. Here, as throughout *The Christian Story,* the term refers to the range of universal human sensibilities beyond the boundaries of the Scripture and the Christian community — "the world" outside of "the Bible" and "the church," access to which is in principle open to all.[60] "World" so understood has its affective, rational, and moral dimensions — "thinking," "doing," and "feeling."[61]

Of course, the world is much with Bible and church; Scripture and

---

57. Jürgen Moltmann, *The Trinity and the Kingdom: The Doctrine of God; God in Creation: A New Theology of Creation and the Spirit of God; The Way of Jesus Christ: Christology in Messianic Dimensions;* and *The Spirit of Life: A Universal Affirmation* (San Francisco: Harper & Row, 1981, 1985, 1990, 1992 E.T.).

58. Wolfhart Pannenberg, *Systematic Theology,* vols. 1, 2, trans. Geoffrey Bromiley (Grand Rapids: Eerdmans, 1991, 1994).

59. Karl Barth, *The Göttingen Dogmatics: Instruction in the Christian Religion,* vol. 1, ed. Hannelotte Reiffen and trans. Geoffrey W. Bromiley (Grand Rapids: Eerdmans, 1991).

60. Following the distinctions Barth makes in *Church Dogmatics,* IV, 3, 1, trans. G. W. Bromiley (Edinburgh: T & T Clark, 1961), 96ff.

61. As adapted from Friedrich Schleiermacher's division of "knowing," "doing," and "feeling" in *The Christian Faith,* vol. 1, ed. H. R. Mackintosh and J. D. Stewart (New York: Harper & Row, 1963), passim.

the Christian community are inextricable from universal human experience. The key here is the qualification "universal." For example, to the extent to which Scripture or the church entails scientific worldviews or cultural premises, it is enmeshed in the world of human experience and subject to analyses from the same. From the early christological controversies on, classical Christian faith has rejected Docetism, recognizing the earthy rootages of its revelatory claims.

In the current examples of this type of systematics, "experience" functions both normatively and descriptively. Its exponents see it operative negatively and without acknowledgment in alternative theological programs, and a form of it, positively, in their efforts in theological reconstruction. The major current expression of experiential systematics rises out of an ethical protest against both received interpretations and restatements of faith. Descriptively — "the way things are" is analyzed by a "hermeneutic of suspicion" — traditional theologies (conservative or liberal) are viewed as the creatures of social, economic, or political power. Normatively — "the way things should be" is stated through a victim-oriented hermeneutic — the texts and traditions of the Christian community are reframed in terms of the experiential concerns of the powerless.

Rosemary Radford Ruether's 1983 *Sexism and God-Talk* is one of the first and clearest expressions of a protest systematics, revising traditional content and categories in terms of the experiences of oppression and liberation.[62] Many of the standard loci are visited and their content reread in the light of feminist premises, with "women church" or its liberation equivalents as the community of privileged discourse. The more recent *Lift Every Voice,* edited by Susan Thistlethwaite and Mary Potter Engel, is a reconstruction of the received tradition along similar lines.[63] In this case, "constructing Christian theologies" is undertaken by feminist revision of some doctrines and the reformulation of other standard teachings "from the underside" of Native American, Asian, Latin American, gay and lesbian, and other marginalized or emerging communities. With closely related liberation and feminist concerns, Dorothee Sölle's *Thinking about God* contrasts her liberation construal

---

62. Rosemary Radford Ruether, *Sexism and God-Talk* (Boston: Beacon Press, 1983).
63. Susan Brooks Thistlethwaite and Mary Potter Engel, eds., *Lift Every Voice: Constructing Christian Theologies from the Underside* (San Francisco: Harper & Row, 1990).

of many of the loci with "conservative" and "liberal" interpretations of the same.[64]

James Cone's 1970 *A Black Theology of Liberation* was the manifesto of a new movement.[65] A case could be made that it was the first of the new wave of systematics works, covering as it did, albeit briefly, most of the standard loci. It was, as well, the initial venture in this period of the experientialist genre, redoing the classical teachings in the categories of African-American experiences of oppression and liberation and repudiating earlier readings as the ideology of white wielders of power. James Evans's recent *We Have Been Believers* asserts biblical authority, but holds it to be open-ended, inviting the imaginative "conjuring" of its meaning in terms of the African-American struggle for justice.[66]

Experientialist systematics have recourse to determinative philosophical as well as social-ethical frameworks. Process perspectives supply the orientation points in the earlier volume of Marjorie Hewett Suchocki, *God Christ Church*[67] and the recent small work of Robert Neville, *A Theology Primer*,[68] although each has other issues (Suchocki, feminist concerns, and Neville, Methodist accents). Ninian Smart and Steve Konstantine's *Christian Systematic Theology in a World Context* espouses a "soft relativism" for religiously pluralist times, with attention to the contributions of religious studies programs.[69] Paul van Buren also ventures a pluralist revision of standard topics, in this case vis-à-vis one religious tradition, Judaism, reconceiving the loci in a post-Holocaust framework in three of four projected volumes, *A Theology of Jewish-Christian Reality*.[70]

64. Dorothee Sölle, *Thinking About God: An Introduction to Theology* (London: SCM Press and Philadelphia: Trinity Press International, 1990).

65. James Cone, *A Black Theology of Liberation* (Philadelphia: J. B. Lippincott, 1970 and Maryknoll: Orbis, 1983 [rev.], 1990).

66. James H. Evans, Jr., *We Have Been Believers: An African-American Systematic Theology* (Minneapolis: Fortress Press, 1992).

67. Marjorie Hewett Suchocki, *God Christ Church: A Practical Guide to Process Theology* (New York: Crossroad, 1982).

68. Robert Cummings Neville, *A Theology Primer* (Albany: State University of New York: 1991).

69. Ninian Smart and Steven Konstantine, *Christian Systematic Theology in a World Context* (Minneapolis: Fortress Press, 1991).

70. Paul M. van Buren, *Discerning the Way: A Theology of the Jewish Christian Reality* (New York: Seabury, 1980); *A Christian Theology of the People Israel*, part 2 (New York:

Peter Hodgson in *Winds of the Spirit,* wary of evangelical and ecumenical retrievals, takes a "revisionist" tack shaped by pluralist and praxis interests.[71] In *Reconstructing Christian Theology,* edited by Rebecca A. Chopp and Mark Lewis Taylor, fifteen authors approach the loci from variously the points of view of pluralism, deconstruction, reenvisioning, and praxis.[72] Gordon Kaufman, who wrote a widely used seminary text when few others were available, *Systematic Theology: A Historicist Perspective,*[73] subsequently judged the enterprise no longer viable. However, his 1993 *In the Face of Mystery: A Constructive Theology,* returns to the task with the tools of "deconstruction" and "imaginative" reconstruction of the loci.[74]

Conclusion

The current outpouring of systematics is a sign of energy in the Body of Christ. This quest to see things whole is a new *state of mind* that goes beyond the 1960s moratorium on systematics, which declared only for theological "bits and pieces."

As can be seen by this survey, the surge is also marked by a great diversity of perspectives. What will this mean for the Christian community? Does it portend a theological pluralism in which each camp associates only with its own constituency and "does its own thing"? Or will we enter a period of tribal warfare, mounting periodic assaults on one another?

An alternative to relativism and imperialism is a new *state of soul.* The catholicity that Paul urges on the Corinthian church is a "more excellent way." It recognizes the richness of the theological gifts in the Body of Christ.

Seabury, 1983); *A Theology of the Jewish Christian Reality* (San Francisco: Harper & Row, 1987).

71. Peter C. Hodgson, *Winds of the Spirit: A Constructive Christian Theology* (Louisville: Westminster/John Knox, 1994).

72. Rebecca A. Chopp and Mark Lewis Taylor, eds., *Reconstructing Christian Theology* (Minneapolis: AugsburgFortress, 1994).

73. Gordon D. Kaufman, *Systematic Theology: A Historicist Perspective* (New York: Charles Scribner's Sons, 1968). John Macquarrie's *Principles of Christian Theology,* 2nd ed. (New York: Charles Scribner's Sons, 1977) was the other standard text in mainline seminaries in the period between the giants and the subsequent surge in systematics.

74. Gordon Kaufman, *In the Face of Mystery: A Constructive Theology* (Cambridge: Harvard University Press, 1993).

And it knows that "the eye cannot say to the hand, 'I have no need of you'"
(1 Cor. 12:21). Separate existence is impossible, for the parts require each
other to be a living organism. The first step in this direction for the
systematics renewal is an invitation to conversation extended to those of
different perspective. One of the features of the volumes to come in the
Christian Story series will be, therefore, an attempt to understand, and to
enter into both appreciative and critical dialogue with, the variety of points
of view found within the community of Christian theology.

Index

267